Rogue's Progress

Books by John Burke

WINGED LEGEND
DUET IN DIAMONDS
BUFFALO BILL
THE LEGEND OF BABY DOE
ROGUE'S PROGRESS

Rogue's Progress

THE FABULOUS ADVENTURES
OF WILSON MIZNER

by John Burke

G. P. Putnam's Sons, New York

75-033190-2 Γ © 1975 BY JOHN BURKE

SBN: 399-11423-8

Library of Congress Catalog Card Number: 74-16879

PRINTED IN THE UNITED STATES OF AMERICA

CONTENTS

INTRODUCTION

"WHY," Wilson Mizner once remarked, "if I ever start to tell the story of my life, it will be interrupted by the blowing of a million police whistles."

He may have been exaggerating slightly, but his career did include a variety of questionable activities such as confidence games, cardsharping on luxury liners, operating gambling joints, and selling Florida real estate not entirely above sea level. A lively sense of opportunism carried him to such hectic scenes as the Klondike gold rush, a Central American banana plantation, San Francisco's Barbary Coast, Broadway and Fifth Avenue during their most expansive periods, and Hollywood during its pharaonic phase when the vast biscuit-colored studios seemed as enduring as the temples of the Nile.

At the very least Wilson Mizner was an American original. His life was a series of panels illustrating the Rogue's Progress. Dastardly though many of his misdeeds, which left in his wake a rabid concourse of victims shouting for the constabulary, he contributed much to the gayety of the nation. His whole life seemed a series of jocund anecdotes; he was Peck's Bad Boy in his boyhood and equally wayward in his manhood; the Katzenjammer Kid, Scaramouche, the man who corrupted a dozen Hadleyburgs, an O. Henry grifter, and the All-American picaroon wrapped up in one outrageous package.

Nothing was too sacred to be turned into a sardonic little comedy starring Wilson Mizner with a supporting cast of lesser knaves, dupes, and bumpkins. Witticisms, epigrams, and deflating one-liners came whirling off the top of his head like sparks from a pinwheel. Every presumptuous aspect of American life was subjected to the acid bath of Miznerian wit.

The wisecrack is supposed to be a uniquely American contribution to humor, and Mizner was a master and leading innovator of the form. *Bartlett's Familiar Quotations* (13th Edition) stubbornly ignores his claim to eminence while finding room for the wit and wisdom of Calvin Coolidge and Herbert Hoover. The trouble, perhaps, was the company Mizner insisted on keeping. Great truths are not supposed to be uttered in Broadway cabarets and all-night restaurants, Klondike saloons, Barbary Coast deadfalls, or the other settings in which street-level aphorisms are minted. He lacked the dignity which should mantle the humblest philosopher or lowliest humorist; furthermore, he never committed anything to paper, if he could help it, and there is nothing like print to certify a man's claim to stature. Yet H. L. Mencken rightly credited him with spinning off more jests, as casually as a man tossing away a cigarette butt, than any other citizen of the United States. He was not the conscious, conspicuously literate fabricator of bitter aphorisms that Ambrose Bierce was with his *Devil's Dictionary*, but Mizner's home brew of humor, delivered at vaudeville speed, embedded itself more deeply in the American lexicon.

His style of humor was in the American tradition. It was not drawled out by highborn gentlemen in drawing rooms,

or lisped by recumbent ladies in a French salon, or discharged with loving malice by coffeehouse intellectuals in
the Middle European style. It was indigenous to the bar-
relhouse, the loungers holding up a Broadway lamppost, the
wings of a vaudeville stage, the parlor of a brothel, the back
room of a gambling joint.

Like most exemplars of oral humor, Mizner was prodigal
with his special talent. His object was to amuse a select
circle of companions, not to bedazzle posterity. Probably
many of his best quips simply vanished into a bellow of
laughter, a momentary appreciation of his auditors, and a
swirl of cigar smoke and whiskey fumes. If Mizner was sort
of a Samuel Johnson of lesser illumination, he unfortunately
lacked a James Boswell earnestly recording his ad-lib remarks. There is a justifiable suspicion, in fact, that Mizner
sensed that his efforts were being dissipated, that he was
enough of an artist, like one of his more distinguished ancestors, to regret this, and that later in his life he recalled some
of his more memorable offerings for the benefit of Damon
Runyon, Walter Winchell, and other newspaper columnists
who served in a Boswellian role.

Time and changing fashion have tarnished what seemed
like brilliance to his contemporaries. His wit was of the
bitterly laconic type bearing little resemblance to the sly
convolutions of Irish humor, for instance, or the gallows
view of Jewish humor. Nor did it rely on the understatement
prized by his Anglo-Saxon forebears. His observations stung
like a whiplash and were laced with the hyperbolic over-
statement which afflicted Westerners overwhelmed by the
sheer incomprehensible size of their habitat.

His off-the-cuff witticisms have been recycled so many
times that they have become a part of folklore, if not folk
wisdom—clichés worn to the nub—so in judging their

quality, it is important to remember that he said them first. Cold print, too, deprives them of the sardonic quality of their delivery. "Be nice to people on the way up because you'll meet them on the way down. . . . Treat a lady like a whore and a whore like a lady. . . . He'd steal a hot stove and come back for the smoke. . . . If you copy from one author, it's plagiarism. If you copy from two, it's research. . . . The first hundred years are the hardest. . . . Most open minds should be closed for repairs. . . . The life of a party almost always winds up in a corner with an overcoat over him. . . . I never saw a mob rush across town to do a good deed. . . . Hollywood almost made a good picture once, but they caught it just in time. . . ."

Obviously the Mizner view of the human condition divided people into two categories: the wiseacre and the sucker. His own life was one long confidence game which confirmed his earnest belief that a masterpiece wasn't a work of art but a fake you sold to somebody who didn't deserve to own a masterpiece in the first place. There was something salutary about trimming a sucker, beneficial to the victim as well as the trickster. Naiveté must be punished. If you sold a man the Brooklyn Bridge, his education would be advanced immeasurably; at least he wouldn't buy another bridge.

His outlook on humanity was broadened and further confirmed by his experiences as a nonwriting but highly successful playwright and screenwriter, as a nondigging Klondike prospector and a promoter of waterlogged Florida real estate. He had seen his fellow Americans and caustically deplored their behavior during their most memorable fever dreams, all of them filigreed with gold, and had noted that a man is never more off-balance than when he is reaching for the goodies at the top of the money tree.

Certainly he would have agreed with Somerset Maugham that "Impropriety is the soul of wit." The thrust of his humor, the oblique outlook on human behavior as viewed from the brawling pit of a Beggar's Opera, took into full account the general foolishness of his species; nor did he spare himself and his colleagues from its penetrations. Its angle of vision was from the underworld.

If statelier observers like Dean Swift looked down on humanity from a satiric mountaintop, he looked up from the gutter level. The readings taken from both positions were pretty much the same.

This book was gleaned in part, years ago, from the recollections of a number of men in Hollywood, New York and elsewhere. They include Seth Clarkson, Stanley Rose, Mark Kelly, Marshall "Mickey" Neilan, Gene Fowler, and Louis Stevens. I hope they are all reunited with Mizner in some all-night Valhalla bar and grill where the tab is paid in advance. This book is dedicated to them; also to Tom Caton, my old friend and executive city editor of the Los Angeles *Herald-Examiner*, and David "Spec" McClure, who was Hedda Hopper's chief of staff and is an expert on Hollywood in the thirties, both of whom were of great assistance in writing this book.

1

MAMA'S ANGEL BIRDIE

"TO my embarrassment, I was born in bed with a lady," was one of Wilson Mizner's more celebrated quips.

That event took place in 1876, the same year Custer was miscalculating the risks on the Little Bighorn, which is not to say both occurrences were equally disastrous.

It was the last occasion on which Wilson Mizner would admit to being embarrassed. It was also true that the first lady with whom he shared a bed was indeed a lady and a most imposing one. She was a society figure of matriarchal eminence not only in Benicia, where she gave birth to Wilson and had produced his five brothers and one sister, but thirty miles down the bay in San Francisco; she never hesitated to remind pushy newcomers that the Mizners had been lords of the California earth when the newly rich silver magnates were still pushing wheelbarrows. Strong-mindedness was characteristic of the female side of the house. His sister Minnie later was an imperious matron of peninsular society. She objected to a newly rich family who

1

occupied a mansion on a cliff above her own palatial home in Burlingame. When her neighbors gave a garden party, she burned huge piles of trash and watched the thick black smoke drift upward to disrupt the festivities of the newcomers and send their guests reeling and choking back into the house.

All of Wilson's brothers were brought up under a system of strenuous discipline applied not only by Mrs. Mizner but by her husband, Lansing, a lawyer-politician who for many years presided over the State Senate of California. Wilson's siblings were surprised and somewhat annoyed that he was not subjected to the same ironhanded supervision. But Wilson was her youngest son, the last child she would bear, and she spoiled him, happily unaware that the effects of her coddling would be borne for more than half a century by a large number of his bedeviled contemporaries.

"You," she often told Wilson, who cringed, "are Mama's Angel Birdie."

"More likely a jailbirdie," remarked one of his skeptical brothers.

Yet if Wilson went spectacularly astray, it may have been traceable not only to maternal tolerance but to the fact that he was surrounded by so much rectitude and family distinction. An atmosphere of traditional high-mindedness can produce, through the alchemy of human perversity, some amazing exceptions and biological sports. A study of the later careers of clergymen's offspring is instructive in that regard. The more sanctified the atmosphere, the greater the temptation to defile the bloodlines.

The Mizner clan, as Wilson was endlessly reminded, was one of California's First Families, preeminent among the Native Sons of the Golden West, and had been meritori-

ously involved in the state's affairs ever since the flag of the
Bear Republic was hoisted.

Every time young Wilson misbehaved, he was ad-
monished that he was letting down a long stately line of
ancestors going back into English history. His great-great-
uncle was Sir Joshua Reynolds, the celebrated painter, and
Wilson's middle name was Reynolds. His great-uncle on his
mother's side, Dr. Robert Semple, had founded the towns
of Benicia, Vacaville, and Colusa. Two of his uncles were
general officers in the regular army. Another kinsman had
been the first governor of Illinois and gave Abraham Lincoln
his first political appointment. A cousin was the leading
meat-packer of St. Louis.

Nor did it appear that the present crop of Mizners was
likely, until Mama gave birth to Angel Birdie, to besmirch
the family honor. Lansing, named for his father, was
likewise a lawyer. Edgar was a mining engineer and executive of the Alaska Commercial Company, in charge of its
operations in the Yukon Valley, of which good things would
soon be heard. William was a San Francisco physician. And
brother Henry was the family saint, an Episcopal clergyman
and rector of Christ Church, St. Louis. A man of unearthly
goodness, of suffocating holiness, the Reverend Henry
would write his brothers epistles offering corrective advice
whenever word reached him that they had erred.

If there was any doubt of the worthiness and stability of
the present generation among the family elders, it was
concentrated not only on the spoiled and undisciplined
young Wilson but on the next youngest brother, Addison,
who had developed artistic tendencies and would soon skip
off to San Francisco to set up an atelier and announce, with a
flippancy his family could only deplore, "I'm a descendant of

Sir Joshua Reynolds, and I josh and I paint." Nothing good,
it was felt, would be heard from that boisterous sprig until
he stopped daubing paint on canvas. It was one thing to have
a famous ancestor who painted and another to have a contemporary member of the family taking up the smock and
beret.

Addison and Wilson did not greatly resemble each other
—Addison fought a little harder against his demons—but his
slightly older brother would always be the human Wilson
felt closest to. That kid-brotherly regard, as Addison often
groaned, was the greatest burden of his life.

Despite the fondness of sociologists for the theory that
environment is everything, Wilson Mizner's contained nothing that would encourage a lifetime of delinquency. The
respectability of his background and upbringing should
have brought forth a statesman, a bishop, an admiral, not a
man dedicated to skinning the human race. Benicia, located
on San Francisco Bay between the estuaries of the Sac-
ramento and San Joaquin rivers, was known with some
justification as the "Athens of the Pacific." The Mizners
were its foremost family. Around their dinner table almost
every evening, to satisfy Mrs. Mizner's lust for culture and
the Honorable Lansing Mizner's pursuit of political glory,
were gathered a dozen luminaries, either regional or visiting notables.

The Mizners presided over the local social life which was
partly military, owing to the presence of the Benicia Bar-
racks, and partly academic, a number of girls' seminaries
(including the seedbed of Mills College) and a number of
boys' preparatory schools having located there.

Wilson began his education in one of the local private
schools, where his prankishness and aversion to discipline
made the masters sigh for the English tradition of birching.

An invariable truant in the academic groves, he was more interested in the local fascination with pugilism, a sport which then attracted the patronage of society gentlemen as it had in England during an earlier period. Prizefighting had become almost a craze around Benicia during Wilson's boyhood. It had sent John Heenan, "The Benicia Boy," on to a notable career as a heavyweight contender. In 1880 Heenan had fought Tom Sayers, the English heavyweight champion, to a draw, and every saloon in Benicia was plastered with pictures of his thirty-seven-round bout with the Englishman. In those days fistfighting, instead of being deplored as a sign of humanity's aggressive tendencies, was known as the "manly art of self-defense" (a semantic evasion similar to changing the name of the War Department to the Department of Defense). All the Mizner boys, except for the pacific Henry, who was destined for holy orders instead of unholy disorders, were encouraged to learn how to handle themselves in the ring, a gym having been built into the tank house at the rear of the family property. The Mizners boasted of fistic skills with or without the padded gloves; Wilson's handiness in a saloon brawl was legendary, and his brother Edgar (according to Addison) once laid out twenty-six opponents in a Klondike saloon fracas.

The most memorable event of Wilson's boyhood was the celebrated and much-harried fight between the two most promising young heavyweights on the Pacific Coast—James J. Corbett, who would dance and jab his way to the heavyweight title, and Joe Choynski, a close contender for that prize—which one commentator called "the most picturesque land-and-sea action since the Texas cavalry captured the Mexican navy in 1836."

Prizefights were illegal in California and had to be staged with the utmost clandestine care; otherwise they would be raided by sheriffs' posses which rode out under the battle cry "Confiscate the stakes and turn 'em loose." Them, or 'em, referred to the spectators, who were likely to number among them the governor, an assortment of mayors and police chiefs, bankers, and industrial magnates. In 1889, however, various sportsmen from San Francisco and the peninsular towns were determined to stage a bout between Gentleman Jim Corbett, the boxing instructor at San Francisco's Olympic Club, an elegant stylist who waltzed his opponents into a state of exhaustion and then cut them up with a hurricane of left jabs, and Choynski, a rugged Slav with a durable chin and a powerhouse punch with both fists, a veritable windmill in the ring. (Later Choynski got a draw against Jim Jeffries and knocked out Jack Johnson, under what were described as suspicious circumstances.) San Francisco sportsmen raised a purse of $20,000 to settle the question, argued in male sanctuaries from the clubs of Nob Hill to the saloons of the Barbary Coast, whether the fistic artist personified by Corbett could prevail over the sturdy artisan chunkily embodied by Choynski: the rapier versus the bung starter.

A barn in the backcountry of Marin County was the site of the first Corbett-Choynski meeting on May 30, 1889. The decision went to the sheriff, who raided the barn in the sixth round and sent everyone fleeing into the foothills, fighters and spectators alike. Fortunately the stakeholders were among those who escaped the posse.

Greater canniness was employed in rescheduling the fight, which was set for June 5. A huge wheat barge was leased and towed to an anchorage in the bay near Benicia, which was located exactly on the boundary between Solano and Contra Costa counties. If the authorities somehow learned of the bout—so its promoters reasoned—they

would be too embroiled in a jurisdictional dispute to inter-
fere. The 200 spectators allowed to buy tickets were men of
established honor, further sworn to secrecy, and obviously
men willing to go to considerable lengths to watch a couple
of young men belabor each other with their padded fists. At
1 A.M. on June 5 they would board the tugs *Richmond* and
Sea Queen on the Embarcadero and be transported to the
barge off Benicia. The fight would begin at dawn.

The night of June 4, as Jim Corbett related in his autobiography, "they put me on a train for a little country town
called Benicia. From the station I was taken to the home of
Wilson Mizner"—by which he meant Mizner's father,
whose dignity as presiding officer of the California Senate
was evidently unimpaired by conspiring in an illegal activity.

Corbett and his opponent boarded the barge before dawn
with their handlers. Everything was ready, except that the
paying customers hadn't arrived. Their tugs had gone
aground on the mud flats along the shore of the bay and
finally they had to be transferred to a fleet of rowboats.

Then, just as the weary and mud-spattered subscribers to
the fight clambered over the side of the barge, every red-
blooded and able-bodied youth in the vicinity of Benicia
headed out to sea on skiffs, rowboats, rafts, and dinghies and
tried to board the barge. The legitimate spectators stoutly
resisted the invasion, and the brawl between the San Francisco sportsmen and the Benicia gate-crashers served as the
curtainraiser to the main event. Two prominent politicians
were dumped overboard before a truce was arranged, the
agreement being that the gate-crashers would be permitted
to watch the fight from their various craft surrounding the
barge.

Among the prefight combatants was thirteen-year-old

Wilson Mizner. Since senior males in his family hadn't seen fit to buy him a ticket, he joined the amphibious assault launched by the lower classes of his hometown. The strapping young Mizner gave a good account of himself during the brawl but got his right hand bashed by a boat hook in the melee, the first of many reproofs life had in store for him now that the fledgling felt himself strong enough to fly from Mama's nest.

Wilson and his comrades then settled down to watch a masterly exhibition of fistic ballet presented by young Mr. Corbett. During the early rounds, Choynski kept charging like a bull bedeviled by a matador but for his pains was stabbed repeatedly by Corbett's left. Choynski began leaking so much blood the canvas got slippery. Pirouetting around his opponent in a classic demonstration of Celtic guile vs. Slavic doggedness, dancing in and out, bobbing up and down with his patent-leather hair still slicked down, Corbett was so enraptured with his swanlike grace that he got a bit careless. A Polish fist thudded against the profile which would later make Corbett a matinee idol in the theater. Corbett's eye was closed, but he had learned to be less contemptuous of his opponent. Round after round he kept wearing Choynski down with his jabs and his flitting movement around the ring. In the twenty-seventh round Corbett followed up a left jab with a right cross that left Choynski inert on the canvas.

It was shortly after that naval battle off Benicia that Lansing Mizner, Sr., as a loyal Republican chieftain of the Western provinces, was appointed by President Benjamin Harrison as minister plenipotentiary and envoy extraordinary to the five Central American republics, with his headquarters in Guatemala City. Mrs. Mizner felt that she had to introduce her daughter, Minnie, to San Francisco society, but

Wilson and Addison were sent along with their father. No doubt the two years they spent in Guatemala as lordlings in an ambassadorial villa, with a valet and tutor in attendance on each, contributed much to the sheer presence Wilson and Addison could summon on occasion, a habit of command which Addison would use to overawe multimillionaires and Wilson would wield against less privileged folk as an occasional bunco artist.

Wilson at thirteen and his brother at seventeen were treated with deference by generals, diplomats, and politicians. As sons of the U. S. representative in what gringos referred to as banana republics, they were vouchsafed extraterritorial rights which would have encouraged mischievous tendencies in even less boisterous boys. Undoubtedly they could have slain a peasant or two with impunity, but with a forbearance which Wilson, at least, would seldom display in the future they confined their criminal activity to malicious mischief and destruction of public property.

After two years of suffering their prankishness, Guatemalans were relieved to learn that first Addison, then Wilson were being sent back to California to continue their schooling.

With his father still in Guatemala and his mother engrossed in Nob Hill social maneuvering, Wilson spent his summer vacation in a district far below the hilltop mansions. Not cotillions and the gilded youth of Nob Hill but the Barbary Coast, the squalid hell-raising underside of San Francisco, held a magnetic attraction for young Wilson. He was being reared to be a gentleman, but his inclinations led him to the lowlifes, the whores and boozers and opium smokers, and despite civic restraints placed on the section—one was no longer likely to wake up on a tramp steamer bound for Shanghai after having a friendly drink in one of its resorts—the Barbary Coast was still one of the sin capitals of the United States. Later Wilson claimed he held down a summer job collecting from a string of brothels, riding a high-wheeled bike from one bagnio to another. No doubt that was purely a literary image, irresistible to a man who became one of the more creative American raconteurs. He also claimed that, at the age of fifteen, he learned to smoke opium in various Chinatown pads. Opium smoking, like prizefighting, was technically illegal, but there was many a respectable citizen with calluses on one elbow from lying on the bunk of an opium dispensary.

Apparently Mrs. Mizner reclaimed her erstwhile Angel Birdie from his unwholesome pursuits in time to place him in one of the Benicia prep schools. For the next two years his academic career was a disgrace to the family and an ordeal for his preceptors; his stay in Guatemala, under the umbrella of diplomatic immunity, had fostered a lifelong conviction that laws were made for other people. Wilson entered and was discharged from a number of the local prep schools, until it seemed to his family that he considered an educational institution no more than a revolving door. The schoolmasters reported that he not only disrupted discipline but led other, more innocent youths astray.

An anguished family decided to send him to Santa Clara College, a sort of high-class reform school in those days with the reputation for taming the most ardent of delinquents. Wilson felt as though he were being dispatched to the Dry Tortugas and responded with his usual spirit. Santa Clara's atmosphere was prisonlike with large and ferocious dogs turned loose to roam the campus after curfew. Wilson expressed his opinion of such penal measures by tying a large sirloin steak to the rope of the fire bell. The guard dogs, kept on starvation rations to increase their ferocity, rang the fire bell all night trying to snatch the meat. A member of the faculty notorious for his lack of tolerance for wayward youth next attracted Wilson's attention. Somewhere he obtained a cannonball, heated it over red coals for several hours, carried it on a shovel to the corridor on which the disciplinarian's office was located, and sent it steaming down the hallway. As he expected, the educator rushed out into the corridor like a shortstop about to field a hot grounder and was badly burned for his efforts. Long before the cannonball had cooled, Wilson was frog-marched to the dean's office, tried, and summarily expelled from school.

Rather than face another family tribunal, Wilson decided it was time to make a definitive break with the Mizner clan. Running away from home and family was, after all, the classic beginning of what his seniors often referred to as life's great adventure. He was seventeen and, as his brother Addison recalled him in a memoir, was a strapping six-footer with a muscular torso and broad shoulders but rather spindly legs. His large head was supported by a thin neck, or as Addison graphically put it, he wore a size 7 collar and a size 8 hat. Despite those physical discrepancies, he was regarded as extraordinarily handsome, with more than his share of guile, charm, and magnetism, the latter quality especially evident to the opposite sex. If he had one serious handicap, it was the delusion that he had a magnificent singing voice; it would take many vicissitudes and many barrages of overripe vegetables to convince him that, to ears other than his own, his bel canto resembled that of a lovesick jackass.

The year 1893 was not a vintage year for striking out on one's own. The great depression of the nineties had begun, following the collapse of silver's parity with gold, and the railroads were overburdened with free riders, many of them

heading East to join General Coxey's demonstration in
Washington. Wilson, however, made it to San Francisco
without too much trouble. Horrifying reports soon reached
the Mizner family of the errant youngest son's progress: He
was raising his soulful baritone in sentimental ballads at
Spider Kelly's cabaret at Mason and Eddy Streets while
pickpockets worked over the clientele and female members
of the staff solicited after-hours work. It was said that
Wilson's rendition of "You Would Not Insult Me, Sir, If
Jack Were Only Here" was the most mournful braying
heard in the West since Washington announced it was going
off the silver standard. Except for the most soddenly sentimental drunks, he was not popular with Spider Kelly's
patrons.

The master of ceremonies would somewhat defiantly announce that "Mr. Wilson Mizner will now sing."

"To hell with that jackass," a roughneck in the audience
would respond. Male singers were not popular at Spider
Kelly's, soulful baritones least of all.

"Nevertheless," the MC said firmly but with a fatalistic
shrug, "Mr. Wilson Mizner will now sing."

Impresario Kelly finally decided that Wilson was driving
customers away and discharged him. By then the Mizner
family had tracked down the prodigal and reclaimed him
despite a new growth of black fleece. It was decided that
hard labor might make a man of him, though Mizners were
usually considered eligible only for brainwork.

He was packed off to the Gold Star gold mine at Grass
Valley, which was owned by a friend of the family. Digging
gold for other people's profit, at $3 a day, did not appeal to
the youth, nor did being imprisoned 3,600 feet below the
surface of the earth.

The family, he later related, with some exaggeration, "thought they'd get rid of me. I had the feeling some of 'em were praying for a mine accident."

After several weeks' confinement in the Gold Star mine, Wilson escaped back to San Francisco. He caught on as a member of the red-jerseyed entourage accompanying a journeyman fighter named Kid Savage on his tour of the Pacific Northwest's boxing arenas. Wilson served as a second in the ring.

The Kid's punch was good enough, but his jaw unfortunately was the most delicate grade of eggshell china. Since most purses were offered on a winner-take-all basis and the Kid usually succumbed in an early round, he and his handlers were soon reduced to touring Washington and Oregon on the brake rods. The oblique angle at which Wilson viewed the world, from under a freight car, with the scenery going by in a blur, may have contributed to his astigmatic outlook on moral distinctions.

Finally, the group decided that Kid Savage would never learn to protect his fragile chin and disbanded. Wilson was stranded in Spokane, where he sang for a time at the Louvre Café until once again he found himself in violent disfavor with audiences. A patrolman on duty in the Spokane redlight district arrested him on a charge of vagrancy. He decided it was time to let the folks at home know how he was getting along. The telegram announcing that he was a resident of the city jail up north shocked his mother, who had persevered in her hopes for her youngest son, but not his brother Addison.

"I called him my darling little Birdie," she wistfully told Addison, "and I was certain that he would become an ambassador like his father was."

"Ambassador!" snorted Addison, whose affection for his

younger brother was never quite exhausted but who was
always aware of his shortcomings. "We should burn candles
if he manages to stay off the gallows!"

Mrs. Mizner engaged an attorney by telegraph to spring
Wilson, who then sent a series of telegrams home request-
ing money. Mrs. Mizner financed him until her patience ran
out and one day replied to a demand for $100: "I did not
receive your telegram."

Wilson, as Addison later learned, even considered obtaining some sort of honest work now that he could no longer tap
the family exchequer, but the temptation quickly passed,
and he lived for a time as the guest of a girl named Belle.

When Belle's affection became cloying, he caught on with
an itinerant healer who called himself Dr. Silas Slocum, who
was sharing his scientific knowledge with the simpler souls
of the Pacific Northwest. Cynics may have designated Dr.
Slocum and his assistants as a medicine show, but among his
miracle potions was a pill for expectant mothers guaranteed
to produce a male infant—the sort of scientific advance less
imaginative practitioners condemned as charlatanism,
probably out of professional jealousy. Dr. Slocum's success
in dispensing his pill, which was only one of the wonder
drugs he prescribed, was based on birth records compiled in
the communities he befriended. If there was a high rate of
male births after he appeared in a certain place, he
scheduled it for a return appearance; the others he avoided
until memories of his claims had faded.

At Wilson's first interview with the goateed Dr. Slocum
he learned that the shaman did have a position on his faculty
open. One of his confreres, vulgarly known as the spieler,
had quit. What Dr. Slocum required was a pedantic personality who could reel off learned phrases in Latin to impress
the provincials. In addition to his duties as a diagnostician

and lecturer, the spieler was required to act as traveling companion of a trained bear whose talents were employed to attract an audience, the medical symposium alone having been found to lack the requisite drawing power.

"Latin?" Wilson said. "I speak it like a native."

"Let's hear you speak a piece of it," suggested Dr. Slocum.

Wilson, who had spent much time among the lower classes in Guatemala, reeled off a sample of Spanish curses and obscenities.

"By God, you can speak Latin," Dr. Slocum marveled. "You're hired."

Wilson described his adventures with Dr. Slocum's traveling lyceum of the medical arts for a New York newspaper reporter seventeen years later. His recollections may have tended toward the hyperbolic; anything he did was likely to be recounted with the coloration of legend making, at which he was adept, but his experiences were not too dissimilar from those of many others who trouped with the medicine shows. A bastard issue of show business and the patent-medicine industry, the medicine show was a part of rural Americana, as familiar and almost as respectable as torchlight parades, political stump speaking, and strawberry socials. "It was high noon," a historian of the art form has written, "for the sarsaparillas, the celeries, the vegetable compounds; for assorted nostrums certified as cures for every recognized disease and for others that existed only in the fevered imaginations of writers of advertising copy. The chronology of their genesis and popularity extended full across the nineteenth century, and into the twentieth." It had become an $80,000,000-a-year business, and "medicine shows were trouping throughout rural America, among them a score of companies under the hoary banner of Healy

and Bigelow, operating for humanity with Kickapoo Indian
Sagwa. Other shows were on the road for the glory of Old
Doc Hamlin, discoverer and proprietor of Hamlin's Wizard
Oil. There were lesser outfits, often posing as Quakers, like
Hal the Healer, Brother John and Brother Benjamin, all of
whom used Thee and Thou most of the time and never failed
to open with a strong pitch about the inherent honesty of the
Friends and their remedies."

There was nothing Quakerish about Dr. Slocum's little
company of ad-lib healers—they forthrightly combined the
esoteric with the erotic. The former was represented by Dr.
Slocum and his learned young colleague Mizner, the latter
by Bianca the Beautiful, a sinuous brunette who performed
what was billed as the "fire dance." Bianca's husband accompanied her wrigglings on the portable organ and in his
spare time picked pockets. In addition to the performing
bear, the natural sciences were represented by a flea circus.

Dr. Slocum's aggregation set out on a tour of the lumber
towns and mining camps of the hinterland, up in the wet and
wooded mountains of the Northwest. In those forlorn ham-
lets Wilson began his study of the genus American Sucker.
As soon as the medicine show arrived in a town, the torches
would be lit, the organ would begin blaring, and Bianca the
Beautiful would emerge from the canvas curtains to display
her muscle control. When an audience of sufficient size had
been attracted, Professor Mizner would take the podium to
expound on the all-encompassing benefits of Dr. Slocum's
Elixir, a panacea guaranteed to cure everything from the
collywobbles to incontinent bladders.

"Do you experience a gnawing sensation after having
abstained from food for several days?" he would demand of
his audience. "Are you inclined to feel tired after a thirty-
mile walk? Do you suffer from indigestion after a ten-course

dinner? After a sleepless night do you experience a twitch-
ing of the eyelids? Can you walk up a mountainside without
losing your breath?"

The youthful savant would then unroll a series of charts in
primary colors which showed cross sections of the human
anatomy but looked more like a display of cold cuts. Whack-
ing at various points of anatomical interest with his whangee
cane, Wilson would describe how Dr. Slocum's Elixir—"the
discovery that astounded medical science from London to
Budapest"—surged through the system, toning up glands,
revitalizing organs, soothing nerves, enriching the blood-
stream, and clarifying the brain. When he came to certain
regions of his charts, he would switch to Spanish obscenities
purported to be Latin medical phrases. Then Bianca the
Beautiful would return with her own anatomical lesson, the
fleas would perform, the bear would do his tricks, and kindly
old Dr. Slocum and Bianca's husband would pass through
the multitude selling bottles of elixir at $1 a throw.

Wilson reappeared after the commercial activity sub-
sided, this time with a row of large glass jars containing what
looked like boa constrictors or sections of sea monsters
pickled in alcohol. For several moments he allowed the
audience to goggle at the specimens, then would explain
that each was a tapeworm extracted from the insides of
various statesmen, actresses, athletes, and famous divines
by Dr. Slocum's Vermifuge. Lily Langtry would have been
horrified to learn that a tapeworm the size of an eel had
nestled in her innards. Many standing before him, he thun-
dered, were harboring similar parasites. On his honor as a
dedicated scientist, he pledged that they would be purged
of their tapeworms if only they would cough up $1 for his
colleagues just then passing among them with bottles of the
medicine.

Wilson and his colleagues had traveled through half of Washington State by the time word reached Benicia that Wilson was trouping with a medicine show. The report was forwarded by a maternal uncle, Eugene Semple, who had served as governor of Washington and felt the family was being disgraced by Wilson's new career. At an urgent family council it was decided to send Addison to retrieve Wilson from Doc Slocum's clutches before he could sink any lower. It took Addison weeks to search out Slocum's wandering band. By the time he caught up with the troupe Wilson had left it in a huff. It seemed that Slocum had decided Wilson was too young to be entirely persuasive as a medical savant and urged that he adopt a new persona as a saintly Quaker practitioner. Wilson was handed a wide-brimmed hat and instructed to sprinkle his discourse with "thees" and "thous." Wilson felt his personality was being smothered in the new characterization; furthermore, he didn't feel comfortable in a role calling for emanations of a strong spiritual quality.

Wilson's dissatisfaction led him to part company abruptly with Dr. Slocum and his traveling dispensary. In lieu of severance pay Wilson absconded with the performing bear. To all his other crimes, Addison learned, Wilson had added bear kidnapping and was liable to prosecution if Doc Slocum ever learned his whereabouts.

Addison resumed his search and finally got on Wilson's trail across the Montana border. Wilson had converted the bear from toe dancing and juggling to prizefighting. He had taught the bear a few rudimentary punches, equipped him with outsize boxing gloves, and was challenging all comers, human or otherwise, to meet his champion in the ring. Though tied to a stake to prevent him from being carried away by ursine enthusiasm for combat, the bear usually

managed to knock out a human opponent with one or two
swipes of his sheathed paws. That bear, as Wilson often
sighed in reminiscence, was the most dependable confederate he ever found.

When Addison caught up with him in a Montana village,
Wilson had just succeeded in matching his champion against
a local fighter named Breen. The latter was a dog, an out-
sized mongrel that oddly resembled a bear. Wilson had bet
all his funds on the bear and refused to return to Benicia
with Addison until the match was held. Further, he persuaded Addison to bet everything but their return fare on
the contest.

Addison then demanded an inspection of the bear's opponent, whose backers claimed he was the most ferocious
beast on four legs. He was led into the darkened interior of a
barn, in which he was shown a burly creature with gleaming
fangs and a slavering maw.

"What is it?" Addison whispered. "The Hound of the
Baskervilles?"

"Just a stray mutt," Wilson airily replied. "Won't last a
round with my boy."

The bearbaiting contest was scheduled for the next day.
Every male in town turned out for the spectacle. Wilson led
his bear out, tied him to a stake in the ring, and proudly
watched as the bear reared up and flailed the air with his
paws.

Then his ravening opponent was escorted from the barn
to the ring. The gong rang, and everyone waited for the fur
to fly. Instead the two combatants happily sniffed at each
other. Wilson's bear woofed with joy. The other animal
sidled coyly toward him, all but simpering. Some zoologist
in the crowd pointed out that Breen, the dog, was actually a
winsome young female bear. The scheduled fight to a finish

turned into a mating dance. And the two bears scampered
out of the ring and into the wilds.

On the subject of the wagers, a hometown verdict was
handed down. Wilson's bear had refused to fight, it was
pointed out, so all the stake money was turned over to the
local bettors. The brothers Mizner vigorously protested
until it was apparent that they were outvoted 200 to 2, and
besides, the local constable gave them twelve hours to get
out of town.

All they had between them were two return tickets to
Benicia and a brotherly dispute over the wisdom of matching a male bear to fight a female bear, over the question of
whether Wilson was smart enough to tell a dog from a bear.
They were distracted from the quarrel only when starvation
overtook them on the long daycoach journey through Montana, Idaho, and Oregon. In the later stages of their journey,
Addison had great difficulty in restraining Wilson from
mugging the candy butcher.

The bosom of his family proved a bit prickly for Wilson,
who was arraigned before his seniors on his return to Benicia. It was a family custom to support one of its rare
delinquents with constant moralizing and to keep him under
round-the-clock surveillance. At nineteen Wilson found it
irksome to be bathed in so much solicitude. Mama's former
Angel Birdie flew the coop again and fetched up on the
Barbary Coast as the resident pianist of a parlor house,
meanwhile looking for a cabaret to employ his talents as a
singer. The donkeyish timbre of his voice when he hit a high
note refused to dismay him; the boos and catcalls with which
his repertoire was received, it seemed to him, always came
from the males in his audience. The adverse masculine

reaction he laid to jealousy or a lack of appreciation for the finer things in life.

On quitting the staff of the parlor house, he resumed his singing career on tour with a vaudeville troupe as an "illustrated-song artist." He sang tear-jerking ballads while magic-lantern slides thrown on the screen behind him illustrated his themes; the female part of the audience snuffled in appreciation, and the males yearned for a supply of rotten vegetables. In the entertainment business such a performer was regarded as a filler between the worthier acts and was ranked, professionally and socially, somewhere between the Japanese acrobats and the slowest learner in the trained-dog troupe. Some fellow performers questioned whether an illustrated-song artist shouldn't be required to dress out in the alley.

Later Wilson kept this phase of his career, lasting about a year, a carefully guarded secret. He would admit to anything from mopery to operating a badger game, but not that. It came to light during the twenties, when Mark Kelly, the sardonic redhead who was then sports editor of the Los Angeles *Examiner*, wrote a column about the seamier aspects of the Mizner past. Kelly was a friend of Mizner's, but that didn't prevent him from exulting when, shortly after the column appeared in print, he received a letter from a man in Fresno enclosing an old vaudeville program in which the youthful Mizner's photograph was published. "Is this man Mizner the six-fingered thief who came to Fresno under the name of Gerard Salvini, the Golden-Throated Thrush?" Kelly's correspondent wanted to know. The Fresno man went on to explain that Signor Salvini had attempted to elope with the daughter of a prominent man, a girl of tender years and hitherto-unblemished reputation, had been thwarted, and had escaped sentencing to San Quentin only by skipping town before he could be arrested.

Confronted with that documentary evidence, Mizner confessed to having been billed as the Golden-Throated Salvini and added, "I didn't think there was another man alive who knew about that." He implored Kelly to keep it a secret. Only after Mizner's death did Kelly reveal that episode.

Wilson's singing career was terminated, in any case, when one of his older brothers sent out a call for a gathering of the clan. A sub-Arctic gold rush was about to begin, and there was no reason the Mizners shouldn't assume a proprietary interest.

2

WILSON'S ONE-MAN GOLD RUSH

FOR years rumors had been drifting down the long jigsaw coastline from Alaska that there were fabulous gold deposits in the creeks and hillsides of Alaska and Yukon Territory. Veteran prospectors said it was only a question of time before the new Golconda was uncovered. It had been a long time since the California Mother Lode, Pikes Peak, the Dakota Badlands, and other celebrations of the gold-hunting instinct. America needed a golden shot in the arm after the depression of '93.

The Mizners were among the first to become aware of the lucrative possibilities of a stampede to the Northern territories. Edgar Ames Mizner, one of Wilson's older brothers, was placed in charge of a chain of trading posts which his company, the Alaska Commercial, established in the Yukon Valley early in 1896. Thus, he was among the first to learn of startling finds along the tributaries of the Yukon, principally a forlorn stream in the tundra called the Klondike. Edgar's first thought was that the gold rush he foresaw

should be well manned by Mizners. He telegraphed word to
Benicia to round up all available and able-bodied members
of the family and dispatch them North.

Not all of Wilson's brothers declared themselves eligible
for Northern adventures. Reverend Henry, in St. Louis,
stated that his wealthy parishioners needed him more than
an unwashed and uncouth horde of would-be miners. Lansing, the oldest, maintained that it would be undignified for
him to drop his briefs and torts to take up the pick and
shovel.

That left William, the doctor; Addison, the painter and
determined bohemian, and Wilson, the renegade and
singer—the family culls. William was large and powerfully
built but determinedly lazy. His medical education seemed
to have exhausted him. But he allowed that he might be
willing to go North if reaping a fortune didn't involve too
much stoop labor and manual exercise for hands dedicated
to healing.

When Edgar's bulletin reached Benicia, Addison's artistic career in San Francisco was in the doldrums. Eccentric
even for a Mizner, he had attained a local celebrity for his
sartorial displays, which included appearances on the street
in billowing silk pajamas with a brace of chow dogs towing
him like a barge. People on Nob Hill able to afford to
commission a portrait decided that he was a little too offbeat
to be allowed to set up his easel in their salons. For a time he
had worked in an architect's office, but his expansive style of
living had resulted in the accumulation of a mound of bills,
duns, writs, and summonses. The only remedy was flight.
He had headed for the Sierra foothills and was working as a
miner near Delta when the newsletter from Edgar arrived.

The news from the Yukon caught Wilson at his lowest
ebb, no longer touring as an illustrated-song artist, sunken

back into the tidal flats of the Barbary Coast. He was singing in a dive called the Crenmore, where the drinks were often flavored with chloral hydrate, a specific against sleeplessness vulgarly known as knockout drops. He had also set up light housekeeping with a sloe-eyed, volatile brunette entertainer named Rena Fargo.

An uncle hearing of the plans to ship the three youngest, least promising, and most troublesome Mizners to the frozen solitudes had only one question regarding the project. "Is Alaska," he wondered, "far enough?"

Edgar Ames Mizner's scheme to get in on the ground floor of the prospective gold rush by enlisting the support of his three younger brothers can be explained only by the fact that he hadn't seen them for many years and knew nothing of their aversion for physical labor. Ordinarily astute and hard-headed, with so authoritarian a manner that he was nicknamed the Pope, Edgar based the success of his plan to enrich the whole family on the willingness of William, Addison, and Wilson to stretch their muscles and voluntarily endure countless hardships. He had staked out claims near others proved to be gold-bearing in the vicinity of Dawson, near the confluence of the Klondike and the Yukon. Working them depended on the strong backs of the younger Mizners, but William and Wilson considered themselves to be executive types, if anything, and only Addison, for short periods of time, could be persuaded of the dignity of hard labor.

Equally chancy was the assignment of Wilson to the task of overseeing the logistics of the Mizner expeditionary force. With someone else's credit at his disposal, Wilson was likely to lavish it on laborsaving devices and luxuries better suited to a grand duke's hunting party. Wilson had acquainted himself with the strip of Alaskan coast they would traverse through a study of geography books and commendably had boned up on the high passes, the portages, the chain of lakes and rivers—an obstacle course that would break many a brave heart—which stood between them and the valley of the Yukon. The only practical way to negotiate that rugged terrain was to cut trees, whipsaw them into planks, and build flat-bottomed boats on the spot. Then the voyagers would be confronted by many miles of earnest rowing.

Dismayed at the prospect of coarsening hands dedicated to more delicate tasks, Wilson and William invented a sort of iceboat which would allow them to skim over the frozen lakes and rivers while less imaginative gold seekers holed up for the winter, built boats, and waited for the spring thaw. The Mizner cutter was a shallow-draft craft equipped with two heavy steel runners and a sail. It weighed about a ton. Just how their iceboat could be packed over the man-killing trail that led over the Chilkoot Pass between coastal Skagway and the lakes inland was not part of their deliberations.

Early in autumn '96 the three brothers, with adjurations from parents, older brothers, and uncles to "make something of yourselves" ringing in their ears, left San Francisco with a small mountain of equipment purchased on brother Edgar's letter of credit and including all sorts of little comforts to sustain them on the journey. One of the latter was Wilson's girlfriend, Rena Fargo, who, to the surprise of his brothers, boarded the train with Wilson.

"Just going as far as Seattle, Addie," Wilson assured his brother regarding Rena. Addison was relieved. Surely even the harebrained Wilson wouldn't drag along a female on an expedition like theirs.

In Seattle they boarded the steamer *Tonka* bound for

Dyea, the port of Skagway, and bearing a full load of gold rushers who were equally fast off the mark.

Addison was taken aback to discover Wilson and Rena snugly settled in one of the *Tonka*'s cabins.

"Only going as far as Juneau," Wilson explained. "She's got a job waiting for her in a Juneau honky-tonk."

"Being a Mizner, I showed no surprise," Addison later wrote in his vastly entertaining, though highly inaccurate memoir. He was, however, greatly concerned. Before they left San Francisco, their mother had made Addison swear he would serve as Wilson's moral watchdog and protect him from his known frailties. Rena certainly qualified as a frailty. And Addison couldn't help wondering whether a warm-blooded brunette was really standard equipment for survival in what the newspapers called the Frozen North, and whether Edgar could be persuaded she was rightly a part of the table of organization.

"Were Wilson and Rena married?" Addison recalled wondering repeatedly during the journey. "Or was it better if they were not?"

As he explained in his memoirs, Wilson was his penance—a lifelong cross to bear—for his own misdeeds. Looking back on their relationship, Addison saw himself as Wilson's shield and buckler. "I have been a mother to him all my life. He seldom wrote a letter home and for years I lied for him in mine. At heart, I always hoped he would at any minute turn to the dullness of righteousness and become a God-fearing, outstanding character. He had always been his own worst enemy, thinking it smart to know the doings of the lowest characters and, generally, getting the blame for their indiscretions, where he generally was absolutely innocent. So, it was with this delusion I always wrote to Mother."

Rena failed to detach herself from the party to resume her career in Juneau. When they reached Skagway, she moved into a room with Wilson.

"To save expenses," Wilson blithely explained, surely one of the oddest excuses in the long history of concubinage.

When the Mizners and their female traveling companion landed in Skagway, that gateway to the goldfields was a greater hazard to transients than anything that lay ahead on the journey to the Yukon. S. B. Steele of the Royal Canadian Mounted Police paid a visit to Skagway during this period and reported, "At night the crash of bands, shouts of 'Murder!' and cries for help mingled with the cracked voices of the singers in the variety halls."

One Jefferson Randolph Smith, better known as Soapy, and his gang of miscreants had taken over Skagway and were running it along the lines Al Capone would follow on the South Side of Chicago. He and his associates—Kid Jimmy Fresh, Doc Baggs, Judge Van Horn, Frisco Red Harris, Slim Jim Foster, and other disorderly characters —administered Skagway's affairs from the backroom of Soapy's saloon. Soapy preferred to use his persuasive powers, which were considerable, but he could not always control his colleagues' tendency to settle disputes by pulling a trigger.

Wilson, who studied Soapy's methods with great interest, would always consider him one of the great men in the ancient profession of bunco and its allied arts. Though he was still only in his mid-thirties, Soapy Smith had a lengthy career behind him. He had risen from operator of a shell game to become a dominant force in the Denver underworld. He was a close student of the flaws in human nature which allowed a confidence man to thrive. "When I see anyone looking in a jewelry store window thinking how they would like to get away with the diamonds," he once said, "an irresistible desire comes over me to skin them." One of his own foibles was a hatred for the nickel-in-the-slot music boxes, the prototype of the jukebox. He devised a way of jamming them with a slightly flattened nickel, which would make them play indefinitely. The music box in Denver's Union Station once played "Maggie Murphy" for six hours until Soapy's nickel was jacked out. Soapy was a man of Napoleonic ambition, once having invaded Mexico with the intention of organizing a foreign legion and taking over the country. Angrily expelled by Mexico, he returned to Denver to find that Sam and Lou Blonger had taken over the local underworld and decreed that he would have to give them half of his gang's take if he wanted to operate. Shortly thereafter he transferred himself and his followers to Skagway.

The Alaskan port did not submit without resistance to Soapy's rule, which included a ruthless extortion from every person who passed through on his way to the Yukon. A few respectable citizens organized a Committee of 101 to establish law and order by vigilante methods; Soapy countered by forming the Committee of 303 and putting the Committee of 101 out of business. But he knew how to cajole public opinion. Just as Al Capone would establish soup kitchens in Chicago during the Depression, Soapy handed out money to indigent wayfarers and saw that his benefactions were widely known and thereby excused his more nefarious activities. The Robin Hood legend is perdurable and usually efficacious.

Wilson not only studied his methods with professional interest but always claimed that Soapy was one of his limited pantheon—an assorted lot of heroes which included Governor Alfred E. Smith, H. L. Mencken, Ambrose Bierce, Jimmy Walker, Bat Masterson, and heavyweight champion Jack Johnson, all of whom had one quality in common: style.

And style was what Wilson admired and would endlessly seek to attain.

Later he would admit that Soapy's operations, from the professional viewpoint, could be criticized for being heavy-handed on occasion, usually because of the excesses of his confederates. "No less than fifty people were killed by Soapy's gang," he would recall, frowning over the theory of massacre as an instrument of municipal administration, "and fights were nothing but rough mutilations in which the stranger hadn't a chance. As is usually true, the underlings of Soapy were more vicious than he ever was, but it was his power that made it possible." Eventually Soapy was forced into a shoot-out with a public-spirited citizen, and both were killed in the exchange. The lesson of Soapy Smith's career, to Wilson, was that a decent crook should stay out of politics.

Once Wilson and his brothers plucked up their courage for the assault on the Chilkoot Pass, which towered above Skagway, they found that Rena Fargo, taking up no more than 100 pounds of their total baggage, was highly useful in her special way: exerting her charms on a horde of men deprived of female company.

While they were still in Skagway, the Mizners had been approached by a huge black-bearded man named Betterled who had three four-horse teams that he employed in freighting supplies between Skagway and the summit of Chilkoot. Betterled offered to haul the Mizners' supplies free of charge, for "nothing but friendship." He admitted to being smitten with Rena Fargo. The brothers agreed to accept Betterled's offer, the alternatives being to pack the supplies themselves, including those heavy steel runners for the iceboat, or pay Indian porters the inflated rate of 30 cents per 100 pounds.

They soon learned the motive behind Betterled's gesture. He had mistaken Wilson for his brother Edgar, who, it was known, had staked a number of promising claims up in the Klondike country. With more assurance than discretion, Betterled approached Rena with a proposition. She would induce Edgar (Wilson) to put the claims in her name; they would then be married and would live happily ever after on the profits from the Mizner claims.

Rena, of course, revealed Betterled's plot to her consort. Wilson instructed her to play along with Betterled, since he had already begun hauling their supplies to Sheep Camp, six miles from the summit of Chilkoot.

Somehow Betterled learned that the Mizners were on to his scheme. Abandoning all pretense of friendship, he left them sitting on a mountain of supplies with six steeply upward miles to be negotiated. They were overwhelmed at the task ahead of them. The last half mile of the upper trail through the pass zigzagged along a cliff past dead horses and exhausted men. Murals of gold rushers slogging up Chilkoot like an army of overburdened ants became almost as famous in saloon art as Custer's Last Stand. Yet it wasn't quite the man-killer it was to be portrayed in Arctic literature of the Jack London-Rex Beach school. Young men of determination and in good condition could make it without much difficulty. One Mike Mahoney, in fact, carried a grand piano over the pass on his broad and willing back.

Of the three Mizners only Addison was eager to meet the challenge. He tore into the job of packing their supplies to the summit of the pass with an enthusiasm that wrung a crafty admiration from his brothers. Dr. William, who was six feet three and built like the Terrible Turk, and Wilson, who was an inch taller and equally formidable in structure, mostly sat around and cheered Addison on. Addison's temper finally exploded one day when, pausing in his labors like a blown horse, he overheard the two intellectuals discussing plans for an aerial route over the pass, the basis of which would be a cluster of hot-air balloons which would lift supplies over the Chilkoot and would be equipped with rudders to allow them to maneuver against the tricky winds screeching down the pass. William and Wilson were working it all out down to the last detail, nominating themselves as president and chairman of the board of the Mizner Aerial Navigation Company, the affairs of which would be dictated from the Riviera, when Addison blew up. He forcefully suggested that they expend their hot air on helping him haul the components of Wilson's collapsible iceboat.

During their labors on the trail, they witnessed the crude workings of frontier-style justice, a summary affair which convinced Wilson that he would have to keep a tight rein on his acquisitive instincts. A miner's court had been convened to try three men charged with stealing food, a crime in that country considered worse than murder or even claim jumping. One of the defendants was found not guilty, another committed suicide, and the third, having been convicted, was flogged by a sadistic dwarf and sent reeling back down the trail to Skagway with a sign attached to his lacerated back: "Thief: Pass him along!" The suicide was dumped into an unmarked grave along the trail while a minister in the throng quoted over it, "But he that maketh haste to be rich shall not be unpunished." Wilson thought it a curious choice of text to be hurled at a mob determined to "maketh haste" for the gold of the interior.

Hauling the iceboat slowed up the Mizners' progress so much that they, with Rena Fargo still in tow, arrived on the shores of Lake Bennett just in time to be trapped by the winter. There was nothing to do but hunker down against the icy blasts and the endless snowfall. Wilson's iceboat, it developed, sounded better than it could perform. There would be no breezy sail into Dawson past the camps of stranded fellow stampeders. The snow on the chain of lakes leading to the Yukon Valley was too deep for iceboating. Their only recourse was to go into winter quarters.

Meanwhile, the Mizner group seethed with recrimination. Wilson was roundly denounced for his iceboat theory. Addison realized that he had been conned into doing most of the donkey work thus far and announced that he was going into hibernation. William and Wilson, he told them, would have to spend the winter cutting down trees and whipsawing them into lumber for shelter, firewood, and boatbuilding.

Only Wilson and Rena were on speaking terms, for reasons which also didn't sit too well with his brothers. Why hadn't their selfish junior considered the matter of female companionship for them, too?

The irritations of living together at close quarters all winter—a complex malady known as cabin fever, often more lethal than a cholera epidemic—soon frayed the fraternal bonds beyond immediate repair. William refused to take part in the lumbering operations, pointing out that they were a job for more youthful muscles, and besides, he couldn't risk injuring hands trained for surgery. So Addison had to give up hibernation and help Wilson in felling and trimming spruce trees and then sawing them into planks. The trimmed tree trunks were placed on a scaffold six feet off the ground. One man stood on the scaffold and pulled the two-man saw upward; the other pulled it back down. Possibly the bitterest controversy in the Yukon country that winter was over whether the top man or the bottom man had the tougher job. The top man had the muscle-straining job of hauling the whipsaw up, but the bottom man got a constant stream of sawdust in his eyes. Lifelong friends quarreled over the subject, split up their possessions, sometimes even sawed their tents and sacks of flour in half to divide up the community property and be quit of each other.

Quarreling incessantly, Wilson and Addison changed positions a dozen times a day. Finally, they came to blows when Wilson called Addison a "big stupid dumb brute" and struck him over the head with a calking iron. Dr. William got off his pallet long enough to stop the fight before more blood was spilled, not because it didn't delight him to see his two younger brothers brawling but because he knew he would be arraigned by their mother if either brother was seriously damaged.

The estrangement between Wilson and Addison was only widened by an incident involving, perhaps inevitably, Rena Fargo. Wilson and William one day decided to relieve the monotony of the camp by exploring the surrounding spruce forests. While they were gone, Addison and Rena mixed up a horrendous punch from twelve bottles of Jamaica ginger and six bottles of lemon extract, a concoction potent enough to paralyze half of Seattle's skid row. "We cemented our friendship," Addison later explained in regard to his drinking companion, "but did not commit incest." It looked mighty suspicious to Wilson, however, when he returned with brother William and found brother Addison and his girlfriend in total disarray.

By the time the ice began breaking up on Lake Bennett the three brothers detested the sight of one another and were constant prey to meditating on the joys of fratricide. "Each day," Addison would remember, "we did something more foolish than the day before, but, as we all hated each

other, anything was better than sitting around scowling and
thinking of new things to fight about."

When the landscape finally thawed out completely, the
Mizners split up, vowing to one another they would never
speak again if some misfortune caused their paths to cross.
Fortunately each had a boat to sail away in his chosen
company. Wilson and Rena pushed off in one boat, with
Wilson shaking his fist from the stern. William took off in
another with a newfound partner. Addison departed in the
third with a character named Och Gott Louie, whose broken
English Addison found immensely preferable to Wilson's
witticisms and William's medical pontificating.

Wilson and his traveling companion sailed down the lakes
and made it over the Whitehorse Rapids in a craft called the
"Klondike coffin," a boxlike improvisation which constantly
sprung leaks and required frantic bailing out. Still in the first
wave of the gold rush, they reached Dawson just as its
population was expanding fortyfold. Wilson figured there
was a place for a man of his capabilities, especially one with
such a toothsome partner.

One thing he was determined to avoid was coming under
the influence of brother Edgar, whose disposition made
even William's and Addison's seem angelic in comparison.
As Wilson quickly learned, Pope Edgar was detested from
one end of the Yukon to the other, and that was a distance of
1,200 miles. His high-handedness had become a legend in
the North Country. Only Addison was willing to fall in with
Edgar's plans to work his claims with his brothers' muscles.
En route to Dawson, Dr. William had turned back down the
trail and headed south for Skagway and California, leaving
behind him the aphorism, "This is a country for the young,

strong, and stupid." He was right on at least two counts.

Everything he heard of Edgar's activities as Yukon manager of the Alaska Commercial Company's interests convinced Wilson that mucking out a Dawson saloon would be preferable to falling under Edgar's domination. In the company's own history Edgar Mizner was described as a notably hard-fisted and overbearing character. Alaska Commercial had some reason for being disenchanted with Edgar; his lack of vision had already cost the company 50 percent of a rich gold strike. An Austrian named Antone Stander had staked out a highly promising claim on Eldorado Creek but needed a little credit to continue operations. When Stander applied at the Alaska Commercial's post at Forty Mile for food and other supplies in exchange for a piece of his action, Edgar coldly turned him down. He was informed that he would have to find a guarantor before Edgar would hand over so much as a sack of flour. Stander then found a Californian named Clarence Berry, a frugal fruit grower from Fresno, willing to back him. The Austrian agreed to trade half of his claim for half of Berry's on a less promising creek. The result was that Berry took millions out of his acquisition, became the biggest winner in the Klondike, stayed out of the honky-tonks, and went home a multimillionaire. The story of that transaction was widely retailed and reflected little credit on Edgar's judgment of men.

Wilson had already decided on conducting his own kind of one-man gold rush, a plan which didn't include slaving away on Edgar's claims. Edgar had made his brothers' journey to the Klondike possible, but Wilson was not overwhelmed by gratitude. In later years it must have galled Edgar to reflect that if he had backed Antone Stander instead of his unreliable brothers, he would have been a lot better off.

As Wilson sized up the possibilities, there were really two gold rushes going on. One was composed of musclebound types hacking away at the frozen tundra; the other consisted of a parasitical element that always formed around such ventures. You could either make your strike in a creek bed, if you worked your fool head off and were extraordinarily lucky, or you could prospect for gold in the pockets of your fellow stampeders. A good share of those who came North were crooks, whores, pimps, dive keepers, madams, gamblers, and speculators. This group, he believed, would come out a lot richer than the suckers who dug for gold, took their dust and nuggets to Dawson, and were gulled, rolled, swindled, diddled, conned, aced, or seduced out of the contents of their moosehide pokes.

The great outdoors and the bleak sub-Arctic vistas held no attraction for Wilson, or as he put it, "Flesh beats scenery." His kind of people were the flimflammers who lay in wait behind swinging doors, under lamplight, with the siren call of ragtime piano, clinking chips, gurgling bottles, sweet-talking bar girls, slip-slap of cards being dealt by expert mechanics, the sigh of gold dust being poured on the scales behind the bar. Dawson was simply the Barbary Coast moved north 1,000 miles. A sucker was a sucker whether he wore Congress gaiters or mukluks.

His refusal to join Edgar and Addison outraged his brothers, who now regarded him as an unredeemable black sheep. The Pope excommunicated him and, worse yet, refused him cash or credit. Addison left Dawson for Edgar's claim, later recalling, "I did have qualms of conscience in leaving my baby brother behind in this den of iniquity." He was further disturbed by reports that Wilson and his girlfriend were staying at Dawson's best hotel, the Dominion, and wondered how Wilson would get the money to pay the hotel bill. Knowing Wilson, he expected his brother would wind up as grist for Canadian justice, if somebody didn't shoot him first.

Actually Wilson's agile mind had turned first, not to crime, as his brother feared, but to artistry. During their first weeks in Dawson, he and Rena teamed up as a singing act which played the circuit of local saloons. In one of the cafés which endured Wilson's baritone for a brief engagement, Alexander Pantages was working as a waiter and laying the foundation of theatrical fortune. Pantages, as Wilson later related, wore leather pockets in his trousers and used them to smuggle steaks out of the kitchen, which he then sold for $10 apiece. He also had the sawdust concession in the café. Volunteering to work as night porter without extra pay, Pantages washed gold dust which had leaked from the pokes of the carefree miners from the sawdust on the floor.

His observations of Pantages' methods convinced him it would be more profitable to handle the miners' gold than to remind them of home with his ballads. Rena Fargo continued as a single while he went to work as a cashier, or weigher, at the Monte Carlo, a combination saloon, variety theater, and gambling hall operated by Swiftwater Bill Gates and Jack Smith. His pay was three ounces of gold a day—gold was worth a lot less in Dawson in 1898 than in Zurich in 1974—plus stealage rights.

A gold weigher held a position of some dignity and trust, often misplaced. He presided with an air of great probity behind a pair of massive brass scales and measured out the dust which was converted into whiskey, poker chips, and dance hall girls' favors.

The trick for the weigher was to make some of that dust

stick to his own fingers. Some weighers cultivated man-
darin-length fingernails to collect the golden grains; others
kept their fingers moist and dusted them off in the leather
pockets of their trousers; still others wore their hair long
and well oiled, frequently running their fingers through it
and ending the night with a vigorous, lucrative shampoo.
Mizner's technique was simpler but more effective: Each
week he placed a new piece of carpet under his feet and
burned the old one, a smelting process which he claimed
(with his congenital airiness about statistics) was worth
$2,500 a week to him. "I weighed a million and a half dollars'
worth of gold dust at Swiftwater Bill's joint," he later told a
New York journalist, "and never made a mistake that wasn't
in favor of the house."

The house apparently caught on to his homemade smelter, possibly because its carpet kept diminishing week by
week, and later that summer he was employed as a faro
dealer in various Dawson gambling saloons. Once again, as
Addison related, Rena was his business partner. In Wilson's
philosophy luck was something that could always stand im-
provement; you couldn't wait around for a handout from the
high table. So Rena, pretending to be a stranger, would
appear at the table where Wilson was dealing and have a
miraculous run of luck. That dodge couldn't be worked too
often, so Wilson kept changing his places of employment.

In the last place where they operated in tandem, Wilson,
carried away by enthusiasm, dealt her such remarkable
hands that she broke the faro bank. The proprietor bustled
over to investigate. He couldn't bring himself to suspect his
jovial dealer was involved, but Rena with all those winnings
had to have cheated. He bashed Rena over the head with a
small log. Always somewhat deficient in chivalry, Wilson

did not attempt to defend her; that would have given him away. Rena was deeply offended by his abstention and broke off their partnership.

It became apparent however, that Wilson didn't need any female inspiration for his misconduct. He was involved in a number of escapades which made his respectable brothers wonder whether they shouldn't arrange for his deportation by the Mounted Police. One scrape that landed him in the Dawson lockup involved a stolen typewriter. That he would have been involved in that kind of heist was unbelievable to his later collaborators on Broadway and in Hollywood, who noted his aversion to the typewriter and laid it to laziness. Possibly it was due to what happened in Dawson. As Wilson explained it, in his roundabout fashion, his difficulties arose from his youthful faith in friendship and his services to local law enforcement, which included nominating an old pal for police chief. "I had faith in that man," he would recall. "He made the first set of burglar's tools ever turned out in Alaska. I elected him chief of police. I paid his expenses and managed his campaign and organized a reception for him the day he took office. I even pinned a gold star on his chest.

"And the first man he arrested was me!

"At that time, there was only one typewriter in town. Somebody had stolen it and sold it to a butcher, who thought it was a cash register. Three friends of mine were in danger of being put away for life. We needed the typewriter to draw up an appeal, and in the emergency I borrowed it from the butcher shop when the butcher was out. My new police chief arrested me—and that was the true-blue comradeship of the North for you."

By his own account, Wilson was always getting in trouble through an excess of humanitarian instinct. In his youth, he would maintain, he often experienced twinges of sentiment.

Thus his involvement in a chocolate robbery. According to the story told by Sid Grauman, then a Klondike scuffler like Mizner but later a Hollywood theater magnate whose cement forecourt immortalized (loosely speaking) the footprints of Hollywood stars, Wilson once held up a candy store on behalf of Nellie the Pig. Nellie Lamore, whose turned-up nose accounted for her sobriquet, was a very pretty dance hall girl. She expressed a raging desire for some chocolate candy, which was then worth its weight in gold.

Wilson put on a black mask, equipped himself with a revolver, and entered the candy store, possibly shouting, "Your chocolates or your life!" The owner shoved his cash register at Wilson and told him to take it and be gone. As for his chocolates, they were locked in his safe and Wilson would have to shoot him before he'd open it. Wilson figured it wasn't worth killing a man for a box of vanilla creams, so he fled with the cash register. Then he stripped off his mask, stashed his gun, and hurried to a nearby saloon, where he began rendering "Sweet Alice, Ben Bolt" with throbbing emotion. His old friend the police chief showed up, having suspected only Mizner would try to loot a candy store, and accused him of being the masked bandit. A dozen witnesses sprang up from the audience to swear Wilson had been vocalizing for hours. The chief left, and Wilson gratefully delivered an encore.

In an informal, unscholarly but perceptive way, he would serve as the sociologist of Klondike gold-rush manners and mores. His insight was never sharper than in detailing the rigorous caste system established by the female contingent in the Klondike. Social barriers did not exist among the men, he explained, and there was a free and easy association between millionaires and barflies, but the women were violently class-conscious.

"The kept ladies," he said, "ignored the dancehall girls,
no matter what their ability might be. In the dancehalls the
entertainers who went to the boxes and did a little light
finger-lifting (that is, pickpocketing), as well as dancing with
the visitors, were a privileged set and very haughty toward
the girls who merely danced without thieving. Dollar-a-
dance girls, they were called, receiving a cut in dust of
whatever their partners drank. Of course, there were girls
in town who had no particular ability on any dance floor and
were what might be termed 'weak.' Everybody ignored
them in the presence of anyone else; but they did a land
office business, always. They included some of the plainest
fancy women imaginable."

Any departures from the strict pecking order, he noted,
usually resulted in one of those hair-pulling, eye-scratching
affrays which were one of the more cherished forms of
outdoor entertainment under the midnight sun. As a case to
illustrate his point, Wilson would cite the occasion when
Seattle Emily spoke familiarly to Bertha the Adder. Bertha
tore off all of Emily's clothing, chased her through the
Dawson streets, pelted her with rocks, and finally drove her
into the shallows of the Yukon.

By autumn, 1898, there was another defection by a Mizner brother. Addison decided he couldn't face another
winter out on the tundra as foreman of the crew working
Edgar's claims, on which no spectacular finds had thus far
been made. Before leaving for the States, Addison sought a
reconciliation with Wilson because he knew he couldn't face
their mother without being able to report on how Mama's
Angel Birdie was doing.

Addison found his younger brother bedded down at the
Dominion Hotel, running a fever, with his cheeks dis-
tended. For once Wilson was utterly downcast and unable

to utter a wisecrack. "Poor kid got the mumps," Addison laconically reported, "and they weren't all in his neck. My heart and sympathy went out to him."

Some of the sympathy evaporated after Addison heard the stories of Wilson's recent capers circulating around Dawson's saloons. Nothing but divine intervention, it seemed to Addison, would snatch that brand from the burning. Reverend Henry was the family's plenipotentiary in dealing with spiritual matters, so Addison wrote the rector of Christ Church, St. Louis, for guidance.

Henry, however, could offer little but a spinsterish hand wringing and a bit of Pollyannaish philosophy. "I am dismayed," he wrote Addison, "that Wilson could actually be dishonest. We must stick to him as long as we can—come what may. Some day this may all be forgotten, horrible as it is now."

Fat lot of good that Epistle from St. Louis did, Addison thought, as he packed up and went back to civilization, leaving Wilson's upbringing and moral guidance to brother Edgar.

Wilson did flirt with respectability just before Addison left Dawson, if promoting a fight falls in that category. One of the local celebrities was Frank Slavin, an Australian so tall and long-armed he was known as the Sydney Cornstalk, who was the heavyweight champion of the British Empire. He was so fearsome a puncher that both Gentleman Jim Corbett and John L. Sullivan pretended to be deaf when Slavin challenged them for the world heavyweight championship.

Slavin trained on whiskey, like most fighters of his day, and apparently was overtrained one night at the Monte Carlo. A local ruffian named Biff Hoffman, also in his cups, tangled with him over the favors of a female member of the staff. Slavin was kayoed by a haymaker.

Wilson saw an opportunity and seized upon it. A "grudge match" between Slavin and Hoffman ought to be box-office magic, though pitting a mere saloon brawler against a sober professional fighter in the ring might be termed conspiracy to abet mayhem. The return match would take place on the stage of a dance hall which Wilson rented for the night.

Although it temporarily enriched its promoter, the fight did little to advance the fistic art. Slavin was so contemptuous of his opponent that he climbed into the ring wearing a white turtleneck sweater and spotless white flannels. A few seconds after the bell rang Slavin maneuvered Hoffman into a corner, launched a right cross that left Hoffman inert upon the canvas, and walked off with $1,000 for his night's work.

A short time later the Royal Mounted Police began rounding up various characters classified as "undesirable" and deporting them from Yukon Territory. It seemed an anti-American measure because so many of the parasitical element were Americans, but the Yukon was Dominion territory, and protest was futile.

On returning from his company's post at St. Michael, Edgar Mizner learned that Wilson's name was high on the list slated for deportation. Wilson's departure would have contributed to Edgar's peace of mind; on the other hand, it would damage Edgar's prestige if Wilson were kicked out of Dawson, which was almost as bad as being exiled from Port Said for general depravity. Just then Edgar was in bad odor with his company over the large number of letters written to Alaska Commercial's headquarters complaining of his tight-fisted attitude toward granting credit at the company's posts.

Wilson would have to be hauled back from the brink of delinquency by fabricating some instant respectability for him. With some understandable misgivings, Edgar appointed him foreman of the crew working his claims, the place recently vacated by Addison. Might make a man of him. Might also get the true empire-building Mizner blood stirring in his veins.

Confronted with the choice of being deported and facing yet another wrathful family council or going to work for Edgar, Wilson reluctantly chose the latter. A remote and isolated mining claim on a frozen creek was, as Wilson suspected, a terrible place to spend the long Arctic night. The nearest log-cabin saloon was miles away. It also distressed Wilson that the miners under his direction had been encouraged, or bullied, into working too hard. He pointed out to them that it was silly to exhaust themselves hacking away at the frozen creek bed for the niggardly pay they were receiving. The proper antidote to overwork, he allowed, was playing poker with the boss.

Later that winter Edgar made a surprise inspection trip to his property and found that operations had ground to a halt, that his whole pick-and-shovel crew were snugged down in their bunkhouse engaged in a marathon poker session with the foreman. Wilson was fired on the spot and sent back to Dawson to take his chances with the Mounties.

Hardheaded and self-righteous as he was, Edgar soon came a cropper himself. In whatever time he could spare from Alaska Commercial's ledgers, he had been wooing Grace Drummond, a beautiful but mercenary young woman known as the "toast of the Monte Carlo." They were more or less engaged when Charley Anderson, known as the Lucky Swede, appeared on the Monte Carlo scene fresh from locating a claim eventually worth $1,250,000 on a 500-foot stretch of creek bed. Anderson was smitten by Grace Drummond. How much cash on the barrelhead, he delicately inquired, would it take for her to jilt Edgar Mizner?

Fifty thousand, plus marriage, she briskly replied. Deal.

Edgar took it hard when Grace and the Lucky Swede left for a European honeymoon. In his weakened condition, he caught the gambling fever endemic in the Klondike and began playing roulette in the style of a Romanov princeling. Inevitably, with the enemies he had made through his hard-nosed attitude toward granting credit, word that he had lost $15,000 in one night on the roulette wheel at the Monte Carlo reached his company's Seattle headquarters. Edgar, who had done so much of the spadework that made the company prosper when boom times came, was fired forthwith.

There was a moral in Edgar's comeuppance for his brother Wilson to take with him on further adventures in the North Country: Serious concern for other people's money will get you no place.

3

AT HOME IN NOME

WILSON loitered around Dawson until the spring of 1899 and finally decided to depart the gold-rush capital without any prodding from the authorities. He took a reading of the portents and came to the conclusion that, as he put it, "civilization had set in." A sturdy jailhouse had been constructed and, even more alarmingly, was "jammed in short order." Spending a few months in jail during the winter months wasn't the worst thing he could imagine, but the Royal Canadian Mounted Police, with a fiendish ingenuity, had instituted a work program for their prisoners. Now one had to work all day chopping wood.

There were other distressing omens, too. A railroad had been built over the passes from Skagway which would bring in tourists and other bourgeois types. Worst of all, the Klondike *Nugget* had started publishing a society column, a sure sign that respectable women were invading the place along with preachers, reformers, and other spoilsports. It had always been thus on the frontier: Lace curtains went up, and signs like Ye Olde Whore Shoppe came down. Soon Lousetown, where the red lights blazed like fireflies on a July night, would be a residential suburb.

During his last months around Dawson, he succumbed to an endemic type of feverish optimism which impelled hordes of men to drop whatever they were doing and rush out on the tundra. The stampedes, which even roused to action such congenitally lazy men as Wilson Mizner, would be caused by reports of a new Golconda located out on one of the creeks. Invariably either the reports proved false, or the stampeders arrived to find all the likely claims had been staked. "When I was in the Klondike," he would later shamefacedly recall, after explaining that there was a little bit of sucker in every wise guy, "I ran more than 300 miles on reports of various gold strikes. Half the people in the world burn out their bearings responding to false alarms."

On his last dash into the frozen wilderness, he had taken off in such a hurry that he brought with him, as iron rations, only a frozen doughnut. He broke a front tooth trying to gnaw on the doughnut. When he returned crestfallen to Dawson, he was given the nickname of the Yellow Kid after a comic-strip character with an incisor missing.

Restless, wind-broken, self-disgusted, he was in a mood for change when reports drifted in from the North that large quantities of gold had been found on the beaches of Nome. That northern outpost had another appealing quality for Wilson: It was in Alaska Territory, therefore part of the United States and beyond the inhibiting influence of the Canadian authorities.

The news of the massive finds around Nome in the midsummer of 1899 caused something like a mass evacuation of Dawson, whose surrounding creeks and one-man sluicing operations had given way to industrialized mining. Few had come North for a lunch-bucket job. "The story was beginning again," the most eloquent of Dawson's chroniclers, Pierre Berton, has written, "like a continuous show at a movie house. In Dawson, log cabins could be had for the taking as steamboat after steamboat, jammed from steerage to upper deck, puffed out of town en route to Nome. The saloon trade fell off; real estate dropped; dance halls lost their custom. Arizona Charlie Meadows announced that he would float his Palace Grand in one piece down the [Yukon] River to the new strike. Jacqueline, the dance hall girl, complained that her week's percentage would hardly pay her laundry bill. In a single week eight thousand people left Dawson forever. . . ."

The Nome rush almost equaled the Klondike in size and enthusiasm and greatly exceeded it in criminality. Thirty thousand people landed there from the summer of 1899 to the summer of 1900. The great attraction was the report of easy pickings; gold rushers used up most of their energy in reaching the scene of a strike. Around Nome the gold was found on the black-sand beaches. It was extracted by a simple process of rocking the gold-bearing sand in a sort of wooden cradle until the gold dust settled at the bottom.

Regarding the Nome rush, in which he participated as a member of the vanguard and acquired the material for several best-selling novels, Rex Beach recalled in his memoir, "So sensational were the reports of this new Golconda that another rush occurred as spectacular in its way as the Klondike stampede two years before. Every available derelict was chartered and inside of ten days after the ice went out of the Bering Sea, Nome grew from a town of three to thirty thousand people. . . .

"When that hysterical army was dumped ashore together with mountains of freight, fuel, mine supplies and building

materials, the chaos can be imagined. Nome itself, a thin
row of saloons, dugouts and canvas shelters, lay like a wagon
track between the surf and a treeless, spongy tundra that ran
back to a low range of inhospitable hills. Into the wet moss
and mud one's boots sank to the knees; aside from the sandy
beach there was not a dry place to stand and, of course,
nobody had time to sit down. . . . That was an exciting show.
There was no law to speak of; bickerings and quarrels went
on everywhere and a person could pick the sort of fight he
preferred. An occasional gun battle filled one with a not
unpleasant sense of insecurity inasmuch as the bystanders
usually suffered. . . ."

Easy and uncomplicated as local mining was, Wilson
arrived in Nome aboard a crowded river steamer with the
determination to avoid any direct metallurgical associations
himself. It was simpler to let other men rock their little
cradles and bring the gold to him for exchange into whatever
rude pleasures he might devise for them. The most profitable mining, he had observed in Dawson, was in other men's
moosehide pokes. "Never was I diverted," he would recall,
with almost the air of a Horatio Alger hero, "from my
intention of setting up a gambling shack and giving the boys
an outlet for their gold dust."

He later claimed that he arrived in Nome with a grubstake
of $20,000, but he offered no explanation of how he had
saved up that amount of money during his hand-to-mouth
existence in Dawson. Wilson was congenitally careless
about fiscal matters and in later life would often claim to
have been a multimillionaire several times during his
career. Those who knew him best subtracted at least three
zeros from any sum Wilson mentioned in regard to his
personal finances.

In Nome, with the rule of law no more firmly established

than in any other boomtown on American territory (in contrast with the wise Canadian practice of sending in hard-
nosed police and incorruptible judges as soon as such an
event mushroomed), Wilson's naturally predatory instincts
were finally turned loose, like a pack of baying hounds.

He opened a ramshackle casino called the McQuestion, a
combination gambling house and saloon with a bunkhouse
at the rear for the accommodation of weary, drunken, or
bankrupted patrons. Admittedly the games of chance were
delicately adjusted in favor of the house; its proprietor always believed in protecting himself against the vagaries of
luck and demonstrated a keen appreciation of the percen-
tages.

The McQuestion prospered amazingly, and if Wilson had
squirreled away the profits, he would have been able to
leave the Far North in a year or two with a sizable fortune.
Instead he succumbed to the high-rolling games at two
other Nome establishments with a classier atmosphere than
the McQuestion: the Great Northern Saloon operated by
Tex Rickard, who would become the leading promoter during the Dempsey/Tunney golden age of prizefighting, and
the Dexter Bar, whose proprietor was the self-proclaimed
ace of pistoleros, Wyatt Earp, of Dodge City, Tombstone,
and other places with half the population buried on Boot
Hill.

The result was that the wise guy got taken by wiser guys,
he lost the McQuestion after a few months, and again was
reduced to living by his wits. His Nome career became a
roller coaster of spectacular ups and downs. One night he
was buying champagne, the next he was stealing coal to keep
from freezing. He sat in on rigged poker games, operated
the badger game with comely acquaintances, and became
one of the founding fathers of the Nome underworld.

Every incoming ship reported to be bearing a cargo of female entertainers (not all of whom sang, danced, or played the musical saw) was met by Wilson and the Nome brass band. He cast himself in the role of the camp's leading bon vivant. One of the local witticisms had it that he could borrow money from a lamppost, or even Wyatt Earp, who kept a death grip on every dollar that came his way. His success with the small but colorful contingent of available women was later recalled with awe by fellow citizens of Nome. One actress said to be the "toast of Nome" during 1901, which was something like being Miss Plowshare of Keokuk, Iowa, afterward claimed that Wilson had married her in some sort of loosely sanctified ceremony. Wilson's reply was a simple, if unchivalrous, statement that he couldn't remember any such alliance.

He had certain advantages over his fellow malefactors, including a fertile imagination, a bold ingenuity, and a riotous sense of humor. It is possible, of course, to laugh your way right into the slammer. Early on, however, he had discovered that you could get away with almost anything if you were impudent enough. The law, like all the world, detests a solemn pinchpenny villain and goes lightly with a fellow who can make it laugh. In the threepenny opera of his Northern nights, Wilson formulated the first principle of lawlessness: Always leave your victims laughing or laughed at.

Outrageousness was the key to criminal success. He never committed small, meanly calculated misdeeds solely for the purpose of fattening his wallet. He was a sort of creative artist in crime who converted each caper, at least by his own recapitulations, into a sardonic little comedy.

Doubtless he was the animating spirit of a quixotic group of outlaws known as the Wag Boys. Certainly several of its members were among his closest associates, and their activities bore the Mizner stamp. According to Rex Beach, they "seldom molested orderly and industrious members of the community, preferring instead to hijack members of the floating population who were as predatory as they, or to aim their depredations at stores, mines or mercantile companies that could absorb a loss. . . . Among the nocturnal habitués of the saloons and gambling houses, however, they were known as perhaps the most extraordinary group of undesirables that had ever invaded the North. . . .

"There were something like eight men in the gang, they bore such monickers as Big and Little Jack Frost, Deaf Mike the Hobo Kid and so on and each had a record for evil-doing. It may well be that they were attracted to each other by a community of interests and banded together for mutual protection during the closed season when an alibi was worth more than a horse. Whatever the tie that united them, they respected it. Actually they outnumbered the agents of justice, and for that reason perhaps the law flew a flag of truce and ignored them as pointedly as possible. They were gamblers, thieves, stick-up men and why they called themselves the Wag Boys was another mystery. Quite likely it was because they possessed a bitter collective sense of humor and were given to unsmiling pranks of which some were fantastic and a few even sanguinary. Their motto seemed to be, 'Anything for a laugh.' "

One of Wilson's early victims in Nome was a young lawyer from Nevada named Key Pittman, later a distinguished lawmaker and chairman of the Senate Foreign Relations Committee. The summer of his arrival in Nome, Pittman sized up the local commodity market and decided to invest in coal futures. When winter came to that treeless tundra, he reasoned, fuel would be desperately needed. He arranged to have several tons of coal shipped to him before winter. As it turned out, the coal was so valuable that he was able to sell it by the pound. His coal was piled up in the yard behind his law office, and he watched it night and day with a loaded shotgun in easy reach.

Pittman's success as an entrepreneur was cagily observed by Wilson Mizner, who sized up the young Nevadan as hardheaded enough for his profession but subcutaneously a sentimentalist. One day he entered Pittman's office with a long face and a sad story which he related with violins sobbing, not quite audibly, in the background. According to Wilson, Rose, one of Nome's more amiable doxies, required immediate surgery; he had tried to borrow $200 from the bank for the operation but was told he would have to find a cosigner for the note. Pittman agreed to back his pledge, later explaining in self-defense that though he was "familiar with Mizner's wiles" he also "knew Mizner could be genuinely unselfish."

Pittman turned away from the window overlooking his coal pile long enough to sign the note and congratulate Wilson on his humanitarian instincts. Just as Wilson was hurrying out the door, he glanced out the window and saw four men known to be confederates of Wilson's fleeing on a sleigh loaded with a ton of the coal.

Later that afternoon, his faith in human nature greatly diminished, Pittman looked up the supposedly ailing Rose at Tex Rickard's casino and asked about her operation.

"What operation?" she inquired.

It came as a further shock to Pittman's self-esteem when the bank forced him to pay off the $200 note he had cosigned for Mizner.

Wilson's trickiness manifested itself in his avocation as a fight manager, an occupation which fascinated him for much of his career not only because pugilism appealed to his sporting instincts but also because of the opportunities it offered for mendacity, intrigue, and low-down trickery.

It was a promising field of endeavor because Nome was fight-crazy like the rest of turn-of-the-century America. Possibly the finest crop of fighters ever seen was then in the ring: Jim Corbett, Battling Nelson, Ad Wolgast, Jack Johnson, Jim Jeffries, Bob Fitzsimmons, a whole galaxy of fist-fighters of all weights and nationalities. In Alaska the gold rushers awaited the steamer-borne news of the outcome of a championship fight with more interest than the dispatches from the fighting fronts in the Caribbean and the Philippines.

Every Saturday night the Standard Theater in Nome was crammed for the matches promoted by Tex Rickard. Possibly the most memorable encounter ever staged at the Standard involved a pair of feuding Irishmen who accomplished a double knockout. One of the contestants was Paddy Ryan, a semipro, who was challenged from the ring by another combative Celt, who shouted that Ryan was a "dirty dog" and dared him to "show his cowardly length" on the stage. Ryan charged into the ring with a roar. It took the whole crew of stagehands to keep them apart until they could be fitted out with boxing gloves and bets laid in the audience. The two warriors met in the center of the ring "with the headlong charge of two buffaloes," as one witness later reported, and laid each other out with simultaneous haymakers.

Wilson acquired a small stable of willing lads, among them a youth from Seattle named Leo McKernan whose aggressive style appealed to Wilson. McKernan, the son of a Seattle sports editor who would change his name to Jack Kearns and become the most celebrated of American mana-

gers for several decades, was so eager to lay hands on the
gold dust reputed to be lying around the beaches that he
jumped off the ship which brought him from Seattle and
swam ashore. Mining, he found, was complicated by the
necessity of locating and establishing title to a claim. He
then joined the Mizner stable and fought a number of bouts
with mixed success. In prizefighting as in gold mining, he
learned from his mentor, sheer eagerness was not enough.

On his last appearance in the ring as a fighter, Kearns
faced a bigger and more experienced opponent. Manager
Mizner decided to equalize the contest by wrapping strips of
lead around Kearns' fists. Kearns' punch hitherto had been
considered of flyweight caliber, but in the first round he
appeared to have developed a paralyzing punch in both
hands. Even a feathery left jab raised a welt on his
opponent's face. But in the second round Kearns grew so
weary from throwing weighted punches that the other man
suddenly knocked him out.

Kearns then decided to bow out of prizefighting. As a
reward for his earnest efforts, Wilson got him a job as gold
weigher in one of the casinos and also initiated him in the
technique of that craft. He poured part of a jug of corn syrup
on Kearns' head and instructed the novice to keep running
his hands through his hair while presiding at the scales. At
the end of each shift Kearns' hair would be stiff with a golden
cement, and a shampoo would usually net him about $100.

Some years later Wilson would take a proprietary interest
in the firm of Rickard, Dempsey, & Kearns, with its
million-dollar gates at Madison Square Garden. He considered himself its unofficial founder. He reasoned that his
money, lost at Rickard's tables at the Great Northern, provided part of the stake Rickard used to promote the
heavyweight championship from the pursuit of a bauble into

one of the glories of American capitalism. His faux pas in mixing metallurgy with fistfighting, furthermore, had set Jack Kearns on a managerial path.

One of Wilson's more profitable sidelines was the badger game, a crude form of extortion which most professional criminals affect to despise. It requires little or no capital, merely a comely female accomplice. Wilson always boasted of his aptitude as an operator of the badger game. In Nome he operated in partnership with one of the more alluring dance hall girls, who played the erring wife, roped in the victims with her charms, and set them up for Wilson's bristling appearance as the wronged husband.

The occasion he often boasted of as demonstrating his quick-wittedness under trying circumstances involved a tomato can which earned him $10,000. His partner had alerted him to break into her room at a certain hour. Wilson, however, lingered too long in a saloon and was so fuddled by the intake of raw whiskey that he had to repair to his room to sleep off the effects. When he awakened, it was long after the appointed hour—and timing, of course, was the essence of such an operation. Worse yet, his revolver, another essential ingredient, was missing. An outrageous bluff was his only hope. On his way over to the girl's room, he picked up a tomato can and tore off the label.

He followed the usual scenario, broke down the door to the girl's room and found her in a compromising situation with the man she had picked up. Wild-eyed with simulated rage and grief, he raised the tomato can over his head, announced it was full of nitroglycerin, and shouted that he was going to blow himself, the "interloper," and his "wife" to smithereens. It was the only way, he said, to mend a broken heart.

The mark (as the victim was known in the argot of Wilson's

newfound profession), babbling something about $10,000
worth of gold dust in his possession which he would gladly
donate to assuage Wilson's outraged feelings, begged him to
reconsider.

Wilson struggled manfully with his emotions, thought
over the proposition while carelessly tossing the can from
one hand to the other, and finally agreed to accept the offer
and let the home wrecker leave in one piece.

Once the sucker had slunk away, the girl suggested it was
time to split the take.

Wilson, with a bemused air, handed her the tomato can.

"What the hell good will this do me?" she demanded.

"I don't know," Wilson said with a sigh, "but it just earned
me ten thousand dollars."

There was no doubt that his sense of opportunism was
extraordinarily well developed; it was almost like an extra
gland which secreted a keen awareness and fertilized an
amazing variety of schemes. Certainly it was functioning
superbly on Christmas Eve, 1900, the night when Diamond
Jim Wilson went to his reward and Wilson presided over the
lightning probate of his estate. In a few hours he demonstrated what legal miracles can be accomplished, even by an
unqualified jurist, if he is determined to slash away at red
tape and eschew legalistic niceties. In formally constituted
courts probate cases often were dragged out for years in an
unseemly atmosphere of greed and recrimination. Wilson
administered the postmortem affairs of the deceased over-
night and spared the territorial courts, all too busy with
other matters, much unnecessary wrangling. The account of
his juridical triumph by Jack Hines, a younger singer and
protégé of Wilson's, may have skimped on the fretwork so
valued by law professors but provided a clear picture of an
ad-lib legal mind in action.

Diamond Jim Wilson was the proprietor of the Anvil Bar, Nome's fanciest after Rickard's and Earp's saloons. Like Diamond Jim Brady, whose sobriquet he adopted, Wilson weighed in at about 300 pounds and festooned himself with diamond rings, tiepin, cuff links, studs, watch fobs, and other bric-a-brac. His mistress was a blonde named Ione, whose mercenary instincts were notable even in that milieu and whose tongue was reputed to be sharper than an Eskimo's harpoon. On this final day of Diamond Jim's gluttonous and self-centered life, he had bought himself a $6,000 ring but had neglected to buy the diamond tiara which Ione felt would dignify her position as queen of Diamond Jim's deadfall.

Late in the afternoon of Christmas Eve Diamond Jim and Ione joined their friends at the Anvil Bar for an all-night spree at Diamond Jim's expense. The company included such local society folk as Wilson Mizner, the Double-O Kid, the Single-O Kid, the In-and-Out Kid, and the Hobo Kid, whose manners were almost as polished as their sobriquets indicated, and such sparkling representatives of the demimonde as Shady Sadie, Frisco Sal, Nellie the Pig (who had come up from Dawson but was no longer intimately associated with Mizner), and Diamond Tooth Lil, who was said to have the most voluptuous figure north of Seattle.

All but the invited guests were barred from the Anvil, which was soon awash in ardent spirits and consequent bonhomie. Twenty cases of champagne were broached. When the champagne ran out, Diamond Jim's guests cheerfully switched to whiskey, rum, gin, and a native distillation known as hootch. Surrounded by his friends, the elite of the Nome underworld, Diamond Jim was a proud and happy man. In the strongbox near his desk, at which he sat in a chair specially constructed to hold his bulk, was approxi-

mately $100,000 in gold dust and currency. He wore the key
to his strongbox on a gold chain around his size 20 neck.
Banks, he had often publicly observed (an observation
which Wilson found interesting), were downright untrust-
worthy.

Later in the evening Diamond Jim took his friends, all
whooping and singing now, on a tour of the Front Street
bars. In each he bought a drink for the house and was
rewarded by a rendition of "For He's a Jolly Good Fellow."
As they passed in triumph through Rickard's, Earp's,
Boozer Brown's, Gus Seigert's, Joe Jourdan's, Diamond
Jim's complexion assumed an alarming shade of puce, which
only grew purpler when the party adjourned to the Café de
Paris for a banquet washed down with more wine and
spirits. "More champagne," Diamond Jim kept bellowing,
and corks popped like a battery of howitzers. They topped
off the feast with a rum omelet and a final round of brandy.

The banqueters then staggered back to the Anvil. Someone, noting their host's tortured breathing and congested
arteries, suggested that they join in heaving Diamond Jim
onto his bed. Ione, with more malice than compassion
aforethought, wouldn't hear of it. A few more drinks would
straighten Jim out. Whiskey and cigars were passed around,
the ladies partaking of both, and Diamond Jim requested
that Wilson, still an earnest vocalizer in sympathetic company, sing his favorite ballad, "Tom and Ned." Wilson obliged, while boozy tears fell down whiskered cheeks and
mascara dissolved into muddy streaks. In his donkeyish
baritone, Wilson bawled:

> Tom and Ned were next-door neighbors
> In a little country town;
> Two better pals than they were seldom seen,

Till the pretty face and roguish smile
And the laughing eyes of brown
Of the little village beauty came between. . . .

Overcome by emotion, Diamond Jim lurched to his feet and proposed a toast to "the best damned songbird in Alaska." He knocked back the last drink of a well-soaked life, swayed for a moment like an elephant with a bullet in his brain, and then toppled over with a resounding crash. It looked very much as though "Tom and Ned" had served as his requiem.

The Hobo Kid, volunteering himself as house physician, suggested that they carry him upstairs to his bed. With some difficulty, considering the state of the medical-aid team, this was accomplished. The Hobo Kid then pronounced him dead.

Ione, having decently waited for her cue, flung herself on the elephantine corpse and wailed, "Oh, my poor darling. Oh, poor, poor Jim!"

"Poor Jim," Wilson thoughtfully echoed. "Or more accurately, rich Jim."

They all drank a toast to the corpse. A wake was about to commence when Wilson brought them all to their senses.

"There's a hell of a lot of money," he remarked, "in that safe downstairs."

Ione checked any further demonstrations of grief and in a steady, reasonable voice chimed in: "It's true, what Wilson says. We all have to go some time. Jim was lucky—he died among his friends. And we were his friends, all the way back to Dawson in '98."

"He wouldn't want a lot of lawyers pawing over his assets and cutting in on the swag," Wilson murmured.

"Jim often told me," Ione recalled, "that if he was taken

suddenly like this, he wanted his friends to share in the
estate. You've all heard him say that, haven't you?"

There were no dissenting voices.

With the lugubrious sigh of a man performing an unwelcome duty, Wilson began distributing the dead man's possessions: diamond stud to the In-and-Out Kid, cuff links to
the Single-O Kid, other trinkets to the ladies present. A
diamond ring which Wilson decided was Diamond Jim's
bequest to the Hobo Kid had to be wrenched off a pudgy
finger by force, almost as though the corpse were resisting
the summary distribution of his estate.

There was a slight disagreement when Probate Judge Pro
Tem Mizner awarded himself Diamond Jim's diamond-
studded watch with its heavy gold chain and ornately bejeweled fob. The question of a conflict of interest was raised,
with several gentlemen's hands slipping toward their hol-
sters. Before an unseemly affray could result, they all were
distracted by the sudden and unwelcome appearance in
their midst of the Anvil's head bartender, Blackie, who
came bounding up the stairs and began making rude remarks about people "robbing the dead."

Blackie was quickly pacified when Wilson recollected that
Diamond Jim, with his dying breath, had willed Blackie
$1,000 in cash and his job behind the bar in perpetuity.

"Jim also said he wanted Ione to have the Anvil," Wilson
added.

Ione also took charge of the key to the strongbox and the
next day assumed management of the Anvil, presumably
with an irksome number of silent partners, the exact
number being those willing to certify his dying testament.
The day after Christmas Jim's funeral was held. Since he
held the post of fire chief among other civic duties, his grave

was decorated with a large paper wreath bearing the rather sinister prophecy "Gone to his last fire."

Word apparently reached the Mizner family headquarters in Benicia that Wilson was disgracing them again. They were not encouraged by a story in the San Francisco newspapers reporting that he was the "best-dressed man in Nome," but failing to indicate how he was supporting himself in style. (His wardrobe was periodically replenished by Bullock & Jones, a San Francisco tailor, which did not manage to collect until years later, and then only with the assistance of a writ of garnishee.) Naturally Wilson's stylishness worried the family, knowing his tendency to cut corners, ethically speaking.

Addison, as usual, was nominated to investigate his younger brother. Remembering Wilson's activities in Dawson, he naturally expected to find Wilson up to his neck in criminality. Instead, on his arrival in Nome he was astounded to learn that Wilson was regarded as the local hero of law enforcement and the "bravest man in Nome." Even more surprisingly Wilson had been appointed a deputy sheriff which, to Addison's mind, was something like appointing Jack the Ripper as the superintendent of a home for wayward girls.

He hurried out to the cabin Wilson had built according to his own specifications. Even after a long career of decorating the landscape with some of the most outlandish specimens of American architecture, Addison would remember that cabin as one of the most eccentric habitations he ever saw. It "resembled a small cathedral built by an inebriate," with ridge joints cut at such a narrow angle that it was "all gable and two-thirds attic."

Addison immediately braced his younger brother on his latest apotheosis. The latter confessed his sudden fame as a muscular arm of the law was not entirely deserved. It was something of a fluke, Wilson added with an unexpected but becoming modesty.

About three o'clock one morning, Wilson related, he was awakened by three friends, Scurvy Bill (whose nickname applied to his character rather than any dietetic deficiencies), Two-Tooth Mike, and Mit. They had been involved in a robbery in which Two-Tooth Mike was wounded.

About a month earlier Wilson, who could always use a respectable cover, had been appointed a deputy sheriff, possibly on the theory that it would keep him out of trouble. It was now his clear duty to turn his three friends in, but that would violate an overriding oath he had taken a long time before: Never squeal. So he hid the three miscreants in his attic which, according to Addison, was big enough to accommodate Quantrill's Raiders and all their camp followers.

A few minutes after Wilson had tucked his friends away the sheriff arrived at the head of a posse. They had information, the sheriff told Wilson, that three desperadoes had tried to jump a claim on Anvil Creek and were now holed up in a cabin on a nearby hillock. Wilson was ordered to join the posse.

He rode with his fellow manhunters to the desperadoes' supposed hideout. They surrounded the cabin and scared the wits out of one another by pointing to imaginary faces and rifles glimpsed at the windows. They'd have to rush the place, the sheriff announced.

Wilson bravely offered an alternate plan. "One man should walk up there, tell them to surrender and save bloodshed."

"Fine," the sheriff retorted, "but who's going to risk a bullet between the eyes?"

"I," said Wilson, squaring his shoulders, "will go."

While his fellow possemen watched with admiration for his cool courage, Wilson strolled up to the cabin door and shouted, "Come out, you rats, or I'll blast my way in!"

He then kicked in the cabin door and rushed inside. His comrades waited for a blaze of gunfire.

Instead, having paused to light a cigarette for the nonchalent affect, Wilson came strolling to announce, "Nobody there—just some blood splashed around."

With the sheriff's and his fellow manhunters' praises still ringing in his ears, Wilson hastened back to his own cabin and helped the fugitives he had concealed in his attic make their getaway.

Addison returned to Benicia to report that Wilson hadn't changed much, although his public image had improved. He had succeeded, however, in persuading Wilson to come home for a visit in 1902. Home life and the family circle, with "black sheep" on the tip of every tongue, soon palled.

Early in the spring he boarded the steamer *Portland*, Nome-bound from San Francisco, and unwittingly became involved in a saga of the northern seas. There had been an early thaw, followed by a sudden freeze-up, and on May 7 the *Portland* was frozen solid in the ice floes and drifted helplessly toward the North Pole. For two months the ship would be listed as missing, its passengers mourned for dead. Aboard the *Portland*, however, the worst privations suffered were ennui and an occasional surfeit of Wilson's manic impersonation of an impresario. At last Wilson, the failed vaudevillian, had a captive audience.

"Wilson's high spirits were greatly appreciated, at first,

on that hapless voyage," it was recorded. A large assortment of costumes consigned to Nome theaters was included in the ship's cargo, and Wilson did his best to alleviate the fears of his fellow passengers with a daily revue of which he was the producer, director, sketch-writer, librettist, and star. Routine labor fatigued Mizner quicker than almost any living vertebrate but he always seized energetically on any chance to entertain people—a fortuitous streak of ham for the *Portland's* worried company, which gratefully applauded even his deafening baritone raised in ballads and sea chanteys. Survivors afterward claimed that Mizner's rendition of *Blow the Man Down* rang in their ears for years afterward.

"Not the least of his kindly offices was performed for a Professor Blankenshrift, a roving practitioner of astrology, hypnotism and the occult arts. The passengers denounced him for a charlatan because he had not foretold their fate in the stars and jeered when his attempts to mesmerize various subjects failed, possibly because they were already paralyzed with fear. . . . The professor's plight aroused Mizner's sympathy. One day, when the ice began breaking up, he leaped overboard into the freezing waters, swam to a neighboring ice floe and howled for help. After he had been rescued, Mizner accused the professor of having hypnotized him and having ordered him to jump overboard. This heroic evidence restored the professor to the somewhat fearful esteem of his fellow passengers. . . ."

It makes a nice story, the source of which undoubtedly was Wilson himself, but experts in such matters say that anyone who leaped into the North Pacific at that time of year was not likely to survive long enough to swim to safety.

The *Portland* finally freed itself from the ice and, three

months after leaving San Francisco, arrived in Nome on July 2, 1902, to be greeted by bonfires on the beaches and an all-night carouse.

In Benicia the news that the bad penny had turned up again was received with mixed emotions. His mother was overjoyed that her Angel Birdie had fluttered away from another disaster, but there were those who felt a splendid opportunity had been missed for Wilson to make an honorable exit.

Few things, in later years, would enrage Wilson faster or make his gorge rise higher than a discussion of literature on the subject of the Northern gold rush. The mere mention of Jack London or Rex Beach would bring a roar out of him. In the London and Beach novels the gold rushers were depicted as supermen contending at tremendous odds with brute nature; Wilson remembered most of them as toasting themselves around a fire except when it was necessary to make a trip to the woodpile. He scoffed at tales of heroic treks by dogsled, at solitary contests against the Arctic winter, at epic labors in frozen creek beds; miners were the laziest, most comfort-loving sods in the world. Two other tenets of Arctic literature—that friendship was more precious than gold and that the quality of manhood, not the weight of a man's moosehide poke, was all that counted —were also vigorously disputed.

"I never knew the meaning of ingratitude," he often said, "until I had one of those Arctic pals."

As for the absence of crassly commercial aspects to life in the gold camps, he would cite an incident that occurred after one Jack McCloud went bankrupt in a poker game at Tex Rickard's Great Northern.

McCloud was convinced that he had been cheated and sent Rickard, who had been a town-taming marshal in Texas, the traditional gunfighter's challenge: "Come out, and come out smoking."

Acting on an impulse he could ill afford, Rickard strapped on his gun belt and checked the condition of his shooting iron. Then he paused to consider his net worth, his prospects, the actuarial tables on gunfighting, the fifty-fifty odds. Not good enough for any sensible gambler. "Tell Jack I can't afford it," he said finally. "Here I am, worth three hundred thousand, and he's broke. I won't stack that up against nothing. It ain't business."

McCloud grasped the sense of Rickard's argument. "Tex is right. It ain't business."

Recalling that episode, Wilson would add his own commentary: "Here is a wronged man with revenge in his heart, but the standards of commercialism were too strong for him. He went off to the mines with the idea of making a pile equal to Rickard's, so that he could shoot it out with him on business principles."

On another claim made for the gold rushers by their chroniclers, Wilson was also scornfully in opposition: their reputation for being dead shots. "I was in a saloon with a lot of those Yukon marksmen," he would recall. "They all agreed that there was no sport like bagging ptarmigan with a rifle at two hundred yards when you could see nothing but their eyes, their white feathers being invisible against the snow. They began to talk about throwing half dollars and quarters into the air and shooting them on the fly. One man won the undisputed championship of the saloon by telling how he tossed a dime in the air and barely grazed the rim, so that it would remain spinning for a couple of hundred revolutions before it touched the ground.

"Just then a big Husky dog came in foaming at the mouth. Everybody began shooting at it. They hid behind the bar and made barricades of chairs and tables, took careful aim, and blazed away. The floors, the walls and the ceiling were peppered with bullets. Every shot missed the dog by a mile. Finally the bartender came out with a bungstarter and killed it with one blow of the mallet."

For the most part, Wilson maintained, the gold rush was a concourse of emancipated ribbon clerks, ladies' hairdressers, and absconding bookkeepers—gutless fellows who sat down and wept when buffeted by adversity. The women were tougher than the men, "slammerkins in long red underwear," who could outfight and outdrink the lot of them. His observations on this turnabout in sexual roles caused Wilson, as an amateur sociologist of some perception, much concern about the future of American manhood, and he foresaw a time when the American scene would be dominated by Amazonian women and sissified men.

He was a scornful witness of what became known as the Nome Claim Steal, the victims of which drew his unreserved contempt for their failure to resort manfully to the anarchical rope and torch as a remedy for the injustices inflicted on them. It was engineered by a ring of carpetbagging politicians and their corrupters, a scandal to rank with the Crédit Mobilier as "the most flagrant prostitution," in the words of a federal judge sitting on the case, "of American courts in our history." The trouble around Nome with claim jumpers was exacerbated by the fact that most of the original claimants were Swedes and Lapps, much resented by the late-coming Americans, who proceeded to steal their claims as a lesson in elementary Americanism.

Into this murky situation, with property rights violated on every hand, leaped the figure of Alexander McKenzie, an

influential politician and one of President McKinley's prin-
cipal advisers. With various confederates in Nome and
Washington, McKenzie formed the Alaska Gold Mining
Company to acquire all disputed claims on the Seward
Peninsula. Then he got his own man, a drunkard named
Noyes, appointed United States district judge. Judge Noyes
promptly ordered disputed claims transferred to Alaska
Gold Mining. His edicts were backed up by troops from the
U.S. Army's Alaskan command. There was rioting and occasional armed resistance, but McKenzie and his henchmen
succeeded in confiscating claims and even the gold taken
from them before the court ordered their seizure. For
months Nome was as "paralyzed as by a Central American
revolution," a local historian wrote.

The victims of the wholesale claim steals eventually
banded together, obtained restoration of their claims, and
saw to the conviction of McKenzie, Noyes, and the federal
district attorney at Nome. They disgusted Wilson, however,
by failing to act in the colorful tradition of the old frontier.
"Most of the fellows up there," he would recall, "were the
worst sissies on earth. I was in court when two hundred of
them were robbed of their rights by a crooked judge and a
set of thieving politicians. Did they string up the judge, as
the Forty-niners would have done? Did they tear the politicians limb from limb? No. They just sat there crying in their
beards. Then they slunk back to their cabins and had to be
treated with smelling salts."

From this experience he formulated what might be called
Mizner's Law of Comparative Criminality: An honest crook
doesn't stand a chance against a political crook.

Late in the summer of 1902 he was further discouraged by
the fact that cardsharps and tinhorns were beginning to

outnumber the available victims. His field was over-
crowded. One night at a poker game in the Great Northern
he rang in a stacked deck containing nothing but aces.
Dealing from this pack, he studied with sardonic interest
the frantic attempt of each player to get rid of his extra ace
without letting the others know what he was up to.

"Well, boys," he roared, "what are you betting? Time
flies—you thieves!"

There was prolonged, overhearty laughter at the table
when his fellow players realized they'd been had.

His own laughter was tinged with a mordant reflection: A
place that's too crooked is not a profitable scene for a hardworking crook. It was time to check out of Nome and look for
another money tree. This decision led him, in the curious
way that fate had of toying with Wilson's life, to a banana
plantation in Central America, where the money was supposed to grow in bunches.

He returned to the States with a gambling partner he had
acquired during his last days in Nome. Between them they
had a bankroll of about $10,000. To make sure they had a
grubstake when they reached San Francisco, the two men
entered into a solemn pact not to jeopardize it by gambling
on shipboard.

Wilson, however, couldn't resist the lure of the pasteboards crisply slapping the table. On the second day of the
voyage Mizner came bustling into the cabin he shared with
his friend, the gambler's gleam in his eyes.

"Peel me off a couple of grand," he told his traveling
companion. "I've got a sucker waiting in the card room."

There was a brief but spirited argument over breaking the
pact they had made, but his partner was persuaded to deal
out the greenbacks.

Just as Wilson started to leave the cabin, he turned and asked, "Say, how do you play pinochle?"

Further instruction was supplied by the "sucker" Wilson had found, and he and his partner arrived in San Francisco with severely depleted resources.

4

THE ADVENTURES OF
THE CANDY KID

EARLY in the 1900's there was a widespread belief that money, in the shape of bananas, did indeed grow on trees. The golden fruit, still rather an exotic item on most American tables, was enjoying a boom. It didn't quite match the excitement of bringing in a gusher in the Texas oilfields, but Americans were rushing to the jungles of Central America to make their fortunes just as they had to the frozen tundra of Alaska and the Yukon a few years earlier.

A rush of any kind was irresistible to Wilson, and Central America was attractive because his family had connections there. Apparently through those connections he was hoisted into the banana business. At twenty-seven he was still capable of a boundless optimism. He could picture himself as the master of plantations, lounging on his veranda with servants bringing him drinks while his work force harvested the fruit the year around. In a few years he would return to the States

with a fortune from the banana bonanza, still young enough
to enjoy being a millionaire.

Reality was harsher than he fancied in his Benicia day-
dreams. He soon learned that as overlord of a plantation in
Honduras his role was that of a slave driver, the boss of a
tropical sweatshop. He was supposed to exert himself
tirelessly at making others work hard, though his own con-
cept of labor relations, as demonstrated when he was the
foreman of his brother Edgar's claim near Dawson, was just
the opposite. The thought of physical labor had always
appalled him. In connection with himself it was unthinkable; he had the aristocratic attitude toward toil and sweat.
Being a part-time humanitarian, he was distressed to see
others driven hard at unrewarding tasks. The repugnance
he felt for such a role was only magnified by the consideration that the profits wrung from such effort all went tinkling
into the treasury of the United Fruit Company.

Wilson soon proved himself a total failure as a banana
grower. Instead of cracking a figurative whip, he went
around the groves urging people not to work so hard, not to
strain themselves lifting the huge stalks of green bananas . . .
or at least this was his account of how he had proved disap-
pointing as a planter (United Fruit's version might have
differed). The production on his plantation slacked off to the
point where the executives in Tegucigalpa suspected that a
mysterious plant disease or insect plague had struck the
place.

Long before his one-year contract expired, his superiors
decided that he could be replaced without serious damage
to the company's future.

So Wilson returned to San Francisco and resumed the
lay-about career of a gambler, playboy, and man-about-
town. From all accounts (including that of the period's

chronicler, Evelyn Wells, a San Francisco journalist) he was a prominent figure in the city's more sportive circles, an ornament of those lively years just preceding the earthquake and fire.

The range of his gambling interests, then and always, was nothing short of spectacular. He would bet on anything, though never without a lightning calculation of the odds. "Never gamble," was his motto, "without a little of the best of it." The operative word was "little." The professional gambler looks for the small percentage in his favor; hoggishness about odds only drives the clients away. Thus he would recall that on the occasion in Dawson when the Mounted Police caught him improving his luck he had five *deuces* in the deck. The extra deuce was his modest hedge against ill fortune. A tinhorn, as he pointed out, would have slipped in an extra ace.

His willingness to cover any sort of wager became part of the legend of San Francisco's underside one day when a ferryboat on the Oakland run came churning to a stop with the cry "Man overboard!" When the crew lowered a lifeboat, they found it was Wilson Mizner treading water a hundred yards away and clocking the operation on a stopwatch. He had made a bet on how much time it took to be rescued if one toppled off a ferry.

Through such ventures he had acquired a sizable stake when reports circulated around town that gold had been discovered in a new location in Nevada. Despite his occasionally harrowing experiences in the North Country, Wilson couldn't resist joining another stampede. He hastened to the mining camp of Goldfield after learning that Tex Rickard and Wyatt Earp, two of the cagiest operators he had known, had acquired leases there. (Whatever his televised apotheosis, Wyatt Earp, except for a few risky years in his youth, was primarily an operator of gambling houses and wound up a rather Babbitt-like Southern California real estate speculator in the twenties.) Wilson bought up a number of claims, but none of them panned out. He returned to San Francisco broke.

Early the next year, 1905, he decided to try his luck in New York, where, it was said, the action was. Perhaps it was time to abandon the Western provinces and find out whether it was true that you had to match yourself against New York if you wanted to make it in the big time. New York was then at the apogee as the pleasure-seeking capital of the continent, brilliant with the light of a million new mazda bulbs. Broadway was the Disneyland of its time, combined with the Boul Mich' and the main arcade of a Levantine bazaar. "The Gay White Way," social historian Lloyd Morris wrote, "was a fever in the blood of Americans, breeding hallucinations of forbidden delights."

Hallucinating, often with the help of alcohol or some less respectable chemical agent, was one of Wilson's favorite pastimes. It was inevitable that he would have to try the New York brand of hallucination, and the Big Town was only the more attractive because his brother Addison reportedly was making whalelike splashes in Eastern society and might give him a leg up in New York and Newport.

Addison had journeyed to New York a year earlier and set himself up as a society architect under the patronage of Mrs. Herman Oelrichs and Mrs. William K. Vanderbilt, Jr. He had also won the approval of the third member of what was styled as the Great Triumverate that reigned over the Four Hundred, the acerb Mrs. Stuyvesant Fish, along with that of their tactician, the cotillion-leader Harry Lehr. That entrée to the highest social circles was easily explained. The Mizner brothers had known Mrs. Oelrichs, the former Tessie Fair, daughter of one of the Comstock Lode magnates, ever since she and her sister Birdie were girls going to a fashionable private school in Benicia. Their older brother Edgar, in fact, had been madly in love with Tessie and been rejected by her, which to Wilson and Addison demonstrated her intelligence and good taste. Tessie Oelrichs was now a widow and was being courted by Addison, a courtship which (owing to Mrs. Oelrichs' social and financial position rather than Addison's) the society pages speculated on at length.

Immediately on arrival in Manhattan, Wilson looked up Addison and announced that he was willing to branch out as a society gentleman. Addison was not overjoyed by the news and made it plain that he could not visualize Wilson, with his erratic behavior and his taste for low company, blossoming out as an adornment of the Four Hundred. Wilson, he said, would have to provide proof that he had become civilized and had "stopped associating with ragamuffins" before Addison would act as his sponsor. Until that improbable day, he added, Wilson should not expect to be recognized or greeted if they met in polite society.

The suggestion that Addison's social standing would be imperiled by the merest acknowledgment of acquaintance, let alone kinship, naturally irked Wilson. And Wilson, who viewed his brother's ultimatum as a challenge, was an expert in arranging public embarrassments. He would see to it that Addison regretted his exhibition of snobbery.

Wilson learned that one of the adornments of Addison's social career was an arena-side box at the National Horse Show, to which he invited only his most imposing and elegant friends. The box, like his cultivation of the reigning dowagers, was part of his self-promotion campaign; now that the eminent Stanford White had been laid low by a shot from Harry K. Thaw's pistol ("they shot the wrong ar-

chitect," the current gibe had it), there was room for another
artistic adviser at society's high table. Richard Morris Hunt,
who designed so many of the lordly follies on Fifth Avenue
and in Newport, had also gone to his reward. Addison saw
himself taking their place if he could only preserve his
recently cultivated grand manner.

Like most of the Mizners, however, Addison was an
eccentric mixture of high purpose and wayward impulse.
He presented himself to his younger brother as a model of
sobriety and dignity, for whom he had often been instructed
by their mother to provide an inspiring example. Yet only a
few months before Addison had been arrested for resisting
the efforts of the personnel at the Waldorf-Astoria to heave
him out of the bar. And back in San Francisco a year or two
before, when his proposal of marriage had been turned
down by a local beauty, Addison decided on the classic
remedy. He went to Golden Gate Park to shoot himself. Just
as he was raising the pistol to his temple, he remembered
that his underwear had a hole in it. The idea of the morgue
attendants finding him with ragged underpants was so repellent that he lowered the pistol and gave up the plan to
commit suicide.

One night during the horse show, resplendent in evening
dress and congratulating himself on his hard-won respectability, he was seated in his box above the tanbark at the
horse show. His guests included Tessie Oelrichs, Mrs.
Stuyvesant Fish, and Harry Lehr. His box was the center of
attention from lesser creatures in the surrounding boxes.
He was a proud and happy man until the moment, out of the
corner of his eye, he observed Wilson strutting up and down
the tanbark during an intermission. His only hope was that
Wilson wouldn't catch sight of him or, less likely, would
remember the admonition against public acknowledgment.

Wilson, magnificent in white tie and top hat, with a gardenia in his buttonhole, was attracting considerable attention from the society girls in the boxes above. Despite a pumpkin-sized head, as Addison had always called it, he cut an impressive figure, and the debs and post-debs twittered with speculation.

Some of the twittering, in fact, came from Addison's box. "Who," demanded Mrs. Stuyvesant Fish, always on the lookout for a presentable extra man to grace her dinner table, "is that fine-looking man down in the arena?"

"I don't know," Harry Lehr admitted, though he carried the *Social Register* in his head, page by page, pedigree by pedigree. "His face looks familiar. I notice that he keeps glancing up at this box. Do you know him, Addison?"

"Never saw him before," grunted Addison, who was crouched down in his seat.

A few seconds later his words were vigorously belied. Wilson was staring up at him, then let out a squawk of delight. In a moment Mama's Angel Birdie was heading for Addison's box like a nestling flapping his way home, was clambering over the rail and screeching, "Well, for Gawd's sake, Ad! I've been looking all over town for you. Where the hell are you living anyway?"

Addison, as he later recalled, was about to manhandle him out of the box before he could give away the fact of their relationship, but Tessie Oelrichs recognized him from her girlhood visits to the Mizner household in Benicia—and besides, Wilson would probably have put up a struggle and caused a dreadful scene.

There was nothing to do but introduce Wilson to his guests and silently pray that he would behave himself.

"And where are you stopping, now that you're in town?" Addison asked, forcing politeness into his tone.

"In a cathouse at Broadway and Forty-second Street," Wilson loudly replied. "I just sit there all day reading my beloved books and smoking opium."

Addison turned purple, knowing Wilson was probably telling the exact truth, but his guests took it for a joke and laughed heartily. With some difficulty, he restrained himself from strangling Wilson when the latter insisted on accompanying the party to supper after the show.

Among those fascinated by the scene in Addison's box, once Wilson had invaded it, was a gorgeously attired and lavishly bejeweled woman in the adjoining box. She was no longer young, she was separated but not as yet divorced from her extremely wealthy and predatory husband, but she was susceptible. Her name was Mrs. Myra Adelaide Yerkes. Thanks to a new miracle discovery called peroxide, she was still a blonde. Being an acquaintance of Addison's, she insisted that he introduce her to his brother. From that social seedling blossomed, in garish headlines which caused Addison to regret that he hadn't been suffering from lockjaw that night, what one of the racier New York newspapers called the romance of "the Merry Widow and the Candy Kid."

Soon after their meeting, which was like that of magnetized particles, Myra with her need for a man about the house, Wilson with his need for food and shelter and walk-around money, Wilson became a familiar at the vast rococo Yerkes mansion at 864 Fifth Avenue, which was modeled after an ancient Roman villa, perhaps that of one of the more lunatic Caesars, and furnished in a style that could only be termed Imperial Bad Taste.

The last person in the world to object to Wilson's presence in that house was its master, Charles T. Yerkes, the man who made the title of traction magnate an epithet. At the moment Yerkes was trying to persuade Myra Adelaide to grant him a divorce. He had fallen in love with a beautiful young actress named Emma Grigsby, whom he advertised to the world as his "ward." (During that period there were many such rich and protective guardians with lissome young female wards; it was easily the most popular form of philanthropy among the well-heeled.) The point at issue wasn't Myra's broken heart or bruised pride but the immense fortune which Yerkes had wrung out of the streetcar and subway systems of several American cities. The newspapers reported that the fortune amounted to $50,000,000, but in the soberer calculations of the probate courts it was subsequently determined that his holding had been reduced, through his penchant for young females in need of a protector, to approximately $7,500,000.

That remaining plunder, whether it was $7,500,000 or seven times that, was also a matter of consideration to Wilson Mizner in his role of correspondent-presumptive. It must have been, because Myra Adelaide was twenty years older, a social disaster, and a heavy drinker. "I had never considered marriage, but I had an open mind," as Wilson explained his attitude, "and I was to learn after a brief try at it that most open minds should be closed for repairs."

Yerkes is remembered today for the observatory bearing his name, which he donated to the University of Chicago, and even more signally, perhaps, for serving as the model for the character of Frank Cowperwood, the hero of Theodore Dreiser's novels *The Titan* and *The Financier*. In his own time Yerkes was better known as a man-eating shark of the transportation industry whose formula for success, as he bluntly stated it, was to "Buy old junk, fix it up a little and unload it upon other fellows." He also laid down the First Commandment of Rapid Transit: "It's the straphanger who

pays the dividends." His ruthlessness was remarkable even
in an era when a financier considered himself a failure until
he had plundered several city or state treasuries and was
charged with responsibility for a dozen suicides.

The Yerkes method was to buy up various trolley lines,
bribe the mayor and city council, and obtain a municipal
franchise to operate all public transportation. Once he obtained a local monopoly, he ordered large increases in fares.
His career not at all hampered by a youthful conviction for
embezzlement, he became Chicago's most imposing tycoon
until Samuel Insull did for public utilities what Yerkes did
for public transportation. "To protect the value of inflated
stock holdings by assuring themselves continued franchises," a Chicago historian wrote, "Yerkes and his backers
put through the state legislature a group of 'Eternal
Monopoly' bills which would have given Yerkes unques-
tioned rights to the streets for ninety-nine years. After
turning down a bribe of half a million dollars from Yerkes,
Governor Altgeld vetoed the bill. At the next session of the
legislature, Yerkes had a new plan which would have extended his franchise for fifty years without additional com-
pensation to the city. This bill failed in the legislature but
Yerkes did succeed in putting through another bill, the
Allen Law, permitting the City Countil to give him the
rights which the legislature had refused. Even this gesture
cost him several hundred thousand dollars in bribes."

By the time Wilson appeared as a minor irritant in his
busy life Yerkes had built the Chicago elevated system, part
of the London Tube (subway), and the street-railway system
of his native Philadelphia. He was tied in with the Big Six
syndicate which controlled public transportation and lighting systems in New York, Chicago, Philadelphia,
Pittsburgh, and many smaller cities in the Eastern and

Middlewestern states. One of the links in the Big Six chain was the Metropolitan Street Railway of New York City, which was capitalized at a grossly inflated $260,000,000 and collapsed in scandal and recrimination a year after Yerkes' death.

Yerkes had met Myra Adelaide Moore, now the chateleine of the $4,000,000 brownstone mansion he built on Fifth Avenue, when she was a seventeen-year-old farm girl living near Egypt, Illinois. Their romance was something to gladden those readers who made *Daddy Long Legs* a bathetic best seller. One day Yerkes' private train was halted in the Egypt station by a washout in the tracks up ahead. Myra, oval-faced and winsome, with a fresh milkmaid's complexion that appealed enormously to the jaded appetite of the magnate staring glumly from the window of his train, came dancing down the platform with a lunch bucket for her brother Thomas, the station's telegrapher. Thomas got his lunch, and Yerkes gobbled up the country girl and swept her off to the big city just like one of the heroines in a Dreiser novel. A year later they were married, an event which testified to little Myra Adelaide's tenacity, since Yerkes had never been lured into matrimony before.

Myra was happy enough as the consort of one of America's leading financiers until she learned that Yerkes regarded women as something like streetcar franchises. When you saw one that looked promising, you bought it (her). When you decided there was no more profit in the relationship, you unloaded as expeditiously as possible. Against this knowledge Myra consoled herself by insisting that Yerkes lavish jewelry, art treasures, and fine houses on her. One thing he couldn't buy for her was acceptance by the Chicago society ruled by Mrs. Potter Palmer and her associates, though it was hardly as exclusive as New York's Four Hundred. Yerkes' methods of making money, even more than his status as an ex-convict, was considered a trifle too buccaneering. His sultanlike dealings with women were also frowned upon. In his subsequent research for his novels featuring Yerkes/Cowperwood, Theodore Dreiser learned that Yerkes kept a staff of fifteen lawyers on an annual combined retainer of $150,000 to handle the transactions with "wards," mistresses, and ex-mistresses in their various legal and emotional stages. If a woman proved to be too clinging, Yerkes' lawyers would hire a man to seduce her and arrange that she be found in a compromising situation. The Yerkes legal battery would then threaten her with exposure if she persisted in her demands on the magnate.

Myra and her hyperactive husband moved to New York in the hope, mainly Myra's, that Eastern society would be less squeamish about his financial and sexual affairs, less appalled by her habit of making scenes in public at the top of her piercing voice.

So Yerkes built the Roman villa on Fifth Avenue, hopeful that it would still Myra's clamor, and furnished it lavishly. The money was his, but the taste in decor was that of the Cleopatra from Egypt, Illinois. Yerkes, after all, had other places to hang his striped pants and clawhammer coat. There were nine baths at 864 Fifth Avenue, one of solid onyx that cost $30,000. Marble couches and paintings optimistically valued at $2,000,000 lined the walls. The inner courtyard alone cost $150,000 with its fountain, marble facings, and balustrades. Yerkes' bed had once cradled King Leopold of Belgium, Mrs. Yerkes' was the former property of the Mad King of Bavaria and was placed on a dais with velvet steps. Overhead its occupant could study an enameled Goddess of the Night surrounded by gold cupids.

Overripe in its opulence, gorgeously decadent in the *fin de siècle* style, the House of Yerkes attracted much journalistic attention but little except scorn from the Four Hundred. Society betrayed its feelings about the ill-matched couple when Yerkes, after much pressure, was given a ten-day guest card to the Metropolitan Club; the member who arranged it was brought up before the club's board of governors. After months of brazen campaigning for recognition, Myra found the female sector of society equally closed off. Later Wilson Mizner cracked that she couldn't buy her way into the Haymarket, one of the less exclusive deadfalls in the Tenderloin. Society might have forgiven Myra her husband's activities if she had possessed a gentler or more genteel manner. Unfortunately she was not only an unabashed and aggressive parvenue but had the social style of a steam calliope. Wilson was rather forbearing when he described her approach to the guardians of the Four Hundred as "web-footed." Her constant thirst for and public consumption of scotch highballs didn't help her cause in a day when female boozers nipped brandy in the closets of their boudoirs.

Addison Mizner was an expert at sizing up the social and financial qualifications of his contemporaries, and he tried to warn Wilson off the Yerkes property, whatever his motives in trespassing might be. Mrs. Yerkes, he pointed out, was loose-lipped but tight-fisted. There was nothing wrong, in Addison's code, with a young fellow marrying a fortune, but he had better make sure he would get more out of the venture than having his tailor's bills stamped paid.

Addison cited his own first meeting with Mrs. Yerkes as an example of what Wilson might have to put up with in public; what happened in private, he added with a shudder, was unthinkable.

He met Mrs. Yerkes on what would later be called a blind
date, which was also, as he subsequently learned, something of a joke on the part of the person who arranged it. He,
Myra, and the other couple attended the performance of a
Lillian Russell musical comedy at the Casino Theater. Myra
had an "elegant skinful" when the party arrived at the
theater, and Addison noticed that when he nodded or
bowed to acquaintances, they pretended not to have caught
the gesture. As the performance proceeded, Myra began
making audible comments on the players and their costumes, and unfortunately "her voice always rose when a
considerable time had passed since her last highball."

Addison tried to "creep through my own armhole," as he
put it, when Myra really opened fire on the performance.
"She did not rise to make an address from the box," Addison
recalled, "although she might have under the circumstances
if she had thought of it, but she did say emphatically in a
voice clearly audible from backdrop to box office that the
Lady Teazle of this production was not *the* Lady Teazle.
'Because,' Myra explained at the top of her magnificent
lungs, 'I have a picture of Lady Teazle right in my mansion.
It's an original, it cost a *lot* of money, and it's *right*. Lady
Teazle wears a yellow dress in that picture. This woman
here has a pink dress. She is *not* Lady Teazle.' "

Wilson, however, was undeterred by his brother's recollection of a ruined evening at the theater. You could always
shut a woman up, he maintained by clapping your hand
firmly on her mouth—a theory which indicated unsus-
pected traces of naiveté in Wilson's makeup. He not only
continued to squire Mrs. Yerkes around town, laughing at
the ostracism designed to wither the fortune hunter and the
object of his intentions, but also moved into the marble
monstrosity on Fifth Avenue. Just as an escape hatch

—frequently needed—he kept his room at the Hotel Claridge a few doors off Times Square. Mr. Yerkes by then had moved to the Waldorf-Astoria and was pleading with Myra for a divorce.

Late in December, 1905, Yerkes died suddenly before he could be divorced, remarried, or change his will. The last circumstance was a matter of rejoicing to Wilson, who considered himself in the direct line of inheritance through Myra.

Myra went into deep mourning for several weeks, then abruptly decided that widow's weeds didn't go with her complexion and began pleading with Wilson to legalize their relationship. Or as Wilson put it, she made use of "the most efficient waterpower in the world—women's tears."

Her dowry, he admitted, was also a consideration. "After all, I was born eight dollars short."

On January 30, 1906, they eloped crosstown in a hansom cab and were married at St. Andrews Methodist Episcopal Church. One of Myra's female drinking companions served as matron of honor. The groom was attended by several lads who looked as though they had been leaning against a Bowery lamppost a few hours earlier.

It was a very private ceremony held in the rectory. Myra wanted it kept secret because of the extreme brevity of her mourning period; it was one of her few concessions to public opinion. For that reason, apparently, the honeymoon was postponed—or, to be more accurate, suspended—and the bride went back to her Fifth Avenue mansion while the groom repaired to his cramped quarters at the Claridge.

Three days later the metropolitan press was tipped off to the marriage and gave it front-page attention under such wink-and-nudge headlines as:

CALIFORNIA CANARY
CHIRPS ''I DO'' TO
WEALTHY WIDOW

There was a general suspicion among the wiseacres of Broadway that Wilson had leaked the story himself. An inveterate member of the creditor class, he was thus able to still apprehension over bills long past due. It seemed unlikely that anyone would sue the consort of $50,000,000.

He must have been distressed when a posse of journalists three times stormed the Yerkes mansion to demand of Mrs. Yerkes whether or not she had married Wilson Mizner —and three times she denied it.

On February 2, however, they tracked Wilson to Sherry's, where he was lunching alone and on the cuff (now immaculate), and quoted him as replying to the same question: "Alas, it is true."

Taken aback by his ungallantry, the reporters demanded proof of his statement, so he engaged three victorias and took the whole clamoring crew to 864 Fifth Avenue.

Wilson, according to accounts published in next day's newspapers, bounded into the entry hall, cupped his hands around his mouth, and cut loose with the mating-moose call of "Coo-ee—ee!" which he had learned in the Klondike. A moment later Mrs. Yerkes—Mizner, that is—appeared on the balcony above the hall in a lavender tea gown.

"Where did you find him, boys?" she trilled. "It's more than I could do."

"Then you're married?" one of the reporters asked.

"Who could resist him?" she replied, flinging out her arms in an operatic gesture. "He's the greatest lover and singer in the world."

During the next few days the press declared high carnival over the story. It was repeatedly pointed out that Mrs. Yerkes—no, Mizner—was forty-eight to the bridegroom's twenty-nine; that she had inherited millions and he had only a bizarre reputation as a Klondiker, gambler, and songbird. The groom, it was recorded, sported a tan topcoat with gong-sized pearl buttons, olive-green spats, and a bamboo cane. He described himself as a man of affluence with Alaskan mining properties and a racing stable. (Corrective dispatches arrived from San Francisco. The only horse he had "owned" was a famous racer named Geraldine, which was alleged to be the legal property of Lucky Baldwin, the spectacularly successful San Francisco speculator, and which Wilson was accused of having taken with him when he joined the stampede to Goldfield, Nevada. The dispatches just missed calling Wilson a horse thief.)

The reporters posed a number of impertinent questions for the rather evasive bridegroom, among them:

Was it true that, until the day before the wedding, Wilson kept a girl in a $2-a-week room on Twenty-eighth Street?

Was it true that, as widely rumored, he was a "penniless adventurer"?

Was there any foundation to reports that Wilson had moved into the Yerkes mansion some weeks before Mr. Yerkes' demise and that neighbors had complained to the police about noisy all-night parties?

With a fine show of indignation Wilson denied everything. Regarding the neighbors' charges of all-night revelry, he replied, "It must have been taking place in the servants' quarters."

With a proprietary manner that might have alarmed the new Mrs. Mizner, if she had not withdrawn from the press conference pleading a sudden headache, Wilson showed the reporters around the gallery and described the paintings almost as though he were making a sales pitch.

The New York *Sun*'s representative, in fact, observed him "gazing reflectively at a priceless tapestry." He showed off works by Hals, Corot, Turner, Troyon, Diaz's "Gathering Faggots," Millet's "Pig Killers," Rembrandt's "Portrait of a Rabbi," Lawrence's "Portrait of Mrs. Siddons," Van Dyke's "Charles I," and a painting by his ancestor, Sir Joshua Reynolds, titled "Age of Innocence."

His knowledge of the paintings and their presumed value indicated to more than one reporter that he had been taking inventory.

After an hour or two, Wilson managed to detach the journalistic posse from the free booze and sent them on their disorderly way back to Park Row. Now that his marriage was a matter of public record, he would be able to take his seignorial place in society. His only problem was keeping his mother the length of the continent away from her new daughter-in-law.

5

HIGH JINKS ON
FIFTH AVENUE

SEVERAL days after the marriage became public property his brother Addison appeared at the Yerkes, or Mizner, mansion to offer his congratulations and thank Wilson for *not* inviting him to the wedding. He found Wilson ensconced in that atmosphere of combined squalor and luxury in which he seemed to function best. Wilson was flaked out on King Ludwig's rococo bed with the golden cupids fluttering overhead, propped up on massive pillows with peach satin slips, and covered by a lace spread. His *robe de nuit*, however, was a suit of long woolen underwear, and he was rolling a brown-paper cigarette.

"Why the hell did you do it?" Addison demanded. He was plainly enough referring to the recent marriage.

"Well, the service is good here," Wilson explained after a moment's thought. "I'll show you what I mean." He yanked on the bell cord near his head.

In strolled a familiar figure in San Francisco's less exclu-

91

sive circles, Johnny Bray, whom Wilson had imported as his valet and "companion." Johnny's regular occupation was bartender, usually in one of the tougher joints on the Barbary Coast. He had figured in one of the legends of that quarter. In one of the places he had worked the house rules forbade serving drinks to either blacks or policemen. One day a black police sergeant lurched in and demanded service. Johnny eight-sixed him, citing the fact that his color and his occupation were against him. The black sergeant, anticipating civil rights legislation by half a century, roared that if he couldn't be served, he would be damned if anyone else was. He then started to take the bar apart and was doing splendidly when a minor quake struck the city. The barstools danced, glasses rattled, and pictures of Lady Godiva and Frankie Bailey were shaken from the wall. "My God," gasped the cop, heading for the bat-wing doors, "don't tell anyone that I did this!"

At Wilson's languid command, Johnny Bray went down to the pantry and fetched three drinks on a silver tray—one for the master, one for his guest, and one for himself. (When less respectable callers than his brother were present, according to the recollection of one of his friends, Wilson sometimes received silver-tray service of a less conventional kind. He occasionally liked a touch of morphine to ease the cares of a rich woman's consort. Johnny Bray would bring him a loaded hypodermic on the silver tray, which the Broadway crowd cited as the last word in high-class living.)

Lunch was also served informally in the master's bedroom while Wilson outlined the dilemma confronting him. The life of a licensed gigolo wasn't all it had promised to be. His bride had turned out to be, as Addison had warned, very stingy with the pocket money. She'd even had the effrontery to suggest that Wilson might consider gainful employment and hinted that with a little exertion he might provide her with a fortune as her first husband had.

Wilson's need for immediate cash naturally had turned his thoughts to all those art treasures which crammed the place and which could be smuggled out and discreetly sold once their provenance was established. That inspiration had been blighted by a reading of Yerkes' last and apparently valid will. Through either some quirk of conscience or an attempt to evade inheritance taxes, Yerkes had bequeathed his paintings to the city of New York. Why, moaned Wilson, had Yerkes spent most of his adult life looting cities and then, in his final days, perhaps unwittingly, struck at his successor in the Mad King's bed by handing over millions to the municipality? Now those paintings couldn't be flogged without involving him in a nasty dispute with the authorities.

The course of Wilson's first and last marriage struck a number of snags at the outset, some of them cropping up as the result of disorderly aspects of his earlier career. His past was encumbered by an alarming number of people who were not inclined to wish him the best of luck.

Within days after news of his supposedly lucrative marriage reached the Pacific littoral, letters began arriving at 864 Fifth Avenue with California, Alaska, Hawaii, and Honduras postmarks. Most of them were signed "A Friend" or "One Who Knows," and all were addressed to the new Mrs. Mizner. They accused Wilson of everything from murder to mopery. One correspondent alleged that Wilson had strangled a girlfriend in Honolulu, though he had never been west of Point Mugu. Others warned that if she didn't take measures to protect herself and be wary of allowing Wilson to serve her morning coffee or keeping rat poison around the place, her bridegroom would soon be a self-made widower.

Wilson affected surprise that so many of his old acquaintances were literate, but those communications made his bride a bit edgy, now that she was a wealthy woman in her own right. She became so upset by the volume of correspondence from the Coast that Wilson threatened to exile himself to Patagonia unless the mail was opened by a secretary and all anonymous letters destroyed.

"They're all from the Black Hand," Wilson airily explained to Myra. The Black Hand, which was the terrorist seedling from which the Mafia grew in America, was then planting bombs all over New York when its victims refused to comply with threatening letters.

Wilson almost believed in his own bogeyman one morning when he awakened with a hangover and every ganglion quivering. He headed for the Caesarian bathroom with its sunken pool of green onyx and gold faucets. On one of the tapestries which decorated the wall was a grimy hand print. The Black Hand was threatening to strike; one of the servants was probably a secret member of the organization. Before ordering the mansion searched for hidden bombs, he solved the mystery himself. The day before he had been visited by a prizefighter friend badly in need of a bath. Rather than have the house fumigated, he ordered his friend into the bathroom. On his way into the sunken tub the fighter had steadied himself, apparently, by grabbing at the tapestry.

He had almost come to believe that it would take the best terrorist squad the Black Hand could muster to separate enough money from Myra to fend off his creditors and keep him in the style he believed he was entitled to. He was a consummate con artist, but Myra was impervious to his supplications. Later Johnny Bray would tell of watching through the boudoir keyhole while Wilson, on bended

knee, protested his love for her and urged her to prove her
own affection by signing the blank check he kept waving in
her face. After an hour of desperately honeyed pleading,
Wilson came out crumpling the unsigned check.

His preoccupation with money, ironically never more
intense than during his months of being domiciled with one
of the wealthiest women in the country, which should have
sounded a cautionary signal for all other fortune hunters,
was interrupted only by news of the San Francisco earthquake and fire on April 6, 1906. His mother, sister, and
several brothers all were caught in that disaster. And no
matter how wayward his behavior, no matter how much he
scoffed at conventional feelings, his familial ties were strong
and abiding. He would always be secretly shattered by a
death in the family, much as he pretended indifference. He
may have been one of the outstanding rule breakers of his
time, but he loved Mama Mizner as much as any homesick
plowboy wandering down a city street and humming
"Mother Machree" to himself.

Two nerve-shredding weeks passed before he received
the news that the Mizners had survived the disaster without
a scratch. His mother's masterly handling of the situation in
which she found herself, in fact, provided a sidelight or two
on how her sons managed to bulldoze, charm, or persuade
so many of their contemporaries. Few escaped from the
shattered city, as Mrs. Mizner did, aboard a steam yacht.
She wrote Wilson and Addison that her first concern, when
the predawn quake struck as she slept in a Sutter Street
hotel, was whether she was properly dressed for the occasion. "Fortunately, I had on one of my nicest nightgowns
with hand embroidery, for in the halls people were running
about in very common lingerie. One lady I knew had on a
cotton affair that was quite horrid. . . ."

After that initial shock her first concern was her more prized possessions. "I had a large trunk in my parlor with my fine old laces. This was covered over with some fine old Guatemala brocade and looked very genteel. It acted as an extra piece of furniture and gave me a place to keep more books and articles on top. I also had a smaller trunk in my bedroom treated in the same way. When one lady came in to tell me that the city was on fire in several places, I decided that I had better sort out my finest things, as I had been told by the management that the fire was coming our way very rapidly and that it would be possible to take only one trunk. Edgar [one of the few men to be caught, profitlessly, in both the Klondike gold rush and the San Francisco earthquake] came in about nine and thought the trunk I had selected was too large and that I had better take the smaller one, so again I sorted and packed, for hours." She must have been one of the few people unaffected by the panic which swept the city.

Her other sons, Lansing and William, also dropped by to make sure Mama was making out all right, Edgar hauled off her small trunk, and Mrs. Mizner set out alone to find refuge. "You must remember," she wrote Wilson and Addison, "that I am getting old and that I have never thought it very elegant for a woman to be seen alone on the streets, so you will see I was very much out of practice. But it was Hobson's choice. Everyone was so laden with their own things that I did not have the heart to ask anyone to help me. . . .

"I am sure you would have laughed, had you seen your mother sitting on odd people's steps from time to time. I had only gone ten streets when I saw a fire engine coming slowly up the hill, so I hurried out into the street and called to the driver to give me a lift. He was a very respectable young man, who told me that he had a mother himself, which he seemed to think odd. So I had him drive me to Mrs. Bourns. I got my gown quite soiled, as the engine seemed to be covered with soot; but as it was better than walking with a heavy bag I said nothing. The driver was such a nice man and had been so polite that when he set me down, I offered him a dollar (a taxi would have been at least two dollars), which he would not accept. He said that he still remembered his mother. . . ."

In a postscript Mrs. Mizner added that she had persuaded a Mr. Hayden to place his steam yacht at her disposal, and she sailed away from the burning city in imperial style. Wilson must have reflected that any man born to a mother who could commandeer a fire engine and a yacht to escape from a catastrophe ought to do well in the world.

With that worry off his mind, Wilson was able to resume working out the problem of how to extract money from Myra. She kept her own collection of jewelry under lock, key, and personal surveillance. The city's pawnshops did, however, make Wilson's acquaintance. In rummaging around the four-story mansion on a daily treasure hunt, he managed to locate a number of his predecessor's knick-knacks: bejeweled watch fobs, studs, cuff links, stickpins, and pinkie rings. The late Mr. Yerkes was partial to necktie pins with snake eyes, one of ruby and one of emerald. The only official complaint Wilson ever made to the police—and that undoubtedly was submitted to befog the issue of his own larceny—detailed how he was robbed at the Hotel Cadillac of several pearl studs, two snakehead pins, and three loose diamonds valued at $7,500. Presumably those had formerly been the property of Myra's late husband, and evidently Wilson had probated part of the Yerkes estate in his own informal fashion.

Probably it was the newspaper accounts of Wilson's misfortune at the Hotel Cadillac where he had maintained bachelor quarters, that induced Myra to engage Pinkerton detectives to keep a watch on her various possessions and see that none of them disappeared with her tricky new husband. In later years Wilson would complain to Hype Igoe, the New York *Tribune*'s sports columnist and also a transplanted San Franciscan, that life as Myra's consort had been more difficult than anyone could imagine. He may have been succumbing to hyperbole, however, when he added, "It's a damned unpleasant experience, Hype, to be stopped by two Pinkertons when you're walking out of your own house with a lard can full of jewels."

Despite her alcoholic vagaries and her social pretensions, Myra was a hardheaded Illinois peasant when it came to protecting her treasures. It took all of Wilson's ingenuity to pry an occasional bauble out of her grasp. In one of his more elaborate schemes, he persuaded her that it was the custom of the socially elect to present diamond links to any ambassadors who dined at their tables. He then engaged a bartender of his wide acquaintance to impersonate the ambassador from Spain, decked out in white tie and tails with a crimson sash across his chest. The scheme worked, but necessarily it was a one-shot idea. Too many ambassadors suddenly appearing at her table would arouse Myra's suspicions.

So far he had managed only to nibble around the edges of the Yerkes fortune. He would have to be more diligent and inventive, or he'd have nothing to show for his marriage when the inevitable day came that Myra had him heaved out into Fifth Avenue. Her stubborn refusal to understand the financial problems of a rich woman's husband occasionally brought on embarrassing public uproars. One evening they were sitting at a table in Peacock Alley at the Waldorf-Astoria, having what he described as "one of those little battles which so often terminate in death to bystanders, supplemented by great headlines." The cause was, as usual, money; Wilson complained bitterly of having so little pocket money that he couldn't tip the waiter and announced that he was seriously considering suicide.

Myra flew into a rage and employed the first object she could lay hands on—an envelope stuffed with currency which she kept in her purse. She began belaboring him with the envelope, and the bills of various denominations flew in all directions.

"I can assure you," he would tell his cronies, "that I was the first on my knees in the scramble that followed and did very well indeed." Myra screeched at him that he could keep the money if he was willing to crawl for it. "I'd picked up eight thousand dollars," he recalled, "before I realized that I had been insulted."

But he couldn't depend on being flailed with $100 bills during one of Myra's tantrums. The old masters on the walls of the Yerkes-Mizner mansion kept preying on his mind, a constant challenge to his demonstrated ingenuity in dealing with knotty problems of probate. The city's representatives had passed along the word that in consideration of allegations that he was a California horse thief, he would be held personally responsible for the masterpieces which Yerkes had left to the city. If any proved to be missing, Wilson would be flung into jail. The value of Yerkes' bequest to the city was estimated at $1,000,000. Later, in tranquillity, Wilson could philosophize over his dilemma. "Larceny and art have never been wholly disassociated," he would put it. His own artistic perceptions, he admitted, were limited to "the greens and golds to be found on currency."

One thing he had noticed about New Yorkers was that they sprang at any supposed bargain in stolen merchandise.

And anything "hot," *ipso facto*, was a bargain. Necessarily
operating on a shoestring, he opened an art gallery at 431
Fifth Avenue. While he sang the ballads she loved so much
in Myra's boudoir, in the throbbing baritone she now considered the only worthwhile quality in her bridegroom, Wilson had a small group of impoverished artists copying the
paintings in the Yerkes collection. The copies were placed
on sale at the Mizner gallery, and word circulated that a
bargain in genuine old masters was available to anyone who
didn't mind owning something which nitpickers might clas-
sify as stolen property. Wilson didn't claim the works on sale
at his gallery were the originals; only his confidential manner, his conspiratorial tone, his frequent glances out the
shop window indicated the buyer was joining in a plot
against the city treasury. It was later claimed that Wilson
and his confederates grossed about $200,000. Among the
copied masterpieces he peddled was one of Sir Joshua
Reynolds' "Portrait of Innocence," a transaction the man
who provided Wilson with his middle name would probably
have approved. Later he admitted that, since his Greenwich
Village corps needed steady employment, he had branched
out a little and sold four copies of the "Mona Lisa" from his
Fifth Avenue gallery.

If he had begun to prosper commercially, the course of his
marriage was getting rougher week by week. He would
always blame the eventual breakup on the continuing influx
of mail from the West warning Myra that she had married a
ruthless desperado. "They came on the costliest stationery,"
Wilson said later, "and really indicated the first social attention she ever had."

Some of the poison-pen letters, he charged, were coming
from people interested in the disposition of the Yerkes

estate. "There was litigation, mind you, and the presence of any adviser was not welcome in many quarters."

Another and equally constant irritant was the discord between Johnny Bray and members of the original domestic staff. Johnny won a score of fights, he said, "during the period in which I was incarcerated in the mansion." Brawling sounds erupted regularly from the servants' quarters and echoed through the neighborhood. Thomas Fortune Ryan, one of Yerkes' partners in the Big Six traction syndicate, lived next door, and nearby there were Fricks, Goelets, Vanderbilts, Whitneys, Goulds, and other important personages trying to maintain standards of gentility and decorum. It made an unseemly impression on that high-toned neighborhood that the Mizners' servants' hall sounded like a beer cellar in Yorkville just before closing time.

Aside from anonymous letters, dissension belowstairs, and Myra's parsimony, Wilson felt for a time that he might be able to settle in comfortably at the Romanesque town house at Fifth Avenue and Sixty-fourth Street. To thin-blooded aristocrats, the departed Mr. Yerkes' taste may have seemed those of the parvenu and vulgarian, but Wilson had always admired the baroque, in manner as well as substance. He felt a growing kinship with his predecessor, sensed that their methods of self-aggrandizement were similar (though Wilson admittedly lacked Yerkes' scope), and that if Yerkes' ghost made an occasional, sardonic appearance at 864 Fifth, it was a friendly presence.

He felt particularly at ease in the Clock Room, in which Yerkes' collection of approximately 2,000 timepieces was kept on display. When Wilson arrived, the collection was neglected and had long been unwound. Perhaps as a gesture to the memory of the man who had provided Wilson with such a salubrious setting, he ordered Johnny Bray to see to it that the other servants kept the clocks wound and exactly on time.

On the hour, the Clock Room reverberated mightily, a shock wave ran through the neighborhood, and people a block away felt their sinuses temporarily cleared. It was a tintinnabulous uproar. Chimes rang, bells tolled, and cuckoos spoke in their eldritch tongue. There was a clock in which a whole cage of stuffed birds twittered when the hour struck; on another, toy peasants came out of their thatched hut and called the cows home, and on yet another a whole string section sawed at their violins. The twenty-four-hour clangor from the Clock Room only increased the household's unpopularity in the neighborhood and therefore made it more valuable in Wilson's eyes.

Friends suffering from a hangover were always invited to inspect the Clock Room just before the hourly barrage went off.

He became such a clock fancier that he installed one of the more raucous cuckoo clocks in his bedroom as a fitting totem to the ménage. He liked to listen to its hourly comment on humanity. One morning, however, he came home sober, therefore out of sorts, and in no mood for birdcalls. The clock awakened him at 3 A.M., and he fancied that he detected a sneering note in its commentary, an impression heightened by the fact Wilson had lost heavily at the gaming tables that night. He tried to take the clock down but found it had been placed too high up on the wall.

Wilson trudged up to the gun room on the fourth floor, found a double-barreled shotgun and brought it back to his bedroom, where he waited grimly for the cuckoo's 4 A.M. performance. One squawk, and he let go with both barrels.

That incident caused Myra to wonder if Wilson would ever be housebroken, even by her amiable standards, as she later disclosed to a sympathetic reporter from the New York *Press*. Further doubt on that score arose when he converted one wing of the mansion into training quarters for prize-fighters in whom he took a commercial interest. She was naturally upset when Wilson's gladiators began doing their roadwork in her Italian garden and the sounds of sparring, of the rough camaraderie of the ring, came up the stairwell to her boudoir.

One character to whom she especially objected was Willus Britt, one of those ubiquitous "old pals" from San Francisco and Nome who seemed to be having a free run of her household. Willus' manners were deplorable, even as viewed by members of his own hard-bitten milieu. He was then managing his brother, Jimmy, a promising lightweight who had been matched with Terrible Terry McGovern in a bout at Madison Square Garden. A few months earlier Jimmy Britt had fought Packy Farland in San Francisco and been knocked down. "Get up, you unnatural son of a bitch," Willus roared from the safety of the managerial perch. "Have you no respect for my feelings?"

Wilson conceded to Myra that Willus Britt was "a bit picturesque," but she could not be dissuaded from ordering the Britt brothers out of her house. "Right," snapped Willus. "This joint ain't classy enough."

When the Britt troupe moved from Fifth Avenue to the more reassuring ambiance of Coney Island, Wilson followed them in his role as special consultant, though he and Myra were not formally separated. He apparently served as the staff psychiatrist. Jimmy Britt suffered constantly from homesickness for the fogs of his native San Francisco. Wilson's remedy was to engage a youth named Julius Marx, who aspired to a career in show business despite a voice better suited to hawking Coney Island red-hots, to sing ballads to the languishing pugilist and restore his morale. Julius, later known as Groucho, Marx went on to better things.

The sportswriters frequenting the training camp seized upon the fact that Wilson, though now a society gent, put on the gloves and sparred daily with Sam Berger, a heavyweight also managed by Willus Britt.

Back on Fifth Avenue Myra was outraged by the stories and photographs of Wilson mixing it with the riffraff on Coney Island. She was trying to move her name off the front pages and into the society section, and she regarded the sports section as a bad detour. Simmering more briskly in her mind now was the question of how much more time and money she should invest in a character who preferred low company and whom the newspapers kept referring to as the Candy Kid.

When Wilson came traipsing home from Coney Island, he was confronted with an ultimatum: Either his valet-companion, Johnny Bray, was to be discharged, or both of them would be evicted. The other servants were threatening to quit en masse if they felt the back of Johnny's hand again. Wilson agreed to send Johnny packing. The next morning, however, another batch of letters arrived from the West warning Myra that Wilson was capable of uxoricide.

Domestic warfare broke out again, and as Wilson related, "in the midst of it I tiptoed out." He tiptoed all the way to Washington, where Myra's lawyers caught up with him and made arrangements for a divorce. A month later the marriage was terminated in court.

Wilson assumed a philosophical stance. "People speak of the matrimonial bark," he told his friends, "but believe me

I've heard it. But I can't complain. After all a telephone pole never hits a joyrider except in self-defense and I was the one who agreed to be married." He simply wasn't geared to life on Fifth Avenue and joyously returned to Broadway and bachelorhood.

6

"NO OPIUM SMOKING
IN THE ELEVATORS"

WILSON'S six-month marriage convinced him that matrimony, from the male viewpoint, was a sucker's game. If marriage to a rich woman was hell, how much worse it would be with a poor one. He did not become a misogynist, he was later found in flagrant delectation with a series of females, but he was adamantly opposed to long-term attachments. Women, he had learned, were better appreciated if a certain intervening distance was maintained.

All he got out of the brief marriage to Myra, according to his brother Addison, was an enameled Russian spoon. He was so broke immediately after the divorce that he had to work for a living, an experience which so damaged his pride that he was resolved never to repeat it.

Broadway was in the summer doldrums when he returned from Washington, to which he had fled after the breakup with Myra, and he removed himself to San Francisco for a reunion with his mother, sister, and brothers and

with the city struggling to recover from the April disaster.
He learned that brother Edgar had distinguished himself
just after the quake by taking charge of the "dynamite
division" which blew up buildings in the path of the fire.
Perhaps it was through Edgar that he obtained a job with
Emile Brougiere, a friend of the Mizner clan, who had
obtained a contract to clear the debris left by the quake and
fire. Wilson was placed in charge of 200 carts engaged in
hauling off rubble.

There was plenty of time to spare from his supervisory
duties to reintroduce himself to San Francisco society, high
and low, from the Barbary Coast to Russian Hill. It would be
his last prolonged stay there; Broadway was the big time,
and he could not quite agree with his friend Willus Britt's
pronouncement that "I'd rather be a busted lamppost on
Battery Street in San Francisco than the Waldorf-Astoria."

Wilson always kept one foot in the underworld and the
other in more respectable society. He would carouse with
the Britt brothers and slip away to Chinatown for an occasional pipe of opium, but he was also on display at dinner
parties and cotillions. One of his fancier friends was Ned
Greenway, the veteran cotillion leader, a short fat man with
protruding eyes and a gallant white mustache, who held the
local title of king of the wine bibbers. Champagne drinking
was a professional as well as social duty for Mr. Greenway,
since he was the San Francisco agent for Mumm's Extra
Dry. It was his oddities rather than his social position that
attracted Wilson. Greenway consumed an average of
twenty-five bottles of champagne every day, with an occasional bottle of beer as a chaser. Once, on a hungover
morning, he was asked how he felt. "No gentleman," he
crossly replied, "ever feels well in the morning." His diet
was another Greenway eccentricity, according to Evelyn

Wells, the chronicler of postquake San Francisco. "He was getting stout and found it difficult to prance as nimbly as before in the cotillions. Despairingly, he was trying to diet, but only after midnight at the end of the evening's festivities. Then at the 'midnight snack,' from which it was his duty as a wine salesman to send everyone home as inebriated as possible, while others reveled in oysters and steaks and turkey and duck, the plump Mr. Greenway ate pickled limes and lady fingers with his champagne. It was his own dietary invention. So far the sacrifice had been in vain."

San Francisco's charms faded for Wilson when a newspaper published an account of how Wilson Mizner, playboy and bon vivant, had turned to honest labor and was helping clean up the debris left by the earthquake and fire. Wilson was highly offended by the story; it damaged his reputation, he said, as a lay-about, black sheep, and wastrel; the job was only a passing whim and had already lost its charm for him. Work, he added, was a rotten way to make a living. "I hate work like the Lord hates St. Louis," he told a man from the San Francisco *Bulletin*. St. Louis, by no coincidence, was where his sanctimonious brother Henry was laboring in the Episcopal vineyard.

Wilson was so disgusted by what he regarded as a gross libel picturing him as a worthy citizen that he prepared to flee the city for New York.

But not before undertaking a farewell binge, at the end of which occurred his celebrated misadventure with the multicolored rats. The scene of his spree was Tim McGrath's saloon on the verge of the Barbary Coast.

He was just weaning himself from the sauce when he happened to look out the rear window of the saloon into McGrath's backyard. Blearily, he saw a red rat romping around among the empties. A moment later a pink rat joined the red rat. Then came a green rat and a yellow rat. They all danced a rigadoon on the rubbish heap.

Delirium tremens! screamed Wilson as he dashed out of the barroom and down the street in search of medical consultation. He found a doctor willing to listen to his troubles and his plea, "Put something in my brain fast," he implored, "because I'm seeing red, pink, yellow and green rats. I'm on the wagon for good."

The physician prescribed bed rest and a strong sedative. Wilson returned to his apartment and holed up there for five days until he read in the newspapers that the health department had dyed rats in various colors to trace their movements during the current flu epidemic on the suspicion that they were spreading the disease. He then felt strong enough to leave for New York.

In the next half dozen years he would pursue a career of extraordinary versatility with New York as his home base. During that period he would serve as manager-referee of the rowdiest hotel in the Times Square area, branch out as a gambler and confidence man, play the Atlantic luxury liners as a cardsharp, and become a celebrated playwright.

He lived by his wits, which were sharp enough to make him an outstanding member of that raffish and hedonistic society which coagulated around Broadway and Times Square and extended one block eastward to Sixth Avenue. From 1906 on he rapidly attained the status of a quasi-celebrity for his streaming wisecracks, his hard-bitten philosophy, his Falstaffian humor, and a studied irreverence which conveyed the cynical materialism of the Edwardian years. He became one of the jets in the fountainhead of American humor, the author of quips and epigrams which circulated around New York, then traveled from coast to coast, and finally embedded themselves in the lexicon with a permanence that indicates that verbal, as well as literary, humor can achieve a sort of immortality.

In the predawn hours at Jack Dunstan's hangout near the Hippodrome at Sixth Avenue and Forty-third Street, where the guests were occasionally inspired to fire salt cellars at one another, where the theater, the underworld, and the more venturesome members of Fifth Avenue society had their alcoholic confluence, he created a Vulgate of the unconventional and unruly element of American life, which with professional help he later converted into theatrical works. He was the oral historian and nonwriting philosopher of the demimonde, the wise man of what he called the Times Square Country Club, in which lifting a shot glass or an outlander's wallet qualified as an athletic event, the "Alcade of the Roaring Forties," as Damon Runyon characterized him.

He was an offbeat social leader who, as his brother Addison observed, "knew everyone, from the best homes to the bawdiest houses." His table at Jack's, from midnight to dawn, provided the liveliest and probably the bawdiest conversation in town. It was the place to be seen and heard if one valued his position in the night world. Among those who jockeyed for a place at Wilson's table were Diamond Jim Brady, Lillian Russell, Peggy Hopkins Joyce, Louise Dresser, John W. "Bet a Million" Gates, Irving Berlin, Eddie Cantor, Ethel Barrymore, Nat Goodwin, Al Jolson, George M. Cohan. The latter, as a leading theatrical producer, was so impressed by Wilson's magnetism, his self-assurance, and his imperious presence that he tried to persuade him to accept the title role in *Get-Rich-Quick-Wallingford*.

Irvin S. Cobb, then the New York *World*'s star reporter, noted that Mizner as an Ambrose Bierce of the Tenderloin

was a true original. "He was more than a copycat, infinitely
more than a sidewalk Grimaldi, or a hired contriver of
mildly naughty entertainment. . . . Here was an authentic
wag, an artificer of darting and devastating repartee. But
when he went in for verbal dueling this gaunt stinging
hornet picked on somebody his own size. He didn't show off
his smartness at the expense of some agitated bus boy or
self-conscious novice. . . ."

His sense of opportunism was as keen as his wit. Behind
the barrage of wisecracks were a pair of steady brown eyes
constantly on the alert for anyone with philanthropic tendencies. One of his friends during this low-water period was
young Jack Barrymore, then an underemployed actor whose
theatrically celebrated family was convinced would never
amount to anything. The fact that Barrymore largely survived through the generosity of Frank Case, the manager of
the Algonquin Hotel, who kept Barrymore on one of the
lengthiest tabs in Manhattan hotel history, had not escaped
Wilson. The latter felt that he, too, could use a sponsor of
Case's magnanimity.

"Describe him," Wilson asked Barrymore, referring to
Case, "particularly his attitude toward the meek in pocket-
book."

Barrymore could only resort to superlatives in describing
Case's tenderness toward the disinherited. "Why, he's the
sort of a man who would give you the . . ." Barrymore looked
down at his resplendent shirtfront. "My God, this *is* one of
Frank's shirts!"

Fate, however, stepped in to provide Wilson with a billet
other than the Algonquin.

It was during one of those late-night sessions at Jack
Dunstan's, which specialized in Irish bacon and eggs as a

specific against prolonged roistering and also provided a nightly spectacular when its flying wedge of waiters propelled bellicose college boys into Sixth Avenue, that Wilson made the connection which resulted in his appointment as the manager of the Hotel Rand on West Forty-ninth Street.

The owner of that establishment—which catered to crooks, whores, pimps, kept women and their keepers, and served as shore base for the cardsharps working the Atlantic liners—was a patron of Jack's and one night listened to Wilson recalling his days as proprietor of a casino and hotel in Nome and his methods of coping with an extremely difficult and ruffianly clientele. Just the man to take hold of the Hotel Rand, its owner reflected. Wilson was hired on the spot.

The Hotel Rand is recalled as the most disorderly caravanserai in the history of Manhattan innkeeping, at least in the section north of the Bowery, and Wilson did nothing to upgrade its reputation. His No. 1 rule as Mine Host was to look with tolerance on his guests' foibles. As an occasional devotee of the opium pipe, then jocularly known as a Hong Kong Flute, he could not object to his patrons' indulgence in the poppy. Nor did he regard himself as a standard-bearer for conventional morality.

Even the Hotel Rand had to maintain a semblance of discipline, however, and Wilson felt it necessary to promulgate a few no-nos. The short list of house rules under his management included:

"No opium-smoking in the elevators.

"Guests must carry out their own dead.

"Guests jumping out of windows will try to land in the net placed around the third floor.

"No piano-playing before 5 P.M. as it may disturb the other guests.

"When the gong rings at 3 A.M., all guests will return to their own rooms."

Genial and tolerant though his manner, Wilson was beset by difficulties in managing the Rand. (According to a New York *Morning Telegraph* story which recapitulated his career as a hotelier, "If a man named Butler or Francis subscribed himself as 'Harrison' on the register, Mr. Mizner never gruffily called his attention to the error, but with the courtliness of the Old School affected not to notice it.") Once the pimps who managed some of the girls in residence petitioned for steam-heated fire escapes on which they could wait in comfort while their protégées entertained the paying customers.

Two guests had Wilson arrested on charges that he beat them up with brass knuckles. He denied the charge and was acquitted, later explaining that experience had taught him never to smite a man with brass knuckles because they inflicted more damage on the slugger than the sluggee. A roll of quarters, he added, was more effective.

Shortly after he took over the Rand's management, with Johnny Bray recalled from San Francisco to act as his assistant, he was hauled up before the magistrates on charges of having thrown two disorderly guests into the fountain in the Rand's lobby.

"Nonsense," Wilson replied to that charge. "The fountain will hold only one man."

"But," he added after being acquitted, "I'm going to have it enlarged."

Once when he and Gene Buck, later the founder and president of the American Society of Composers, Authors and Publishers, were strolling down Forty-ninth Street toward the hotel, Wilson guided his friend to the other side of the street as they approached the Rand. "Never walk under the hotel's windows," he advised Buck. "The girls throwing keys down to their friends will knock your brains out."

One of the odder members of Wilson's staff was one Doc DeGarmo, a talented member of the ring of cardsharps which used the Hotel Rand as their headquarters. Damon Runyon said Doc was so skilled a manipulator that "if you gave the doctor a box of soda crackers he can deal you four queens."

As Runyon recounted the misadventure to his friend Gene Fowler, DeGarmo was forced to retire from trimming incautious passengers on the Blue Ribbon liners of the Atlantic because of a Yuletide mishap that occurred in the lobby of the Rand. Wilson had decided that even the Rand should observe Christmas and appointed Doc to take charge of erecting and decorating the Christmas tree. "The Doc," as Runyon related, "is climbing up on a chair to pin the Star of Bethlehem on the topmost twig of the tree, and he loses his footing, which is none of the best whenever he is charged up with three or four nosegays of the poppy. [Runyon meant DeGarmo had been indulging in the opium pipe.] And his luck is the kind that when he obeys Sir Isaac's law—the only one he ever obeys—and he takes a Brodie, he lands on an open shiv, or cutlass, that somebody has left there while pruning a lower branch of the lovely tree. And the doctor's first finger of his best mitt is cut bad. And he has a real doctor snip it off."

A professional manipulator of playing cards with the index finger missing from his dealing hand is as doomed to redundancy as a one-armed paperhanger. Doc DeGarmo was forced into retirement. To keep him off the streets, Wilson appointed him house physician of the Hotel Rand, although Doc was only a nickname and he was unacquainted with the healing arts. It seemed unlikely that he would be called upon to live up to his new honorific, since most misadventures suffered by residents of the Rand were either fatal or ridiculous. In any case, DeGarmo had become so addicted to his Hong Kong Flute that he was seldom able to perform a diagnosis.

One day when Doc was holed up in his smoke-filled room, Wilson and some of his confederates had latched onto a fat Philadelphia playboy whom they bedazzled with one of Wilson's chorus-girl friends, then lured into a poker game at the Rand.

"It was a fine game indeed," as Runyon related, "that Mr. Mizner cooks up for this tubby fellow from Philly. The stranger had at least four chins, one folded over the top of the other, like in that ad for Michelin tires. They let him win a few pots, and everyone is drinking plenty.

"The play lasts three days and three nights. And the sucker has gone to the South Pole with a bundle. He happens to ask if they got a new deck of cards, if you please. And one of the players gets it into his head that this is a terrible insult to the honest deal. And he thereupon picks up a bottle of Old Taylor and lets the fat boy have it right on the melon. The citizen of Philly is cut up something fearful, and there is more blood let than at Waterloo. Mizner is frantic. He sends for the house doctor to come quicker than at once.

"They have a hard time getting the doctor off his hip. But he finally comes down with his black bag. He almost falls across the patient, whose blood now is pouring in the channels between his various and sundry chins. Doctor DeGarmo diagnoses it as a multiple cut throat. One of the drunks threads a needle, and the doc sews all four chins together. And then they take the victim in a cab to Central Park, and stretch him out on the bridle path."

On hasty reconsideration, however, Wilson decided the

police weren't likely to believe the man had been run over
by a horse or a reckless bicyclist. He looked more as though
he had been clawed by a man-eating tiger. With his hulk,
and the alcoholic condition of Doc DeGarmo's assistants, it
didn't seem feasible, however, to plant him in one of the
cages at the Central Park zoo. The playboy came of a prominent family, would undoubtedly remember the Rand as the
scene of the assault, and would bring a swarm of bluecoats
down on the hotel, who would uncover enough evidence of
misconduct to populate a cellblock at Sing Sing. Finally
Wilson decided the only thing to do was to export his
trouble, take the still-unconscious playboy to Grand Central, and put him on the first train out of town. Meanwhile,
he and his friends would have time to cook up an alibi.

The playboy apparently regained consciousness shortly
after he was placed on a train bound for Wheeling, West
Virginia, and he returned to the Hotel Rand to find Wilson
and his friends conferring frantically in the lobby. "His
looks," as Runyon related, "have taken a big turn toward the
grotesque. He is all hunched over, with his head very low
indeed, what with Dr. DeGarmo having basted his many
chins together. He can only look at the floor, which, you can
lay a hundred to one, by now is mopped up of blood, and the
rug put back all nicely and neat. And the card players make a
bolt towards the door. But Mizner has nerves of absolute
zero, and he tells his colleagues to desist and halt.

"And he acts surprised to see his dear sucker again. He
says a friendly hello to him, and so glad to see you, and what
in the world happened to you, sir? And then everybody is
rocked back on their heels when the bent-over fat boy, who
looks like he is saying a long prayer to St. Luke, pipes up. He
says, so help me, he says he has come back here to *thank* Mr.
Mizner and that wonderful doctor *for saving his life!*"

Wilson lasted only about eight months as manager of the Rand, largely because of a multiplication of incidents which dogged his efforts as an innkeeper. One thing he learned as Mine Host was that it was respectable people who caused all the trouble; the bums were easy enough to handle. The case of the lacerated Philadelphian was only one case in point. Another was the Christian Endeavor convention of the summer of 1907. From all over the country Christian soldiers marched on New York and took up all the available hotel rooms. The crusading tide lapped over the Rand and deposited a number of the delegates in Wilson's rooms, though even an innocent from the boondocks should have sensed that this wasn't the sort of establishment where prayer breakfasts were held, that the funny smell seeping into the lobby wasn't churchly incense but opium smoke, and that the females slipping along the corridors in their kimonos weren't bringing calves'-foot jelly to invalid friends. But there was no way Manager Mizner could turn them away; virtue may have been grotesque in that setting, but it wasn't against the law. Soon his ears were ringing with complaints from the Christian Endeavor delegates about the unholy activities of the other guests. He could only suggest a friendly poker game to take their minds off the sinfulness of the metropolis.

Wilson suffered through an even greater ordeal when his brother the Reverend Henry Mizner wrote that he was coming to New York to verify for himself the incredible report from the family headquarters in California that Wilson had redeemed himself through a career in hotel management. His older brother couldn't be persuaded that a hotel outside the Times Square area would be more suitable for a man of the cloth. During the several days Reverend

Henry was visiting, Wilson did his best to create an atmosphere of respectability. Several times an hour he would break off conversations with Henry to rush across the lobby and shout, "Keep the children away from the elevators." He also hired several women and their children, through an employment agency, to sit around the lobby while Henry was there and look respectable. Henry returned to St. Louis with the conviction that Wilson had turned from the primrose path and might yet be a credit to the family.

Early in October 1907, Wilson announced his retirement as a hotelier. It had been fun, he indicated in an interview, but a bit too strenuous for a man of his retiring disposition. The news of his leaving was such "an interesting topic," one newspaper reported, "that half the chorus girls missed their cues last night."

For the next several years Wilson spent much of his time on the high seas working the cardrooms of the transatlantic liners as what he called a "deep-sea fisherman" casting his line for travelers equipped with well-stuffed morocco wallets. In between voyages, at either end of his New York–London axis, he tried his hand at writing vaudeville sketches and blocking out ideas for full-length plays, though he found that actual literary effort, putting one word after another on a sheet of paper, was a tedious occupation. All the literary men with whom he discussed the matter wholeheartedly agreed that writing was a hellish chore. The only thing that kept drawing him to the quill and inkpot—aside from rumors of Klondike-sized strikes made on Broadway—was his natural flair for storytelling. A born raconteur, with the memory of a Scheherazade, he was constantly being told by his friends that he ought to get some of the stuff on paper.

Jack London, a wharf rat from Oakland, had already made his pile with *The Call of the Wild* and other works about the Yukon.

There was no doubt that the theater attracted him, not only because of a stirring of dramaturgic urges but also because of its beautiful women. He attended most of the play openings on Broadway, and from 1907 began displaying himself at Rector's or Bustanoby's with such stage beauties as Evelyn Nesbit, recently involved in the Thaw-White murder, and Grace Washburn. For a time he made a three-some around the lobster palaces with the opulently curved Lillian Russell, who was between divorces, and her fervent but platonic friend the elephantine and diamond-bedecked Jim Brady. Diamond Jim was always protective about Lillian and feared she might succumb to the Mizner charm, despite the fact that she was twenty years Wilson's senior. If Wilson was making a serious play for the blond musical comedy queen, who weighed in at 165 pounds and was so tightly corseted that she couldn't take a deep breath in public, he was thwarted by Diamond Jim's constant chaperonage. The brief friendship did provide Wilson material for one of his quips about Brady's efforts as a trencherman: "Brady likes his oysters sprinkled with clams and his steaks smothered in veal cutlets."

Wilson cut an impressive figure at opening nights, with his towering (six-foot-three) structure draped in evening clothes. Despite his youth, his long, white, solemn face made him look like an archbishop if one ignored the opportunistic gleam in his dark roving eye. After dark Wilson dressed himself in archducal style, wearing white tie and tails and a few fictitious decorations from foreign governments, carrying a long white stick resembling an episcopal staff, and flaunting an Inverness cape with white satin lin-

ing. His manner was equally grand, his attitude conde-
scending, as though he looked on humanity from a condor's
perch. People tended to bow as he approached. All a bit of
japery. When he opened his mouth, the first of a stream of
wisecracks emerged, and the seignorial impression vanished.

There were several results of his early dalliance with the
theatrical/literary world. One was a one-act play titled *A
Loyal Deception* which was staged at an Asbury Park (New
Jersey) vaudeville theater and sank without a trace. He
wrote another one-acter, *The Three Thieves*, apparently
more along the lines he would subsequently follow as an
associate playwright, but it was not produced.

He also became friendly with O. Henry, who had
emerged from an Ohio prison to start a meteoric literary
career in New York. There was a natural sympathy between
the two men, not only because both had danced along the
narrow verge that separates the lawless from the lawful, but
also because both had a keen appreciation of the flip side of
respectable life, of grifters and gamblers and other people
who, as the saying went, "did the best they could." W.
Mizner was, in fact, a sort of O. Henry character in the flesh.
And they both liked to sit up late and tell stories.

As Wilson was spending some time at the London end of
his cardsharp's axis and whiling away his days on shore by
producing skits for a London music hall, he received a
nine-page letter from O. Henry, whose editors found it
extremely difficult to extract nine pages from him on a story
they had paid for in advance. O. Henry playfully wrote that
he heard that Mizner was peddling material stolen from the
estate of a burlesque magnate who had owned the
copyright. Passing himself off as Mignonette Le Clair,
widow of the burleycue producer, O. Henry demanded

royalties on the skits Mizner had written for the London Circus and threatened to expose him as a fugitive from justice. The O. Henry letter, one of the few manuscripts that writer produced without demanding payment in advance, would always be one of Wilson's few prized possessions.

A rather obscure urge to express himself had been awakened, but it would be several years before Wilson, in collaboration with two other men willing to actually sit at a typewriter and do the donkey work of dramatic composition, made a grab for the laurels of Sheridan, Racine, and Shakespeare.

From 1907 to 1910, according to his later recollection, he made about thirty transatlantic crossings, traveling with a school of sharks that included Swifty Morgan, Frankie Dwyer, and other experts. The Cunard, White Star, and North German-Lloyd passenger liners carried a toothsome collection of marks, their inhibitions loosened by the sea air, whom Wilson and his confederates undertook to teach a lesson: Never play cards with strangers. They spent virtually every hour of their crossings either dangling bait in front of the prospective victims or trimming them at the card tables.

Wilson's role as a member of that larcenous group was chiefly to bedazzle the suckers and lay down the psychological barrage that rendered them helpless to defend themselves at the poker table. As the late Alva Johnston, the most definitive chronicler of the Mizner family history, explained it, "Mizner usually won when he played games of chance, by land or by sea, but he never claimed to be a really great cardsharp. He was, however, a supreme artist at taking a lot of people thrown together by chance and quickly converting them into one big, happy family. His power to produce mirth in a small or moderate-sized group of people is said to have been unequalled. On the first night out, he would have the whole ship's population of prospective suckers bellowing. His function was to deprive them of their reason with Mizner gags; once the brain was completely abstracted, it was time for the cardsharps, dice wizards, and con men to go to work. Mizner, his mission accomplished, might then disport himself as he pleased for the rest of the trip. If his crooked friends prospered, they would make a suitable recognition of his contribution to the success of the voyage."

Much of what Mizner and his associates accomplished in the way of latter-day piracy on the high seas is lost to history. Neither victims nor successful crooks care to discuss such matters, though Wilson in later years was volubly candid on the subject. What does emerge from the murk decently enfolding those rigged games of chance and the outcries of their losers are a few sidelights on some classic roguery. Swifty Morgan, later a renowned Times Square character studied with interest by Damon Runyon and other connoisseurs, was a small, wiry man who looked like a jockey. His specialty, as he later defined it, was enticing, then fleecing upper-class English travelers, who were always fascinated by any personage connected with the turf. Swifty, of course, passed himself off as a famous American jockey. The ace of Wilson's group was Frankie Dwyer, one of those eupeptic, beguiling Irishmen. Dwyer's blue eyes and beautiful smile established trust and confidence at the poker table; they even persuaded his victims, on more than one occasion, to drop charges against him when the New York police met the ship and arrested Dwyer in the customs shed. The great detective William A. Pinkerton devoted many painful hours, as a hireling of the steamship companies, to trying to snare Dwyer and send him to prison.

One gambit which Dwyer used to engage the interest of a prospective victim was to shake a pair of dice in his hand, drop one, walk away, then return to study it intently. The steel magnate Charles M. Schwab, an inveterate gambler who once had to be reproached by J. P. Morgan for undermining public confidence in their breed by dropping huge sums on the tables at Monte Carlo, was said to have been taken in by Frankie Dwyer's dice-rattling act. Schwab picked up one of the dice Dwyer dropped and promptly lost $70,000 to him at shooting craps.

Once, Wilson later admitted, he tried to use Dwyer's patented approach play. He kept dropping one of his dice in front of a prosperous-looking Englishman, and the latter kept ignoring the fumbles. Finally, they were introduced by a mutual friend and took tea together. Wilson hopefully kept dropping his cube; the Englishman refused to take the bait. Finally, infuriated, Wilson dropped one of the dice into the Englishman's cup of tea. The latter took a sip, spotted the cube, and roared at the nearest waiter, "Steward, my lump of sugar has specks on it!"

Generally Wilson did right well on a crossing, through either his own efforts or those of his confederates operating in the hilarious, unbuttoned atmosphere he created for their purposes. The marks were well heeled or they wouldn't be traveling first-class on a luxury liner, and usually they could afford their losses without more than a slight quiver of pain. His conscience certainly was never troubled by the methods he used to keep himself in caviar, champagne, and Inverness capes. His attitude toward his victims was not one of pity or regret, but for reasons any amateur Freudian could explain was a fierce resentment. The sucker *deserved* to be taken, *needed* to be taught a lesson, and therefore, Wilson and his fellow sharpshooters were justified in their activities, according to their own reverse morality. He seemed to have a "genuine hatred" for suckers, Alva Johnston wrote. "He regarded them as a corrupting influence. He never showed regret for his misspent life, but his bitterness on the subject of suckers evidently reflected a deep conviction that he would have been a credit to society if he had not fallen into their company. He asserted that confidence men did not find suckers. The suckers, he said, hunted up the confidence men and usually brought them suffering and disgrace. He regarded the sucker as an unconscious *agent provocateur*. The police were never known, he asserted, to catch a confidence man until the suckers found him for them."

Besides such hazards to personal morality as victims forcing themselves on him and clamoring for punishment, he suffered from the comic results of one disguised crook cheating another, the sort of contretemps that made for graceless scenes and ironic recriminations. He was badly confused by a very stylish passenger, who seemed to be dripping money and trailing an aristocratic pedigree, but who was better known to her friends as Deep-Sea Kitty. Another time he lured into a poker game a fellow passenger with a witless demeanor who looked ripe for the plucking. Wilson not only allowed himself to be inveigled into a session of poker with the rube but also let him win a few hands by way of encouragement. Somehow the sucker kept on winning, despite Wilson's most expert manipulation of the laws of chance. In the showdown, Wilson spread out a hand containing four queens which had come into his possession by no accident. His opponent displayed four kings.

"You win," said Wilson bitterly, the truth dawning on him that he had met a mechanic of superior talent, "but those are not the cards I dealt you."

There were more embarrassing scenes than Wilson's occasional comeuppances which finally disbanded the little
group of poker pirates who had been plying the Atlantic
luxury liners. The police on both sides of the Atlantic and
the Pinkerton detective agency were making it uncomforta-
ble for cardsharps because reports had begun widely circulating on how many innocents had been lured into rigged
card games, and that was bad for the transportation business. The steamship companies had not greatly interfered
with the cardsharps—they paid their first-class fares, after
all—until they made themselves notorious. It was yet
another case of success leading to excess, the folly of over-
reaching which Wilson had always warned himself against.

During the crossing of the stately *Mauretania* in June,
1908, there was a scandalous episode involving Frankie
Dwyer and his associates (not including, on that voyage,
Wilson Mizner) and three passengers named Eric Thornton, F. C. Pirkis, and R. L. McLeay. Dwyer was playing
bridge with the three men while several of his confederates
watched the action. Thornton became suspicious of Dwyer's
extraordinary luck with the pasteboards and threw a glass of
brandy in his face.

A fracas ensued, in which the smoking room of the
Mauretania suffered heavy damage. Dwyer's friends
pitched in to help him. The brawl moved from the debris of
the smoking room to the deck outside. It ended only when
Dwyer, whose sojourning in France had provided him with
an expert knowledge of *savate*, rapidly kicked each of the
three adversaries in the groin and put them out of action.

That wasn't the end of *L'Affaire Mauretania*, however.
Bluecoats were waiting at the gangplank to take Dwyer into
custody, and several New York newspapers front-paged the
affray, expanding on what after all was only a matter of

disputed luck at the gaming table. A spokesman for the Cunard line was quoted as saying that anyone who played cards with strangers on a ship needed a nurse or guardian.

Enough heat was created by the newspapers to make deep-sea fishing in the Miznerian sense a rather hazardous occupation. Wilson himself made a number of crossings after that, but Dwyer, whom he greatly admired, went on to other things, including the operation of a diploma mill, or medical institute, which produced a crop of instant MD's. In his lengthy career, which lasted until his death in 1929, Dwyer was never once convicted.

Without Dwyer and other such bright spirits, ocean travel became much less interesting to Wilson. It wasn't crime in itself that fascinated him but the scheming, the honing of wits that accompanied it. After Dwyer and company were discouraged from foreign travel by increased security measures over the first-class passenger list, Wilson as a solo performer was listless, uninspired. He needed other people around to appreciate his capers—even, as events proved, his legitimate ones.

7

IN STANLEY KETCHEL'S CORNER

THE wonderfully varied phases of Wilson's career were usually brief but spectacular and were marked by his unconventional attitude toward the principles and established practices of whatever pursuit engaged him at the moment. Everyone knew that the chief duty of the manager of a champion prizefighter was to keep his man in top form and protect him from all manner of dissipation. Yet when Wilson was briefly the mentor of middleweight champion Stanley Ketchel, he only contributed to the hectic style of Ketchel's young life.

Ketchel once disappeared on the eve of a fight at Johnstown, Pennsylvania. Mizner searched every deadfall and whorehouse until he found his tiger holed up in a hotel with a blonde, a brunette, and a smoldering pipe of opium.

Most other fight managers would have routed the delinquent out of bed and back to the gymnasium, but Wilson took a tolerant view of the situation. For all his fistic laurels,

Ketchel was a mere stripling in his early twenties who had
come out of the smelters of Butte, Montana, and had fought
his way through the ranks in a remarkably short time. Pound
for pound, he was the most ferocious artisan in the prize ring
and, along with Mickey Walker and Sugar Ray Robinson,
would be regarded by boxing historians as the most formidable of the middleweight champions. The boy needed a
little relaxation. Instead of reproaching him, dousing the
opium pipe, and chasing the girls away, Wilson started
removing his clothing.

"What the hell could I do?" Wilson said later in recount-
ing the incident. "I said, 'Move over.' "

He entered the fight game after deciding that cardsharping on the Atlantic run was becoming too hazardous, what
with the ship's personnel sending up signal rockets every
time the more prosperous passengers sat down to play poker
with a strange face at the table. Prizefighting had always
fascinated him from the time he managed the boxing bear on
a tour of Montana, and he'd had some experience as a
manager in Nome. Furthermore, he was an amateur
brawler of some considerable talent. Twice he had been
arrested in New York for barroom brawls, and a San Francisco weekly once published an article detailing a fight in
Spider Kelly's saloon in which Wilson was reported to have
taken on the whole bar and was finally subdued by the
combined efforts of three patrons, a policeman wielding a
nightstick, and a bartender with a bung starter. He once
sparred with the heavyweight Tom Sharkey and performed
so nimbly that Sharkey's manager implored him to turn
professional. His spindly legs, however, would not have
carried him through the thirty- and forty-round bouts of the
time, as he realized, and besides, the spartan routine of the
training camp would have proved intolerable. The disap-

proval of the Mizner clan, from whom he always endeavored
to keep secret his less respectable activities, may also have
persuaded him not to exploit professionally the mulelike
kick he had in both fists.

Wilson sideslipped into the boxing game just at the time
when it was in the worst emotional turmoil of its history. It
was what boxing historians called the White Hope Era,
which began when the great black heavyweight Jack Johnson knocked out the champion of his division, Tommy
Burns, in Australia in 1908. The whole white race, or at least
that segment vitally concerned about who wore the
heavyweight crown, was crushed by the news cabled from
Down Under. Historically, there had been a "color line" in
the prize ring. John L. Sullivan had refused to meet the
outstanding challenger, Peter Jackson, because the latter
was a West Indian black.

A seriocomic half dozen years followed Johnson's attain-
ing the heavyweight championship. Sports pages clamored
for a white man capable of knocking the crown off Johnson,
who was not only huge and competent but also light on his
feet. (The situation for white supremacists was eased only
after Johnson got himself in trouble with the law over a
Mann Act violation and had to flee the country disguised as
the member of a black baseball team from Chicago.) Meanwhile, the gymnasiums from New York to San Francisco
were filled with large, musclebound white youths being
groomed for a shot at Johnson's title and being abjured by
their managers to save the white race from disgrace. Never
have so many innocent bumpkins stumbled down the chutes
to the slaughterhouse; tournament after tournament was
held to weed out the pretenders and find some Caucasian
capable of climbing into the ring against Johnson and not
collapsing from fright before the first-round gong rang. In

1908, just after Johnson won the title, Fireman Jim Flynn
was regarded as the leading White Hope, but unfortunately
he met Sam Langford, a first-rate black boxer who was not
even a heavyweight, in San Francisco. Langford knocked
Flynn right into the lap of the sportswriter who had been
especially vehement in boosting Flynn's chances as the
savior of the blue eyes, saying, "Here comes your champion."

There were many other missteps in the search for a
Caucasian champion, as related by the late John Lardner in
his study of the White Hope frenzy. One Luther McCarty of
Driftwood Creek, Nebraska, was built up as a serious contender and overconfidently matched against a journeyman
named Arthur Pelkey. In the first round Pelkey cuffed
McCarty on the side of the face, and the latter collapsed.
Victor McLaglen, later an Oscar-winning character actor in
Hollywood, entered the lists and was knocked out by one
Sailor White. The big buildup also was given Carl Morris, a
240-pound locomotive engineer on the Frisco Line, who
had distinguished himself in various roundhouse brawls and
was carefully managed through a number of elimination
bouts which ended with his opponents' folding up with
suspicious alacrity after a few rounds. Then Morris was
matched with the old trial horse Fireman Jim Flynn and was
cut up so badly and bled so profusely that the referee had to
change his shirt midway through the ten-round fight.

Wilson first met Stanley Ketchel in Marysville, California, just before he began his amazing rise through the
middleweight ranks. Ketchel was barely twenty, a slender
but wiry blond youth with light-blue eyes, who had
toughened himself by wheeling barrows of slag around the
smelters of his hometown of Butte. The name on his birth
certificate was Stanislaus Kiecal. Like Wilson, he was a

mother worshiper and could whip up the necessary rage to batter down an opponent in the ring only by muttering to himself, over and over, "The son of a bitch insulted your mother."

Ketchel had come to Marysville to fight Joe Thomas, who claimed the middleweight championship, on July 4, 1907. He checked in with the promoter, Tom Fogerty, the owner of a Marysville saloon, a few days before the fight. Wilson was sitting in Fogerty's office when Ketchel strolled in wearing a torn hunting cap, a blue shirt, and a pair of cowboy boots. Ketchel was carrying all his belongings in a satchel: a pair of running shoes worn at the heels, a lumpy pair of boxing gloves, and a pair of red-silk boxing trunks—the capital on which a notable, though brief, career was founded.

Wilson was impressed when the youth fought the veteran Thomas to a draw in their twenty-round bout. But Ketchel faded from his vision for the next couple of years. In 1908 Ketchel was being managed by a San Franciscan, Joe Coffman, who guarded him night and day to prevent other managers from stealing him. Coffman was outwitted and outmaneuvered by Wilson's tricky friend Willus Britt, who had just about given up on his brother Jimmy, the lightweight. Britt climbed a fire escape to the hotel room in which Coffman had locked up Ketchel, gave him a fast line, and made off with the fighter still in his bathrobe.

That was when Mizner came back into Ketchel's life. He and Hype Igoe, the sportswriter from San Francisco now writing a column for a New York newspaper, were engaged as special, unpaid consultants to Willus Britt in managing Ketchel's career. They would advise Britt on the showmanship angles to the buildup they planned for the fighter from Butte.

Undoubtedly, Mizner decided, Ketchel was the kind of
tiger who, properly managed and promoted, would make a
colorful addition to the fight game. He studied the early part
of Ketchel's career and gleaned information to be supplied
the sportswriters and publicity experts for the promoters.
To support his widowed mother, Julia Oblinki Kiecal, the
youth worked as a waiter in a tough miners' saloon in addition to working days at the smelter. One night some drunk-
en miners drew their pistols and forced the piano player to
dance while they fired bullets into the floor under his feet.
The piano player danced until he dropped from exhaustion,
at which point Ketchel tore into the miners and in about ten
seconds laid out the three largest and toughest of the
pianist's tormentors. Every Saturday night for twenty-three
weeks after that exhibition in the saloon he was matched
against all comers in a local arena. Ketchel, a mild-
mannered youth except when he whipped himself to a fury
in the ring, knocked out all twenty-three. The prodigy then
went further afield and began fighting all comers in the
middleweight division throughout the West, until he came
under the management first of Coffman, then of Britt.

Britt managed Ketchel through several more West Coast
fights before deciding to bring him East for the top money.
It was then that Mizner proved his worth as cultural adviser
to the Ketchel-Britt enterprise. A salable persona had to be
created for the fighter; you not only had to win, but you had
to draw the crowds to the box office. Britt bought a Phi Beta
Kappa key at a pawnshop and intended to present Ketchel as
a young man who was fighting his way through a college
education. Wouldn't do, Mizner advised him. Ketchel's
diction more closely resembled that of a roustabout than a
budding scholar, he pointed out. Remembering how
Ketchel was dressed when he first met him before the

Thomas bout in California, Mizner suggested that he be outfitted with high-heeled boots, chaps, a bandanna, and a ten-gallon hat and be publicized as a Wild Westerner. Certainly this more closely matched Ketchel's furious activities in the ring than posing as a member of a scholastic honor society.

Another of Wilson's duties as minister plenipotentiary to the fight world was to guide Britt through the intricacies of political corruption as it pertained to staging boxing exhibitions. Prizefights were then illegal under the New York statutes, as they were in many other states. If you laid bribes on the right people, however, "exhibitions" of the manly art, conducted under the guise of physical fitness programs, could be held at private-membership clubs. No winners were proclaimed in such contests, the decision being left to the sportswriters present. Even so, the police were inclined to raid any "exhibition" for which bribes had not been paid in advance. It was Wilson's job to figure who had to be bribed and could guarantee that the fix was really in.

He often found his job as Britt's grand vizier more than a trifle difficult because Britt, much as he liked the advisers around him, because they fattened his entourage and increased his feeling of self-importance, often failed to act on their suggestions. Instead, Britt made decisions by consulting a pack of cards as a self-taught fortune-teller. If a "bad" card came up, one of the higher spades, it signified he was to back away from whatever move he was considering. Wilson decided to cure Britt of that hocus-pocus type of decision making and substituted a deck of cards containing nothing but the queen of spades. Every time Britt consulted the deck he stared disaster in the face. After being bedded with a case of nervous collapse, Britt decided to give up fortune-telling and relied on the suggestions of his friends.

Thanks to the promotional talents and propaganda making of Wilson, Hype Igoe, and other sports-page connections, Stanley Ketchel was coming to the fore as the fighter
who might carry the banner of white supremacy. He was
light even for a middleweight, about 155 pounds, and was
outweighed by at least 50 pounds by the black heavyweight
champion, but he was being publicized as a future van-
quisher of Jack Johnson. If all those stumbling giants
couldn't prove themselves worthy of getting into the ring
with Johnson, maybe a good little man, particularly one with
the tigerish ferocity of a Ketchel, could turn the trick.
Stanley was willing. He would have fought a whole platoon
of heavyweights if the price were right.

The first step up in class and weight came when Ketchel
was matched with Philadelphia Jack O'Brien, the light
heavyweight champion. The first Ketchel-O'Brien fight was
staged in New York. O'Brien was a dancing master who
flitted around the ring in a flurry of intricate steps and
lightning jabs. Ketchel was a slugger, despite his slender
physique. For seven rounds O'Brien made him look like a
clodhopper who didn't belong in the same ring. By the
eighth round, however, O'Brien had waltzed himself into a
state of exhaustion, and Ketchel began tagging him with
punishing blows. In the tenth round Ketchel knocked him
down. The closing gong sounded when the count had
reached six, but O'Brien couldn't be revived for another half
hour. Some of the sportswriters' decisions favored O'Brien
on the grounds that he had won most of the rounds on
points. O'Brien, who was literate and accounted something
of a prize-ring intellectual, if only on default by most of his
peers, commented in his stately style that Ketchel was an
"example of tumultuous ferocity." Nevertheless, he agreed
to a rematch in Philadelphia some weeks later. In the return

engagement, Ketchel knocked him out in three rounds. Or so the record books say. O'Brien himself, many years later, claimed that he "took a dive" so that the buildup for Ketchel would be enhanced. The suggestion that he might have participated in fixing a fight would not have stunned any of Wilson's friends.

By midsummer of 1909 it was clear to the cognoscenti that Stanley Ketchel was the only one of the crop of White Hopes who could step into the ring with Jack Johnson without courting mayhem. He had won, lost, then rewon the middleweight title in rapid succession with Billy Papke as his opponent. In their last meeting Ketchel had knocked Papke out in the eleventh round.

Despite the 50-pound discrepancy between the two fighters, Ketchel was matched to fight Johnson in Colma, California, on October 16, 1909. At the weigh-in, the scales were doctored so that Ketchel's weight was given out as 170, Johnson's as 195.

Surprisingly enough, the fight went twelve rounds.

For eleven rounds both Ketchel and Johnson contented themselves with sparring in the most gentlemanly fashion. Johnson could hardly have been gentler with his own mother. Ketchel subdued his natural ferocity, an effort immeasurably assisted by the fact that Johnson towered over him. There had been an agreement beforehand that neither fighter was to behave too aggressively for at least ten rounds, so the newsreel company which had the film rights to the fight would get enough footage to make it worthwhile—or so the Broadway wise guys murmured, particularly after looking over the film of the fight.

In the twelfth round white men's hopes surged when, in a sudden flurry, Ketchel managed to knock Johnson down. Johnson went down with a thud that indicated the knock-down wasn't part of the prefight choreography, that Ketchel in a moment of regrettable optimism had decided he might lay out his massive opponent. The black champion spent a few seconds on the canvas looking thoughtful, then got up and threw his Sunday punch at Ketchel. The latter went down for the ten-count, and one more white man bit the dust; it would be years before Johnson yielded his title to Jess Willard in Havana and a white man didn't have to wince every time he heard the phrase "heavyweight champion of the world."

Willus Britt died shortly after the Johnson fight, and Wilson then assumed full charge of Ketchel's career. Its upward trajectory had leveled off by the time Wilson took over. Ketchel had taken a lot of punishment in the three Papke fights and the one with Johnson, but he was only twenty-two years old and still a superb fighting machine. He had, however, acquired a taste for the fleshpots and was going the traditional route—wine, women, silk shirts. A sportswriter charged that Ketchel was "hitting the hop," meaning that he had acquired a taste for the opium pipe. At times Ketchel would train religiously in a camp on Staten Island, but mostly he seemed intent on enjoying his status as a White Hope and middleweight champion.

There were conflicting opinions on Mizner's influence on Ketchel. Certainly no one would have chosen Wilson as a guide to clean living and elevated thought, but one of his more fervent admirers wrote that Wilson did his best to protect Ketchel from the pitfalls of the big city and pointed out that Ketchel was a headstrong young man who could become violent if subjected to too much restraint. "It took plenty of effort on Mizner's part to fend him from the sycophantic parasites and 'idea men'—to say nothing of the multitude of ladies fawning on him. . . . Constantly Mizner induced Ketchel to send fractions of his sizeable earnings to his folks. . . . Even as Ketchel strolled Broadway, a startling figure with his dinner coat, three large diamonds in his stud holes and a huge Stetson hat, the fighter had made it clear he was intent upon returning to farm life when his money made the future secure."

Wilson considered himself Ketchel's mentor in more ways than the strictly pugilistic. He may have served as his guide to the more esoteric pleasures, on the theory that the fighter should enjoy himself thoroughly before succumbing to the head noises which invariably afflicted fighters of his day, but he also broadened the Polish youth's interests, taught him to play the piano, read sentimental poetry to him when he became restless with the routine of the training camp at New Dorp, Staten Island. One poem which never failed to soothe Ketchel, a celebration of bucolic joys by the New York journalist Bob Davis, whose closest acquaintance with rural life was the slaughterhouses on Tenth Avenue, ran:

> I want to go back to the orchard,
> To the orchard that used to be mine;
> I want to stand deep in the wildwood,
> In wildwood the color of twine.
> I want to go back to the turnstile,
> The turnstile that's out by the barn,
> The rocks and the rills—and sweet daffodils.
> I want to go back to the farm. . . .
> I want to go back to the farm.

After hearing Mizner recite the verse in a tremulous baritone, Ketchel would slip away snuffling quietly, and Wilson would remark to his guests, "Just a little attack of whiffle-tree fever. He'll be back. What a holy terror I'm managing."

Ketchel's Slavic sentimentality was a constant wonder to Wilson, whose blood always ran a degree or two cooler than most men's. One night he took Ketchel to the Tenderloin's fanciest parlor house, where they were greeted with the barrage of champagne corks, the madam's flashiest smiles, and the twittering of her protégées, which were reserved for the biggest spenders. Wilson was spreading his charm around the parlor of the establishment when he noticed that Ketchel was missing. Upstairs with one of the girls? No, he was found still in the entrance hall, sobbing over a picture on the wall. It showed a little lamb lost in a blizzard. "Oh, oh," Ketchel sobbed, "the poor little thing."

Whatever Wilson's influence on the fighter, whether he encouraged Ketchel's dissipations or not, Ketchel performed quite well under Wilson's management. His meeting with Sam Langford, the Boston Tar Baby, on April 27, 1910, though only a six-rounder, became one of the legends of the pre-World War I prize ring. Ketchel's talents as a furious brawler were pitted against Langford's boxing skill. Ketchel was outweighed by 10 pounds and was baffled by Langford's style. The latter had very long arms for a man of his dumpy build, and a pile-driver left hook to the body that left many of his opponents with broken ribs. In their Philadelphia fight, Ketchel took a beating for five rounds but came out of his corner in the sixth like a mincing machine and almost laid Langford out. Rarely, it was said, have six rounds between professional fighters been so crammed with action. The decision, as usual, was rendered by the sportswriters. Several gave Ketchel the decision because of his performance in the last round, but the foremost boxing expert, Bat Masterson of the New York *Morning Telegraph*, the retired gunfighter, called the fight a draw.

That was a nontitle fight, but Ketchel also defended his middleweight championship on several occasions with Mizner as the chief adviser in his corner. They journeyed to Boston to confront one Porky Flynn. Just then a number of soothsayers, not yet called psychics, were filling the newspapers with predictions that the end of the world was coming. Unfortunately for Ketchel's peace of mind, the oracles pinpointed midnight on the night of the Ketchel-Flynn fight as the moment when the heavens would open and mankind would be summoned to the Judgment Seat.

Ketchel was a religious young man when he wasn't consorting with blondes, and he took the predictions seriously. On the afternoon of the fight he and Wilson stood on the roof of the Westminster Hotel watching the approaching eclipse of the sun and pondering the significance of the windstorm roaring around the Back Bay rooftops. Wilson tried to laugh him out of his intense concern, but Ketchel told him, "You can joke, but believe me this weather and these winds are pretty queer. If the world is coming to an end, I honestly can't see much sense in beating Porky Flynn tonight. Who's going to pay any attention to it tomorrow and where am I going to send the money? When the world is coming to an end, a guy ought to rest and think it all over. My mind won't be on this fight until tomorrow—and I'm fighting Flynn tonight."

Wilson read reams of sentimental poetry to distract his gladiator in the few hours before the fight, but Ketchel climbed into the ring with a faraway look in his pale-blue eyes. He contemplated eternity and could barely spare a glance for Porky Flynn on the stool across the ring. Despite the abstractions buzzing in his head, he soundly beat Flynn and went back to New York with the title still in his possession. (The world didn't come to an end that night, after all.)

His next-to-last fight was with middleweight challenger Willie Lewis, a bout arranged and privately choreographed with the understanding that neither fighter would try to knock the other out. Whatever the newspaper decision in the six-round bout, therefore, Ketchel would keep his title. Lewis and his manager broke the agreement with Ketchel and Mizner, as often happened with a "fix" when a championship was at stake.

In the first round Ketchel kept missing with his punches, as per agreement. Naively depending on the opposition's word of honor, he left himself open for a moment. Lewis seized the opportunity to launch a paralyzing blow. Ketchel almost went down and barely managed to weather that opening round. During the interval, instead of submitting to his handlers' ministrations with sponge and smelling salts, Ketchel stood on his stool and fixed Lewis with a basilisk stare, the look of a Polish lancer glowering across the Masurian Lakes at a fresh batch of the Teutonic Knights. Wisely, but futilely, Lewis got on his bicycle and backpedaled furiously during the second round, but Ketchel trapped him against the ropes and smashed him to the canvas for a knockout.

Ketchel's last fight, on June 10, 1910, in New York, matched him with a heavyweight named Jim Smith. It was a lackluster bout, in which Ketchel's energies seemed to the boxing experts at ringside to have been dissipated. Ketchel managed to knock out Smith in the sixth round, but he was windblown and close to dropping from exhaustion.

Wilson in all his elegance caught Bat Masterson's hostile eye that night. Masterson wrote in his *Morning Telegraph* column: "Wilson Mizner was on deck, of course, bossing the fight in the champion's corner. He was dressed as though for a party instead of a fight and did not soil his immaculate attire by swinging a towel or dashing water with a sponge." It was Masterson's curious theory that Ketchel was being ruined as a fighter by sartorial excess. Under the Mizner influence, Masterson wrote, Ketchel was becoming a dude, a tailor's dummy, a Fancy Dan. Ketchel, under Wilson's tutelage, was worrying more about the cut of his tailcoat than the precision of his left jab. Why, Masterson continued, he had even witnessed with his own eyes the unseemly spectacle of Ketchel and his mentor, dressed in ambassadorial fashion, leading the grand parade which marked the opening of the season at Hot Springs, Arkansas.

Despite Masterson's forebodings, Ketchel was still more interested in his calling than in the color of his cravat. Though low in funds, he and Wilson decided to go out to California to attend the Jack Johnson-Jim Jeffries championship fight. Jeffries had retired from the ring six years before, but had been persuaded to come out of retirement because the succession of White Hopes had failed to dislodge the crown from Johnson's head. Jeffries had become the Last Hope of all those pale-skinned millions who could hardly sleep nights for worrying over the fate of the white race. When they arrived in San Francisco, Ketchel and Mizner bet all the money they could raise on Johnson—the only practical thing—while harboring the perverse hope that Johnson would get his block knocked off. Naturally they were somewhat aggrieved by their own loss to Johnson the year before.

As Wilson told the story, he and Ketchel bet so heavily they barely had enough money to make it to Reno when the governor of California suddenly prohibited the fight and it had to be transferred out of state. "I remember that Steve, as I always called Stanley, and I went down to the barber shop of the St. Francis Hotel right after hearing the bad news of the switch. He was quick to laugh even in adversity. . . .

"When the barber threw me back in the chair I was just a nervous breakdown with a beard. I had reached the conclusion that we were going to have a mighty hard time getting to Reno to see that fight. 'What can I do for you?' the barber asked. 'Just cut my throat from ear to ear,' I answered."

They made it to Reno on borrowed funds and found that desert town packed with fight fans scrambling for meals and beds. The fight was to be held on July 4, and the heat only contributed to the tinderbox atmosphere. Gun-bearing deputies had to be stationed in the hotels and restaurants to keep order. And the temper of the white partisans was so touchy that Wilson wondered if they could bear up under Jim Jeffries' defeat without starting a race riot. "A vast multitude of negroes," he noted, "had come to see this fight and it was freely predicted that, if Johnson won, all these negroes would not get safely home."

As he recalled, Ketchel was determined to throw a monkey wrench or more accurately a left hook, into preparations for the bout. And Stanley could be very Slavic when he got an idea into his head. He was determined that the fight wouldn't take place after he and Wilson paid an exploratory visit to Jim Jeffries' training camp.

"Stanley knew Jeffries well and liked him," Wilson recalled, "but when we went out to Jeff's camp to see him, Stanley, who had fought Johnson, knew instantly which way this fight to 'maintain white supremacy' was sure to go. Jeff had been out of the ring for six years and looked it. Further, the pressure of this tricky responsibility in which he was literally accountable to the white race for the proper defense of its alleged group superiority, weighed so heavily upon him that he was walking around in a daze. He had done everything possible to get into good condition, but the old boy simply was not there, and knew it. Johnson, the Galveston roustabout, was a cagey, able fighter. Whatever his actual abilities, they had been magnified in Jeff's mind so that, uncertain of his own comeback prowess, he was licked before he ever got into the ring.

"When we came away from that visit, Stanley was preoccupied. We walked away in silence. 'What do you think?' I asked Ketchel finally, although I was pretty sure of the answer.

" 'He's licked,' said Ketchel."

Ketchel brooded over the situation for the several days before the fight, much more concerned about the honor of the white race than the sophisticated Mizner was. Wilson's mind was zeroed in on the outcome of all the wagering they had done; it was never difficult for him to differentiate between sentiment and self-interest. What it came down to was that if Jeffries won, he and his tiger might have to beat their way back East on the brake rods of the fast freights. The less complicated mind of Stanley Ketchel was willing to forgo the profits. The victory of a white man over a black —especially one who had knocked him out—was more important than a few thousand dollars in bets.

The day before the fight Ketchel came to Mizner with a proposition that thoroughly alarmed the latter and made him wonder whether Stanley hadn't taken too many blows to the cerebellum.

Ketchel proposed that at the weighing-in ceremonies,

when various celebrities and other fighters would shake
hands with Jeffries and Johnson, he would lay his best punch
on Jeffries' jaw. The blow would be so devastating in both its
physical and psychological effects that the fight would have
to be called off. Thus, by Ketchel's corkscrew reasoning,
something of the remaining white pride would be salvaged if
yet another white man, especially a former champion,
wasn't humiliated by the black champion.

Wilson vigorously contested Ketchel's proposed action.
Who were a pair of scufflers like Mizner and Ketchel to bear
the white man's burden? The white race, he argued, would
survive even if Jeffries was knocked out in the first round.
Crusader's armor was too snug a fit around the shoulders.
And then he delivered the clincher:

"Think of our dough. We've got everything, including
borrowed money, tied up in Johnson's winning the fight."

Wilson was sweating by the time he persuaded Ketchel
not to go through with his knuckle-headed scheme. Events
proved his was the right, if unsentimental, course. Johnson
toyed with Jeffries for fifteen rounds, then with a triphammer
sequence of malletlike blows from both fists sent him
crashing to the canvas. Rex Beach, who was covering the
fight for a New York newspaper, recalled that the whites at
ringside were drenched in melancholia. A woman rancher
"wept copiously" and turned to the hulking man in the next
seat and said, "Please show me the way out, Mister, I'm
crying so I can't see." Her neighbor was Bull Montana, then
a prizefighter himself but later a movie villain with a fearsomely
brutal visage. "Madam," Montana replied, "you'll
have to lead *me* out, for I'm crying harder than you are."

There were no tears in Wilson's eyes at the outcome,
merely a self-congratulatory smile. He and Ketchel headed

back to San Francisco in the company of Jack London, who had covered the fight for the New York *Herald*. Though he disapproved of London's romanticization of the Klondike, Wilson approved of London's two-fisted drinking style. The three men went on a notable bender. During one leg of their erratic tour of the Barbary Coast they hijacked a hansom cab from its driver and proceeded up Kearny Street with Ketchel holding the reins on the box, and Mizner and London riding inside as passengers. Ketchel was throwing money to the crowds. They surrendered the cab to pursuing officers only when they reached Louis Parente's saloon at Pacific and Kearny.

On recovering from that spree Wilson scheduled a fight for Ketchel with Bill Lang, a heavyweight, for the following month but canceled the bout suddenly. Ketchel's condition was deteriorating, and he didn't want to risk his tiger in the ring until he got straightened out. No more whiskey, opium, or wild women. Under Wilson's orders Ketchel was packed off to a farm near Springfield, Missouri, where it was hoped that rural serenity, the absence of temptation, and hard physical labor would restore him to fighting trim. If Ketchel couldn't get back into shape somehow, Wilson planned to take him on a vaudeville tour.

Unfortunately there were temptations lurking even in rural Missouri. Ketchel shared accommodations on the farm with Goldie Smith, the housekeeper, and Walter A. Dipley, the foreman in charge of the place. Miss Smith and Mr. Dipley were living as man and wife under the assumed names of Mr. and Mrs. Hurtz. When Ketchel showed up, Goldie and the young fighter changed sleeping arrangements in the secluded farmhouse. Dipley so fiercely resented being dispossessed of whatever comforts Goldie could offer that one morning he killed Ketchel with a .22 caliber rifle.

Wilson had been fond of Ketchel in that possessive way of managers with a winning fighter, but he managed to assuage his grief in the new excitements of his budding career as a playwright.

8

WITH PIPE AND PEN
ON BROADWAY

IT must have been coincidental, but Wilson's career as an associate playwright—all four of his plays which reached Broadway were written with one collaborator or another—took its brief but spectular course just at the time he was heavily involved with narcotics. As he was quick to point out, a number of literary men had testified to the helpful creative effects of the juice of the poppy.

In his long flirtation with the less potent drugs on the market sixty to seventy years ago, Wilson was a man of his time. Hitting the pipe in a Chinatown opium pad was regarded as one of the rites of passage for the more venturesome youth. Wilson himself boasted of having smoked opium during his early days of juvenile delinquency. There were many respectable men, and not all of them Orientals, who smoked an occasional pipe of opium throughout their lives. Opium in that form is twenty-five times less potent than its ultimate distillate, heroin.

Narcotics addiction may be regarded now as a phenome-
non of the 1960's and 1970's, but for a generation before
World War I it was an increasingly serious problem. In
1900, it was estimated by United States Commissioner of
Narcotics Harry J. Anslinger, 1 in every 400 Americans was
a narcotics addict, some of them, hooked on opiate-laden
patent medicines, without being aware of their addiction.
There was no legal control over the contents of such remedies. And you could buy narcotics, without a prescription,
over the counter of a drugstore. Genteel ladies resorted to
the laudanum bottle whenever they suffered from the vapors or had a headache. "Along with the rest went the adult-
eration of drugs," Mark Sullivan, the leading chronicler of
the period, wrote, "the use without restrictions, in patent
medicines, of opium, morphine, cocaine, laudanum, and
alcohol; the preposterously false and cruelly misleading
curative qualities claimed. These patent medicines were
sold in every drug store in the land. It was an immense
traffic. In 1900, the total volume of business was
$59,611,355. The patent medicine manufacturers com-
prised at that time the largest single user of advertising
space in the newspapers."

Another expert on the narcotics traffic—so beautifully
disguised in panacea form by a kindly old lady beaming from
the label and offering a spoonful of miracle—has recorded
that addiction was widespread on every level of American
society. "At the turn of the century," wrote George E.
Pettey, "patent medicines containing opiates in some form
were sold in every drug store in the country. They were
offered for relief of headaches, general aches, various pains,
the 'misery' and 'that tired feeling.' School children could go
to a local soda fountain and buy a medicated drink containing cocaine." The distillation of heroin from opium in 1896

was hailed in a magazine advertisement as "the greatest boon to mankind since the discovery of morphine in 1803." Nor was the United States alone in its infatuation with opiates and cocaine; in western Europe, they were regarded, as one Continental physician wrote, as useful in treating "poison, deafness, asthma, colic, coughing, jaundice, fever, leprosy, female troubles and melancholy."

There were no laws against the importation and distribution of narcotics, and even the Pure Food and Drug Act of 1906 merely skirted the problem. Many users were shocked that the drugs which had won so many golden opinions for two decades should be denounced in muckraking journalism as actually injurious to one's health. There was a storm of protest over Samuel Hopkins Adams' conclusions in a series of magazine articles in which he revealed the content of certain widely advertised remedies, "the opium-containing soothing syrups, which stunt or kill helpless infants; the consumption [tuberculosis] cures, perhaps the most devilish of all, in that they destroy hope where hope is struggling against bitter odds for existence; the headache powders which enslave so insidiously the victim is ignorant of his own fate; the catarrh powders which breed cocaine slaves." Restrictions on the narcotics traffic, which was then in hands much more respectable than the international drug-smuggling rings of a half century hence, were only tightened somewhat with the passage of the Harrison Act in 1916.

Meanwhile—though he would learn that the poppy eventually extracted its penalties in agonizing withdrawal symptoms —Wilson was an ardent devotee of the long-shanked bamboo pipe with its tiny bowl and its pellet of bubbling opium. He found that its vapors not only induced philosophical meditation but also inspired schemes for enriching himself, later that it provided impetus for the literary imagination. If everyone from industrial magnates to Chinese laundrymen was hitting the pipe, what harm could there be in opiate relaxation? Booze caused fights in barrooms, as his broken knuckles testified, but the poppy turned the most belligerent into gentle dreamers.

The first time that Howard Emmett Rogers, then a Broadway playwright but later a highly successful screenwriter in Hollywood, met Wilson Mizner it was in a smoke-filled room, and the smoke did not come from perfectos. Rogers was sharing rooms with songwriter Bert Sennigs over Jack Dunstan's restaurant near the Hippodrome, where Wilson fired off some of his more memorable wisecracks. Rogers and Sennigs had an agreement whereby each had exclusive use of the rooms on alternate nights.

On one night supposedly reserved for Rogers, he went up to the apartment and found the door locked. Sennigs came to the door only after a long interval, an opium pipe in his hand. To Rogers' horrified eye the place looked as though it had been converted into a Shanghai opium parlor. A large arrogant-looking stranger, whom Rogers later knew to be Wilson Mizner, was sitting on the couch with a pipe smoldering in his clutch and a lady whom Florenz Ziegfeld had starred in his musicals sleeping with her head in his lap. Another member of the party lay drowsily on the floor.

Rogers was a smallish young man, but he roared with indignation over his roommate's having turned their nest into a den of iniquity. Half fuddled by the heavy reek of opium, he threatened to mop up the floor with Sennigs and his friends.

When he had begun to subside, Mizner stared up at him and quietly asked, "How tall are you, Mr. Rogers?"

"Five foot seven and a half," Rogers replied, bemused by the irrelevance of the question.

"Well," Wilson roared at him, "you are the most unreasonable five-foot-seven-and-a-half son of a bitch I have ever seen!"

Not surprisingly, Wilson's first collaborator on a full-length play was also a roisterer and opium smoker. A new kind of playwright had invaded Broadway to replace the more genteel types who had dominated the theater. He was often an ex-newspaperman or someone like Mizner who had studied life in the raw and was eager to transmit his experiences rather than ape the masters of dramaturgy; Ambrose Bierce had defined a dramatist as one who adapts plays from the French, but all that was changing. The robust and free-swinging newcomers would probably have identified Euripides as the owner of a Greek restaurant on Eighth Avenue. They were the first, as theatrical historians have noted, to infuse a note of realism in the American theater. They also enlivened Broadway with their outsize personalities. Eugene Walter (*Paid in Full* and other hits) was a barroom and newspaper city room veteran who would threaten producers with mayhem if they changed his lines. He and other newcomers brought something cruder, perhaps, but more vital than rewrites of Victorian Sardou to the theater of the first decade of the new century. They "had a greater inclination to mix robust pleasure with hard work," one Broadway historian has noted. "Eugene Walter, with his fondness for bars, spent more time lifting shot glasses than he did writing. Paul Armstrong and his collaborator Wilson Mizner were inspired wits and two-fisted practical jokers. . . . The aim of the new playwrights was to emphasize the play. 'The play's the thing' was their working motto, and

they sought to make the play itself important rather than
merely a vehicle tailored to suit special acting talents. . . .
The new playwrights were trying to make actors *reach*. They
were also writing with flexibility and imagination. In the line
of Ibsen and Shaw, they were switching the channel of
playwrighting from the well-constructed play which Shaw
had called (after Sardou) Sardoodledom. . . ."

No doubt Wilson and his first collaborator, George Bronson Howard, would have been astonished to learn they were
to be viewed as members of a literary avant-garde. They
thought their eye was firmly fixed on a fast buck; their
ambitions were centered on the box office rather than on
future seats in Valhalla.

Separately or in professional tandem, Mizner and Howard made a very odd couple. From the beginning to the end
of their association, they were at odds; it was more of a feud
than a partnership. Howard was a Broadway dandy who
once told H. L. Mencken that he spent half an hour every
morning before deciding on which necktie to wear, whose
silk hats were as glossy as J. P. Morgan's, whose lilac spats
gladdened many a winter day. His dandyism was belied by a
knockabout career. Howard might suffer exquisite agonies
over his rainbow of cravats but he had served in his youth as
a member of the hard-bitten Philippine Constabulary chasing guerrillas around the jungle. He took his discharge in
Manila and broke into journalism on an English-language
paper there, then worked on Philadelphia and Baltimore
journals and covered the Russo-Japanese War as a war correspondent whose traveling wardrobe almost outshone that
of his colleague the resplendent Richard Harding Davis.

By the time he met Mizner and recruited him for collaboration on a play about the seamy side of life Mizner knew so
well, Howard was a prolific producer of essays, short stories,

novelettes, and plays, as well as a regular column in the New York *Morning Telegraph*. He loved controversy and used his newspaper column to start feuds and even old scores. His best known dramatic work was a play called *Snobs* in which many old enemies appeared inadequately disguised for the benefit of the libel laws.

One thing Howard and Mizner had in common, perhaps the only one aside from a taste for playing the Hong Kong Flute, was that each had been very briefly married into society. Wilson's marriage lasted about six months, but Howard's didn't even survive the honeymoon. Howard had married a Virginia society girl in 1907. Subsequently she was voluble and vitriolic on the dangers of any well-bred female's marrying a writer. Even on their honeymoon he had turned out his daily budget of 20,000 words, and when she brashly suggested it was time he paid a little attention to her, he roared that he was writing against a deadline. She further charged that he went to bed at night with his shoes on so he wouldn't have to waste time putting them back on in the morning. What finally sent her back home to mother was his insistence on addressing her, even in public, as "Thing."

Howard was a compulsive worker. When he didn't have anything better to do, he ground out adventure serials for the cheaper magazines at half a cent a word. Howard's compulsive work habits and Mizner's ingrained indolence were yet another cause of personality clashes. "He appalls me by his power of work," the *Dramatic Mirror* quoted Wilson as saying. "He spills words by the gallon. Phrases ooze out of every pore. I have seen him write twenty thousand words at a sitting, get dissatisfied with them, tear them up, and start all over again." Wilson, on the other hand, was verbose in speech but dried up to a trickle when it

came to the written word. His brain, he admitted, succumbed to a form of paralysis when confronted with composing words into sentences to be inscribed on a sheet of paper.

Mizner and Howard got together primarily to collaborate
on a play titled *The Only Law*, its theme contained in one
line of the dialogue: "Being on the square with a pal is the
only law we know." It was a restatement of the supposed
code of the underworld. Mizner's brain teemed with ideas
for offbeat characters with which to stock the melodrama;
Howard's facility for getting words on paper was famous, if
not notorious, and it must have seemed that the talents of
the two collaborators meshed rather nicely. Unfortunately
they had to be locked up together day after day, and their
differing personalities were certain to grate even if their
talents meshed.

Mizner was between careers at the time. Cardsharping on
the Atlantic steamships was becoming a hazardous operation because of the ubiquitous private detectives hired by
the steamship companies. He hadn't yet become Stanley
Ketchel's sole proprietor, and he needed some sort of dry-
land work. The idea of lolling around, letting ideas and bits
of dialogue spin off the top of his head, while another man
put it all on paper, was appealing. If only Howard hadn't
been such a fiend for work, such a neurotic slave to the
proposition that so many pages had to be produced every
day. Wilson barely had time to remove his hat in the brownstone on West Forty-fourth which served as the scene of
their labors when Howard was plunging into a scene they
had left unfinished from their last session. Wilson liked to
approach work diffidently, like a terrier exploring a strange
barn. It took hours for his brain to get revved up and
churning out the ideas which Howard refined and put into
the proper form of dialogue and stage directions.

At least they had their affinity for the opium pipe. When their collaborative labors got bogged down in Mizner's lassitude and Howard's frustration, they took a poppy break and brought out the bamboo pipes. Often they were joined, according to Broadway rumor, by a distinguished literary critic who under a pseudonym wrote a series of highly successful detective novels. Together the three men adopted as their protégée a beautiful girl from Buenos Aires named Teddie Gerard, a stunning brunette who had moved into Howard's brownstone and was adept at preparing the pellets of opium for a gentlemanly pipe or two. A man floating off on a cloud of dream dust doesn't want to be bothered with housekeeping chores. Since Miss Gerard was given a sizeable diamond ring by Howard, as her chief patron, she apparently had other duties in that bohemian household than cooking opium.

In return for her services of one kind or another, Miss Gerard was provided with a theatrical persona by her three patrons, her South American accent was ironed out, her talent for singing and dancing nurtured. With three such promotional talents behind her, Teddie soon became the toast of three continents on the basis of a minimal talent, a striking figure, and the ability to exploit what she had.

She starred in a Broadway musical, *Havana*, and went on to fascinate Paris as La Belle Théodore and London's West End as "Teddie the Great," collecting a string of generous and titled admirers along the way.

Before she could claim her due in the great world outside the opium-fumed house on Forty-fourth Street, however, she had to detach herself from the possessive Mr. Howard. He and his friends had groomed her for theatrical stardom, but he resented the idea of her making use of that education. As Miss Gerard later charged in Magistrate's Court, Howard not only retrieved the diamond ring he had given her by force but had threatened her with a large bowie knife. During the subsequent litigation, Howard was permitted to keep the diamond but was held accountable on the charge of wielding a deadly weapon. Mizner bailed him out, using as security the house he owned uptown (apparently acquired on the proceeds of his Atlantic crossings).

Certainly no greater love hath any man than is demonstrated by putting up $25,000 in bail, yet Wilson and George Bronson Howard were star-crossed collaborators. Nobody had ever succeeded in getting along with Howard for more than a few hours at a time; besides, Howard felt that Wilson had encouraged Teddie Gerard to find her own higher and more spectacular orbit outside the Howard household. And there were other disputes over females, whom Howard alleged Wilson "stole" from him.

The fruits of their collaboration, *The Only Law*, turned out to be equally unpalatable. It demonstrated Wilson's ear for the spoken word; its dialogue crackled with authenticity. That and other plays on which he collaborated were credited with introducing slang, Broadway wise-guy talk, and underworld insights hitherto unavailable to the theatergoer. The trouble was that it was all too authentic, and as one theatrical journal commented, it couldn't be understood by anyone who didn't spend most of his time hanging around Times Square street corners.

The Only Law was the first opening of the 1909 season, and the barrage which greeted it made its authors feel that the drama critics had been storing up invective all summer just for that occasion. The reviewers may also have been offended by a much-quoted Miznerism, "A drama critic is a person who surprises the playwright by informing him what he meant."

Moral standards were loosening, but both the critics and the few audiences which caught *The Only Law* before its scenery was hauled off to Cain's Warehouse were shocked by its unconventional slant. The only character approaching the status of a hero was a gigolo. The others were viewed through a cold prismatic light which reflected Wilson's cynicism about human behavior. Broadway wasn't quite ready for such a strong dose of realism, for such an amoral outlook, and wouldn't be until John O'Hara came along with *Pal Joey*, its hero more than a kissing cousin to some of Mizner's characters.

NO GOOD SERVED BY YEAR'S FIRST PLAY ran the headline over the New York *World*'s review, which complained that the play was crowded with "sluts, scoundrels, and boobies." The *Morning Telegraph* took a kindly view of the play's originality and the "richness" of its slang.

From the moment the lights on the marquee of the theater in which *The Only Law* had unwisely been exposed to public view were doused, the relationship between Wilson and his collaborator deteriorated in the usual recriminations. Howard blamed Wilson for insisting on too dense a texture of dialogue in his pursuit of the real thing, while Wilson believed that he had been let down by Howard's lack of craftsmanship. As Wilson viewed his essays in dramaturgy, he supplied the original genius, the imagination, the atmosphere in which his characters operated. All that was required of his collaborator was an ability to operate a typewriter and supply the scaffolding; it was the wedding of an artist (Wilson) and an artisan (his collaborator).

Some months after the Broadway flop, Howard secured a Chicago production of *The Only Law*. In New York the writing credits had placed Wilson's name first, but in its Chicago manifestation the play was advertised as "by

George Bronson Howard and Wilson Mizner," with the title changed to *The Double-Cross*. As a former vaudevillian with firm ideas on the sanctity of top billing, Wilson violently objected to having his name listed after Howard's. But it didn't matter. Chicago was as scornful of *The Only Law* as Broadway had been.

Howard usually worked off his bruised feelings, resulting from association with inferior specimens of humanity, by using the villains who swarmed through his life as characters in his short stories, novelettes, and novels. Magistrate Joseph Corrigan, who had convicted him on the deadly weapon charge, was the central figure in a Howard novel titled *God's Man* which resulted in damaging litigation against the publisher.

Three years after *The Only Law* collapsed Wilson unwillingly sat for a literary portrait in Howard's busy atelier. The result was a novelette, or long short story, stingingly titled "The Parasite," which was published in *Smart Set*, a magazine edited by Howard's old friend from Baltimore newspaper days, H. L. Mencken. It was a blistering portrait that emerged from the murk of Howard's prose style. Wilson, or Milton Lazard as he was disguised in Howard's story, was "like a giant Brownie—a huge head shaped like a coal scuttle, a heavy round stomach, and the thinnest legs and smallest of feet, which, in one more than six feet tall, made him something of a monstrosity."

Howard evidently had listened closely to the recapitulations of his checkered career which Wilson had provided through the haze of poppy smoke during their period of collaboration. There was some factual basis for Howard's account, and undoubtedly, though magnified by the hyperbolic style American writers inherited from Mark Twain and other members of the literary school which graduated from

Western journalism, it was true in spirit to its subject's life. Milton Lazard/Wilson Mizner had consorted with black-mailers, was a cardsharp and tinhorn gambler, and had once been tarred, feathered, and given a ride out of a Western town on a fence rail. Furthermore, he had once bilked his own mother by having a friend wire her that Wilson had died and asking for a few hundred dollars to spare him from burial in an unmarked grave.

Wilson could laugh off such biographic details—he told equally villainous stories about himself without encouragement—but what really fired up his rage was Howard's allegations that his sense of humor, his already celebrated wit, was mechanical and uninspired. "He worked by formula, was amusing only in certain subjects," Howard wrote. "A detective couldn't catch a cold, couldn't find a third rail in the subway, couldn't locate a Saratoga trunk in a hotel bedroom, and so on, ad infinitum regarding the subject of detectives, a mere reversal of their clever-ness. As for thieves, another class popularly supposed to be clever, a thief couldn't steal a bunch of grass from Central Park, or handful of water out of the East River without getting an icicle down his back; or a swindler couldn't get a biscuit for a barrel of flour. Philanthropists wouldn't give the Lord a prayer, were closer than the next minute. . . ."

Wilson was usually able to shrug off attacks on his charac-ter, but he was stung by Howard's unflattering portrait of him. "Why should I be mad," he told a newspaperman who interviewed him on the subject of his ex-collaborator's dia-tribe, "when I can see the unfortunate results of rage in my adversary? The last time I saw him he was foaming at the mouth like a cream puff. Without his memory for other people's written cleverness, his chief output would have been a letter to his tailor."

He warmed to the task of blistering his former partner and told another interviewer, "Howard thinks that if you stuck a knife in him, he would bleed pure English."

Wilson was even more definite about his feelings toward Howard in subsequent meditations on the unwisdom of getting mixed up with self-conscious literary types.

"There's a type of noisy virtue that I cannot bear," he remarked in a pseudo-philosophical tone. "I don't know how dependable or undependable I may be, but I think there is no meanness in me. Some virtues that sound important are merely tedious. I was in an Alaska camp one night when they were making laws for the little settlement. These laws were not being made by any smug policemen with a hand-out gesture but by the leading blacklegs in town who wanted a little order—and got it.

"While I was standing next to a little gambler who had a habit of being perpetually right, a messenger came to me with a letter. It was about the virtues of a man whom I was to help on his arrival. It said, among other things, something like this: 'This man is conscientious, hardworking, straightforward, and has no bad habits.'

"The little gambler glanced at it and said, 'That's a recommendation for a mule, not a man.'

"George Bronson Howard is merely a mule, who imagined he was working with an ass. Well, I'm a bull, so I gave him a toss or two."

His attempted deflation of Howard lacked the lean symmetry of the classic putdowns. Like most men, he was not at his devastating best when his wit was clouded by passion. Anger, he would learn, blunts the sword. Thereafter he would nurse his sense of outrage whenever he felt he had been unjustly treated—and would be much slower to put up bail money for beleaguered friends. In the future his more acidulous wit would be reserved for targets he could view with cool contempt or fond malice.

The Howard interlude also taught him to be more cautious about falling in with another comrade in the assault on theatrical success. The opening and closing of *The Only Law* was swift as the snap of a crocodile's jaws, and by the time that venture was written off Wilson had become deeply involved in the career of Stanley Ketchel. During that yearlong involvement as Ketchel's sole manager, he could spare little thought to resuming his avocation as an associate playwright. It gave him plenty of time to form a new association—this one quite as hectic as the collaboration with George Bronson Howard, but a lot more successful and somewhat longer-lived.

9

SHAKESPEARE OF THE UNDERWORLD

WILSON MIZNER resumed his career as a playwright of the new and more realistic school, which resembled somewhat the work of the Ash Can school of artists presented in their famous Armory Show, at a time when the public taste was becoming cloyed with the escapism offered by Graustarkian romances. It had even grown willing to accept the theory that criminals were human beings.

A gentleman crook became dramatically if not socially acceptable. *Collier's Weekly's* serialization of *Raffles* had duplicated in the United States the success of that courteous miscreant in his English birthplace.

To the public's fascination with what was loosely categorized as the "crook play," Wilson added a gritty note of skepticism. He didn't sentimentalize his characters or present them as gentle folk forced by circumstance into a life of crime.

In dramatizing the sometimes squalid scenes of his earlier

careers in the Alaska gold rush, on the Barbary Coast, on the
road with Dr. Silas Slocum, in the cardrooms of luxury
liners, he be;ame one of the first to prove that crime could
be made to pay, if it were converted into literary capital.
And if the transmutation of experience into Broadway commercialism could be accomplished with the aid of a collaborator less erratic than George Bronson Howard.

Fortunately, in his penetration of theatrical life, Wilson
had made the acquaintance of Paul Armstrong, known as the
"Hair-Trigger Playwright" for the speed with which he
turned out a play and also accounted the best technician
then operating in the theater. There was no doubt of
Armstrong's ability, even less of his eccentricity. He was a
tall, husky fellow with a ruddy face and a Buffalo Bill goatee.
His temper, especially when sensitized by alcohol, was
formidable, and some of his saloon brawls were said to
match in ferocity the more professional efforts of the late
Stanley Ketchel. Though he affected a Wild Westerner pose
which was enhanced by the broad-brimmed black hats he
wore and might have been expected to dash down tumblers
of raw bourbon, he favored a rather sissyish drink com-
pounded of Amer Picon, grenadine, and a dash of soda, but
that was potent enough to make him truculent over fancied
slights in a barroom.

Armstrong was one of those who believed Wilson was
sitting on a bonanza of literary material which he was dis-
sipating in night-long storytelling sessions at Jack Dunstan's
and other hangouts. The raconteur must be harnessed to the
literary production line; the fountain of witticisms must be
converted into a paying proposition instead of being reserved for Wilson's cronies around a café table. Wilson was
receptive. It was the fall of 1910 when he and Armstrong
became friendly, and Wilson had just lost his meal ticket,

Stanley Ketchel, to a jealous farmhand's rifle shot. Armstrong was further entranced by Wilson's grasp of the practical aspects of a dramatist's life. He was just then extricating himself from a plagiarism suit. After listening to Armstrong's recitation of how easy it was to get involved in disputes over literary property, Wilson delivered a dictum which is still frequently quoted: "If you steal from one author, it's plagiarism. If you steal from two, it's research."

Their association would be marked by many temperamental blowups owing not only to Armstrong's volatile disposition but also to Wilson's waywardness when it came to actual, brain-racking work. Armstrong like most writers had to work by daylight, but Wilson was a night hawk who could rarely be found in his own roost until sunup. As Armstrong said, getting Wilson down to business was a lengthy and nerve-shredding process of "argument, supplication, threat and entreaty." The first job, he later recalled, was to find Wilson. Then the place where he was nesting had to be entered—shoulder to locked door, if necessary, since Wilson refused to answer a doorbell until the sun was down. Then Armstrong would make a pot of strong black coffee —potent enough to wake a pasha after a night in the harem—and pour several cups into his associate. They would talk about everything but the project in which they were engaged. Slowly, then, the conversation would be brought around to Act II, Scene I, and Wilson's brain would begin ticking over. In the last stages of working on a play, it was usually necessary to lure Wilson into a hotel room, lock the door, throw the key out the window, and finish the job in a rush.

Armstrong himself had emerged from a background as picaresque as Wilson's. Born in Michigan, he had begun working as a deckhand on Great Lakes steamers in his teens.

In 1893 he had advanced to the rank of purser on a steamer taking people to the Chicago World Fair. A few years later he had acquired his master's ticket and was captain of a Lake Huron steamer. Early on he had been bitten by the literary bug and started writing short stories while a deckhand, an effete occupation which he had to defend against illiterate shipmates by employing the rough and tumble techniques acquired in Saginaw saloon brawls.

When all his efforts were rejected by the magazine editors, he decided to acquire the necessary discipline and grooming in the newspaper business. He got a job on the staff of the Buffalo *Express*, whose city editor eventually concluded that Armstrong was better equipped to guide a steamboat through a Lake Huron storm. Undiscouraged by his failure in Buffalo journalism, he decided to offer his talents down in New York's Park Row, where he was invited aboard the Hearst afternoon paper, the *Journal*, which appointed him its boxing expert under the byline of "Right Cross."

Between sports-page chores he wrote his first play, titled *Just a Day Dream*. It was unanimously rejected by the Broadway producers, so he used most of his savings in producing it himself. It collapsed on the road. In 1902 he wrote another play, *St. Ann*, and again financed its production himself. It soon became obvious Armstrong lacked the politesse required of a successful producer. During the Baltimore tryout—as H. L. Mencken, then a young reporter for the Baltimore *Herald*, observed in a hilarious series of accounts backstage at the theater where Armstrong was trying to put *St. Ann* on its feet—the company was dogged by one misfortune after another, most of them contributed by their producer-playwright-director's high temper. As chronicled by Mencken, the backstage furor included an affray between Armstrong and his leading man over the affections of the leading lady, following which a sandbag dropped from the flies by a stagehand sympathetic to the leading man's cause narrowly missed fracturing Armstrong's skull. The ingenue eloped with the company's press agent. Another actress was fired for resisting Armstrong's direction, and two other members of the cast quit because of his high-handed methods.

But those were minor disasters compared to the script which Armstrong had written, a "dreadful *réchauffé* of Sardou, Pinero and Augustus Thomas," as Mencken described it. "The first act wobbled, the second was worse, the third became downright maniacal, and the fourth was never finished. . . .

"These proceedings, and especially the bout between Armstrong and the actor, made them excellent newspaper fodder, and it was my sworn duty to describe them in the *Herald*. Armstrong, as a newspaperman, understood my position and did not resent my story. Instead, he seemed grateful that I tamed it down as much as possible, and we straightaway became warm friends. . . ."

The opening night of *St. Ann* was "a nightmare to both audience and dramatist," Mencken recalled, and the play was so riddled by the critical barrage that it was obviously in no shape to proceed to New York for exposure on Broadway.

Several years later, however, having learned not to invest his own money in his creations, Armstrong was launched on a successful career as a playwright. Two roaring successes followed, though they were qualified for years afterward by lawsuits charging plagiarism. His first hit was *The Heir to the Hoorah*, but for sixteen years he was dogged by litigation over its source, the claim being made that the play was stolen bodily from a short story by H. J. W. Dam which had

appeared in *Smart Set*. Armstrong's counterclaim—that the
idea for the story had been stolen from him because he had
discussed it in a restaurant and was overheard—made little
impression on the jury, which awarded Mr. Dam a $23,000
judgment.

Armstrong followed up that somewhat marred success
with *Salomy Jane*, in which Eleanor Robson, who subsequently married August Belmont, Jr., appeared in the title
role. *Salomy Jane* was based on Bret Harte's short story
"Salomy Jane's Kiss." According to Miss Robson's recollection, "Paul Armstrong had been practically locked up in a
hotel room by Mr. Tyler [George Tyler, who produced
many of Armstrong's successes] with a set of Bret Harte's
stories and told not to come out without a play. Gallantly
following instructions, he emerged in two weeks with
Salomy Jane. . . ." Both Tyler and Armstrong, though they
should have known better, apparently were unaware of the
legal difficulties they courted by not having secured the
dramatic rights to the story. Harte was dead, and they
assumed that his work was part of that body of classics which
have ascended into the public domain. Unfortunately, the
Harte estate owned the copyright and its heirs were on the
alert for interlopers. Their claims were settled out of court
after months of negotiation.

Salomy Jane was a resounding success from the moment
the curtain rang down on the opening night on January 19,
1907, its qualities unmarred despite an unsteady appearance by its author just after the cast had taken its bows. One
thing Armstrong dearly loved was to address the opening-
night audience, always provided, of course, that it had given
his work a fittingly hearty reception. Long before the performance started, Armstrong had been dipping his nose into
Amer Picon to soothe his nerves. After the final curtain fell,

he wobbled onstage to make a speech. As producer Tyler recalled in his memoir, "People began to snicker—and a first-nighter's snicker is a sinister thing, believe you me —and I could see our nice new hit falling apart under our noses.

"But at that point the special providence that looks after people in Armstrong's condition came to his rescue and gave him the right hunch just in time. He straightened up and struck up a sort of Daniel Webster pose and said 'But, ladies and gentlemen, I owe it all—every bit of it—to the great soul of Bret Harte!' That fetched them just in time—you could have heard the applause over in Jersey—and *Salomy Jane* was doubly made. Sober or otherwise, Armstrong couldn't have figured out a better climax."

By the time he and Wilson Mizner got together in the fall of 1910 the revenues from *Salomy Jane* had dried up to a trickle inadequate to satisfy the tastes of a successful playwright. He was casting about in all directions for some sort of property to develop and had even taken to dipping into a Gideon Bible, which at least was in the public domain. "What a book, Henry," he told H. L. Mencken. "It's full of plots." But none, unfortunately, that could be adapted to a commercially successful play. Armstrong needed desperately to get back to work. A collaboration with Rex Beach, the novelist who, like Mizner, had received an education in the Klondike, had not resulted in any visible dividends. Beach and Armstrong had holed up in a room at the New York Athletic Club and after about two weeks emerged with a play called *Going Some*, which belied its title and went nowhere. To amuse himself, Armstrong pursued various Broadway vendettas, including one with his producer, George Tyler, which resulted in Armstrong's suing Tyler for 23 cents, the amount the former claimed was missing from

his royalty statement. He also feuded with another producer, Charles Frohman, because he was unable to persuade Frohman to let him write a play for the Frohman star
Maude Adams, an ethereal type whom it would have been
difficult to cast in the robust melodrama in which Armstrong
specialized.

What Mizner offered, at that low-water period, was a new
beginning. Instead of adapting someone else's work, Armstrong could use Wilson's experience of life in the raw to
produce something authentic and original.

With much pomp, Armstrong announced to the theatrical
weeklies that he and Mizner were going to collaborate on a
play titled *The Deep Purple*, which would be a realistic
drama of the underworld. That was the unsensed beginning
of the crook play boom which eventually ebbed away on
Broadway, only to manifest itself two decades later in Hollywood, where the tommy gun would symbolize solvency
for more than one film studio. It was a rage which, as
Alexander Woollcott observed, would "tweak and tantalize
playgoers all over America, England, France, Spain and
South Africa; and which was to breed a very epidemic of
plays in which no self-respecting protagonist would think of
approaching the first act without a murder or at least a bank
robbery to his credit."

Only the realization that they were on to something that
might prove sensationally profitable kept the two men in
tandem. Once they quarreled while still trying to lick the
second act into shape and didn't see each other for a week
until they were reconciled by a mutual friend. They then
greeted each other without any great show of enthusiasm.

"I haven't seen you in a week," Wilson remarked, "but
your face is still streaked with larceny."

"We might as well go on knowing each other, Bill,"

Armstrong sighed. "With me you're merely a thoroughly bad habit."

Later Wilson would recall that "our collaboration was a form of murderous conflict. Paul was up at dawn and I would never yawn until I was sure it was light. Yet he turned day into night for me, however painfully, and abused some of my best work out of this tired hide."

The work went much too slowly for a professional like Armstrong until, in desperation, he lured his colleague to Baltimore and locked them both in a hotel room, swearing they would either finish *The Deep Purple* or the municipal authorities would be charged with removing their emaciated corpses from that room. Removed from the night life of Times Square and other distractions, Wilson, rolling homemade cigarettes from sacks of Bull Durham, began spewing out the situations and dialogue with which Armstrong could construct an ending to the play. Wilson later claimed he was sequestered in the Baltimore hotel for five days, adding, "He got me so used to work that the sight of him would make me ache with exhaustion, but he could always get me up, because he used to make the best damn coffee in the world."

When they returned to New York and gave producer Tyler a look at the result of their labors, Tyler decided certain scenes needed more polishing. Wilson then was relaxing from his monastic five days in Baltimore, certain they had nothing more to do about *The Deep Purple* than take their bows and count the profits. Armstrong knew how outraged his partner would be when he received the news that revisions were in order, so when he called Wilson with the bad news, he had a stenographer listening in on an extension to take down Wilson's remarks verbatim. A moment after Armstrong began telling him it would be necessary to "concentrate" on certain dramaturgic problems again, Wilson broke in with an anguished howl.

"Concentrate be damned! Why don't you stay off the phone and let a man get his rest? If what you do is the result of concentration, why should I ruin a talent?" Wilson paused to ease the strain of shouting on his much-prized larynx. "If you will put a hen's beak on the ground and draw a straight line from it, she will *concentrate*. She will lie in the corner helpless for an hour, like you do. You not only lie in the corner, you lie anywhere and on the slightest liar's opportunity. I'm cutting you off this wire right now, and I'm going back to writing in my own good time not only with nonchalance, but poisonous indifference. Concentration is for day workers. I'm about to throw the covers over a genius."

Wilson added that if Armstrong woke him up again before sundown, "I'll buy you a silk hat and pull it so far down you'll need armholes."

After working off his grouch, Armstrong said, Wilson trotted down and they buckled down to the revisions.

All those harrowing hours spent awake in daylight seemed to have paid off at the opening night of *The Deep Purple*. Producer Tyler may have worried over the public and critical reception of a play built around the badger game, over how an audience would receive characters who talked, not in the stilted language of the nineteenth-century theater, but like people in "real" life.

The first-nighters, however, received the offering with uproarious enthusiasm. Among the critics there was a wide difference of opinion, the more conservative ones deploring its candor, but most of them comparing it favorably with Broadway's more conventional fare. The critical controversy only increased public interest, and *The Deep Purple* was a solid and enduring success. Drama historians would call it something of a landmark in the American theater's advance toward a more naturalistic way of addressing the audience.

And producer Tyler not only was financially rewarded but also got even with Paul Armstrong, who was again feuding with him when *The Deep Purple* opened. "It had been arranged through third parties, just like seconds in a duel, that Armstrong could make a curtain speech," Tyler recalled in his memoir, "but he'd had to promise to wait until I gave him the nod. The applause kept going and the curtain kept rising and falling and Armstrong kept looking at me like a hungry dog in a butcher shop, just ready to burst with suppressed oratory. Finally I nodded at him, just before the applause was going to die down, and he went for the stage like the devil was after him. But he'd waited so long and got so keyed up while he waited that he couldn't utter a word when he got there—couldn't do a mortal thing but stand and stare at the audience and make gulping noises."

Out in the lobby afterward somebody asked George M. Cohan why Armstrong had rushed out in front of the curtain and then just stood there pop-eyed and speechless. "Didn't you know?" Cohan said. "He's not on speaking terms with the audience."

During the months following that opening night, Wilson reveled in discovering the difference between notoriety and fame. If it was better to be notorious than a nonentity, it was better still to be famous, he had decided. He could hardly turn around without someone's begging him for an interview or an autograph, and he was not affronted by such attentions.

The racier newspapers like the *Morning Telegraph* and the *Press* bestowed their wisecracking accolades: He was the

"Shakespeare of the underworld," "the riffraff's delegate to
the respectable world," the "new prophet of the crook
drama,"

Even the somewhat literary New York *Review* took notice
of his eminence and decided to investigate just how a knockabout career like Mizner's could elevate him, at the age of
thirty-five, to being credited (more than his collaborator)
with inventing a new idiom for the stage. Colgate Baker,
whom the *Review* sent to interview Mizner, confessed that
he was dazzled by the magnificent aura Mizner created for
himself. When they strolled into Rector's, Baker reported,
"the headwaiter bowed lower than I had ever seen him bow
before. Even the chef came up from the kitchen to pay his
respects. Ah! It is something to be the author of the dramatic
sensation of the hour." Much of Baker's curiosity about the
newest meteor blazing across Times Square centered on
Mizner's familiarity with the techniques of the badger
game, and as he remarked in his story, "Mr. Armstrong's
taking into partnership of Mr. Mizner upon the exploitation
of a topic so delicate and so technical may be accounted for
upon various theories, none of which need of necessity find
exploitation in this paragraph." Baker bluntly asked Wilson
how he knew so much about the art of extorting money from
unwary lechers, and the latter blandly replied, "You must
remember that I once kept a theatrical hotel," referring to
his tenure at the Hotel Rand. Newly cocooned in respectability, he did not feel it discreet to recall for his interviewer
how he had once cleared $10,000 through what might be
called the tomato-can variation of the badger game under
Alaskan skies.

Wilson enjoyed his status as a celebrity, and only Lillian
Russell herself could rival the pomp and circumstance with
which he entered a Broadway lobster palace. He looked

positively plutocratic when he doffed his silk topper and swept back his satin-lined Inverness cape. And he demanded that the lower orders take cognizance of his new status. One night the waiters in a restaurant were slow in bringing him a pack of cigarettes (he no longer rolled his own from a sack of Bull Durham because one could overdo the picturesque). Finally Wilson went to the telephone and summoned a messenger from the District Telegraph Service, gave him a quarter, and sent him to the restaurant's cigar counter for his cigarettes. The messenger was magnificently tipped. After that the service at Wilson's table was superb.

He and the rising young composer Irving Berlin had become friendly early in Wilson's New York career, but he was slightly offended when Berlin dedicated to him a song rather pointedly titled "Black Sheep Has Come Back to the Fold." Wilson did not want anyone to think that a little temporary respectability had completely reformed him. "I don't know what's coming over me, perhaps I'm getting crabby," he commented on Berlin's dedication. "It's the first time anything but a dinner check was ever dedicated to me, but somehow I can't get happy over it. That title seems to indicate that I've been hanging around, bleeding with remorse over my misspent life. I have returned to no fold whatsoever. I'm the most unfolded guy I've ever known. When I think of the gay dinner party I arranged for Irving, I feel the damn lachrymose title of that little ditty comes under the heading of treason."

During the heady weeks following *The Deep Purple*'s opening night he considered making a solo flight as a playwright. With a couple of bottles of Mumm's sending bubbles to his brain, he could momentarily convince himself that he could sit down and, unassisted, write a play. If only he could make his fingers perform the task his tongue so readily and glibly did. If only the thought of composition didn't paralyze his brain.

He seemingly suffered from a permanent writer's block. His mind took a leave of absence and his imagination petrified when he took a pencil in his hand and tried to guide it across a sheet of paper. "He needed hysterical merriment," as Alva Johnston analyzed his professional dilemma, "faces distorted with laughter, to warm up his inspiration. He felt like a professional mourner in the tomblike silence that surrounded him when he tried to write. He discovered, too, that there were some mean little stumbling blocks to putting words on paper. As a conversationalist, he could change the subject whenever a better one showed up. As a writer, he was supposed to stick to the subject. . . ."

So, struggling with his antipathy for rising before sundown, for wrangling with his collaborator's contentious and demanding personality, he consented to slip back into harness with Paul Armstrong. This time their project was a play titled *The Greyhound* which would be based on Wilson's experiences as a transoceanic cardsharp. In preparation for that effort, he and Armstrong took a trip to Europe on a liner to get the atmosphere right and observe whatever "deep-sea fishermen" were still practicing their profession in the cardrooms.

During ensuing weeks back in New York, sequestered like a cobra and a mongoose, they developed the characters and plot for *The Greyhound* and fought bitterly over just how the play would unfold. The two principal characters would be Frankie Dwyer, Wilson's old friend and confederate, now drydocked by excessive attention from the authorities, and his nemesis on land and sea, William Pinkerton, the great sleuth, who had put in almost twenty years discouraging the marine activities of Dwyer and the like.

Wilson, naturally enough, wanted to make the Dwyer character the hero of their drama and Pinkerton's facsimile the villain.

Armstrong, however, ruled that making a hero out of a crook was asking too much of an audience in which Victorian morality still reverberated. Wilson debated the point vigorously but had to concede that he was the junior member of the partnership (a circumstance indicated by the fact that Armstrong received two-thirds of their royalties).

The Greyhound opened late in March, 1912. Rich in dramatic confrontations and hard-bitten humor, it wasn't as artfully constructed as *The Deep Purple*, was chopped up into too many quick-shifting scenes that strained the capacities of the cast and backstage crew and, worse yet, those of the audience to absorb them. Yet it was well received by the opening-night audience, somewhat more guardedly by the critics, and seemed destined for a moderately successful run.

Wilson had brought his aging father from California to attend the opening performance, certain the old gent would be convinced his son finally had amounted to something.

Someone who asked the senior Mizner what he thought about his son's play learned that Wilson's acerb wit was inherited from the paternal side of his house. "A remarkable play," he commented, "and the most remarkable thing about it is that it took two men to write it."

On April 12, 1912, just when *The Greyhound* was beginning to attract longer lines of ticket buyers, the great new luxury liner *Titanic* sank in the North Atlantic on its maiden voyage. The disaster chilled the more civilized sections of humanity with its implications that mankind was still vulnerable to mischance no matter how massively it prepared

to protect itself. Few regarded a seagoing drama as entertainment at the moment, and the box-office receipts for *The
Greyhound* dropped from $12,000 weekly just before the
Titanic went down to $5,000 to almost nothing. There was
no alternative to closing down.

Just after their play folded, Armstrong and Mizner had a
falling-out. Wilson always claimed that he was coauthor of
Alias Jimmy Valentine, which was an even more resounding
success than either *The Deep Purple* or *The Greyhound*.
Certainly Wilson shared the official program credit. But
Armstrong claimed his contributions were minimal, if not
nonexistent.

Alias Jimmy Valentine was one of the big moneymakers of
the crook drama period on Broadway. It was adapted from
the O. Henry short story "A Retrieved Reformation," based
on material O. Henry gathered while a resident of the Ohio
State Prison. In its theatrical form, it became a drama of
redemption in which a reformed safecracker uses his burglar
tools to open a bank vault in which his fiancée's niece is
trapped. And it provided the springboard for two distinguished acting careers, those of H. B. Warner and Laurette
Taylor.

As Armstrong told it, he wrote *Alias Jimmy Valentine*
while cloistered in the warden's office at the city prison, the
Tombs, in which he absorbed the penitential atmosphere.
Both Mizner's partisans and more objective critics believed
that the authentic crackle of the dialogue, the underworld
slang, the realistic attitudes of the less respectable characters in *Alias Jimmy Valentine* were contributed by Wilson.
(It was nothing new for Armstrong to minimize a
collaborator's contributions. When he and Rex Beach were
writing the aborted *Going Some*, as George Tyler recalled,
they cut each other's lines until "there was no scenario

left—no play at all.") The characters in *Alias Jimmy Valentine* talked like Mizner in the flesh, as various Broadway observers pointed out, so Armstrong had to have been listening to Miznerian echoes, if not to the man himself.

Effectually that was the end of Wilson's career as a playwright, or half of one, to be precise. He might have continued with Armstrong if either man had been more self-effacing, but Armstrong said it took too much energy to get Mizner out of bed, and Wilson complained that Armstrong had to be forcibly prevented from using literary English when the language of the streets should have issued from the mouth of a character. They also differed over dividing the proceeds of their work, with Wilson contending that he was entitled to more than a third of the partnership.

But they never became enemies over their differences of opinion; there was too much respect, affection, and shared tribulation cementing them after two successful years of joint effort. Their mutual friend A. Toxen Worm, the celebrated Danish-born Broadway press agent, reconciled them after several months of ignoring each other's existence and threw a dinner party at Rector's on August 31, 1912, to celebrate the occasion.

Wilson and Armstrong were so thoroughly reconciled over the table at Rector's, and possibly further stimulated by the champagne poured by their host, that they immediately discussed plans to resume their collaboration. The play would be called *The Pirate*, and without developing the scenario for the project, they decided it must provide a starring role for Lou Tellegen, a sleekly romantic Dutch actor who had created a stir in Europe as Sarah Bernhardt's leading man.

Before any work could be done, Wilson suffered a severe attack of appendicitis and was in such distress—with his

fervent distrust of what he called "croakers," or physicians
and surgeons—that he made out his will and instructed his
friends to see to it that the coffin fit well around the shoulders. Nevertheless, he survived the removal of his appendix, flattered to find that his stay in the hospital was front-
page news and by a quip in the *Morning Telegraph*, the
Broadway wise guys' favorite journal, that "Mizner will
never leave this world while there is anything left in it."

During his convalescence he decided that he could not
risk further debilitation by collaborating again with Paul
Armstrong and, to avoid any more encounters with that
hectic personality, took the first ship to Europe on leaving
the hospital.

In London, however, he found himself immersed in the
problems of show business again. The producers of a revue,
Come Over Here, begged for play-doctoring help from Mizner, whom the London papers were lionizing as the American Whirlwind. Wilson was still pale and wobbly from losing
his appendix, but apparently he was eager to prove there
was something in the writing line he could do without help
from Paul Armstrong. Discussing the fast rewrite he did,
Wilson was obliquely referring to Armstrong's reputation as
a literary sprinter when he told London journalists, "I didn't
write the thing in six hours, I merely lit the fuse and the play
was accommodating enough to go off with a bang. I figure
that if I worked twelve hours instead of six it would have
been just twice as bad. . . .

"When you consider that the piece was written to fit
nineteen principal actors, a French automobile, a Russian
ballet, a Hippodrome diving tank, one thousand feet of
motion picture film, and about $50,000 worth of Parisian
gowns, my work was insignificant. It's the first time that I

have collaborated with scenery, and it's the most pleasant theatrical collaboration I have ever had."

His contribution, evidently, was to infuse the libretto with gags and one-liners he recalled from American vaudeville. The show went over with the audience, if not with the more fastidious critics. On opening night there was a clamor for the author to appear, but so many writers had worked on the script that Wilson muttered, "There isn't enough room on the stage to hold all the authors."

Though their professional links were broken, he and Paul Armstrong remained close if argumentative and insult-trading friends. Armstrong's career prospered even without Wilson's collaboration. "He probably earned more money than any other dramatist up to his time," his friend Mencken wrote, "whether here or in Europe. His revenues from a single one-acter, played by two companies in vaudeville, ran, to my personal knowledge, beyond $2,000 a week for two years on end."

Then Armstrong's heart began faltering, and Mencken arranged for his treatment by a specialist at the Johns Hopkins Hospital in Baltimore. He was warned that he would have to avoid the litigious activities that had marked his career, but "he had hardly got back to New York before he became involved in a lawsuit, and before long he was engaged in his usual fights with actors." In his last months, Mencken recalled, Armstrong was still full of ambition and plans for the future. "He was preparing, in his last days, to invade the movies in the grand manner, and if he had lived ten years more he'd have died a millionaire, for he was already master of all the eye-popping, heart-breaking and liver-scratching devices that the movie Shakespeares were to develop only long afterward. At least five years before D.

W. Griffith exacerbated the soul of humanity with 'The Birth of a Nation' Armstrong was entertaining me with projects for historical films on twice its scale, with such excursions and alarms in them that they would have paled it. . . ."

Wilson was stunned by Armstrong's death at the age of forty-six, which only reinforced his views on the physical dangers of overexertion. As usual, he concealed his grief behind a barrage of wisecracks. He would always insist on treating death as a richly comic figure, a clown without wit enough to let good people live and take off the bad ones.

After listening to the eulogy at Armstrong's funeral, Wilson whispered to a friend, "If Paul was up and about, he'd say that speech was his."

But, in his sardonic way, Wilson delivered his own eulogy to the man who made him a successful co-playwright. "I don't know what I will do for another friend like Paul. Nobody will fight from five to eight hours a day with me, and I despise peace. . . . Paul was quick to help anyone who needed it and you can't beat that for an epitaph even if you've got a half block of cornerstone and chiselled all day long. . . . He was a great and able fellow, and I not only take back every quarrel I ever had with him, but I wish I could have them all over again."

10

"HELLO, SUCKER!"

FOR the next decade Wilson Mizner was the reigning wise guy of Times Square and its environs, preeminent among the professional gamblers, sliest of confidence men, fanciest of the dudes, contributor to the American language in its least academic sector.

His epigrams may have lacked the lapidary finish of a Montaigne, but their street-wise cynicism made them as widely quoted. He had a magnetic effect on columnists and feature writers down on Park Row, and often his escapades were emblazoned on page one.

Americans could no longer wholeheartedly admire the captains of industry and buccaneers of speculative finance as they had in the Gilded Age, but an unabashed rogue who operated with humor, imagination, and finesse was forgiven much for his entertainment value.

"Hello, sucker!" he called out in his booming baritone, both to passing friends and the world at large. It was laced with the affection of the predator for his victim, perhaps, but it also reflected his belief that every man was a sucker for having permitted himself to be born. The quality of his "Hello, sucker!" salutation was so infectiously good-humored that Texas Guinan, who presided over the most famous (and expensive) of the Prohibition era's nightclubs, adopted the greeting and made it her trademark.

During the several pre-World War I years, when the mere mention of Broadway and Times Square sent a quiver of envy through Americans unfortunate enough to live west of the Hudson, when the fabulous lights of Broadway had the mellow glow of mazda bulbs instead of the psychedelic fever blush of neon, when the theater was prospering in half a hundred playhouses, Wilson was the philosopher king of that brightly lit world. Hip as they were, its denizens hardly knew what to think on any subject close to their hearts until Wilson had delivered his comments. He described them to themselves, justified their existence, and touched it with glamor with his pinwheeling observations. "Knock a knocker, boost a booster, but with a sucker use your own judgment. I never call a man a fool. I borrow from him. . . . Sure, there's a fool born every minute. And two to take him. . . . Easy Street is a blind alley. . . . The gent who wakes up and finds himself a success hasn't been asleep. . . . Why do women reformers almost always worry about men? . . . Most hardboiled people are half-baked. . . ."

He spent his days sleeping off his nights, his nights in gambling, drinking, talking (endlessly), and touring the hangouts of the Times Square area in which the most pred-atory instincts of his generation coagulated, in which the worlds of the theater, Fifth Avenue society, and the under-world intersected in a smaller but noisier and more amusing Liechtenstein, a principality carved out of the roaring can-yons of midtown Manhattan. He observed the creatures who frequented that world, the special emanations of opulence and squalor which would evaporate in less than a decade after the coming of Prohibition, with the scientific relish of an anthropologist. There were more lusty, eccentric, and roguish characters filed away in Wilson's memory than in the files of M. Bertillon of the Paris police.

One of his favorite observation posts was the Metropole, which occupied the wedge of real estate bounded by Broadway, Seventh Avenue, and Forty-second Street. Among its habitués were one Appetite Bill, whom Damon Runyon described as "a bunco-steerer of the Upper Tenderloin," a rustic in appearance with his ropy mustache and his gunfighter's stalk; Henry Blossom, the brilliantly plumaged playwright who had suits tailored from material other men chose for their fancy vests; and James M. Thornton, the alcoholic and unpredictable monologist whose billing on the vaudeville circuits read "James M. Thornton—Next Week—Perhaps." Buffalo Bill Cody dropped in at the Metropole when his *Wild West Show* was playing the Garden and bellied up to the bar with George M. Cohan, John J. McGraw, Jimmy Walker (before his tenure at City Hall), and Bat Masterson, the gunfighter rehabilitated by journalism. Wilson also favored the Metropole because it served as a drydock for the cardsharps who worked the liners. Once a rubberneck bus pulled up outside the Metropole, and one of the sightseers interrupted the spieler's monologue with the shout "There's the hound that got my bankroll!" According to a New York *Sun* reporter who witnessed the scene, "A party of perhaps twenty young and middleaged men who were sunning themselves in the front door and on the sidewalk dispersed hastily, bruising each other's heels in the grand getaway."

Another regular stop of Wilson's was Doyle's Billiard

Academy, a rendezvous for fight managers and sportswriters, where he could talk shop with Tad Dorgan, Hype Igoe, Sid Mercer, Bill Farnsworth, Patsy Haley, Dumb Dan Morgan, and Gabby Dan McKetrick—and also the Garden Cabaret at Fiftieth Street and Seventh Avenue, another hangout for the fight mob.

Almost nightly he prowled the bars, cabarets, and restaurants which made up what he called the Forty-second Street Country Club, the headquarters of which was the Knickerbocker Bar, in which he was the leading light of a number of informal, self-satirizing debating societies, including the Correspondence School of Drinking. For members of the hard-drinking urban country club, the "first hole" was from the Knickerbocker to the back room at George Considine's Buffet; you proceeded on an increasingly erratic course to Rector's, Shanley's, Churchill's, around Times Square, then up the long fairway to Columbus Circle and Pabst's, Reisenweber's and Rogers' restaurant, to wind up at Jack Dunstan's near the Hippodrome close to dawn. Few foursomes, it was said, ever finished the course.

There were other facetiously organized groups, their titles bespeaking the alcoholic atmosphere in which they were steeped, in which Wilson held gold-card membership. One was the Broadway Poultry Club, to which a number of people were elected to honorary membership on the fowl-like connotations of their surnames—Oscar Egg, the bicycle rider, Judge Swann, Eddie Pigion, Judge Wrenn, Sam Crane, and the famous Chinatown tong warrior Mock Duck.

Wilson was also a founding father of the Broadway Lease Breakers Union, No. 1, which performed a humanitarian function. New York landlords have always been celebrated for the armor-plated leases they inflict on their tenants. The Lease Breakers union was formed to free tenants from their bonds in a noisy but effective extralegal fashion. All fourteen members either sang—with the excruciating and penetrating effect of Wilson's barroom baritone, which could clear sinuses a block away—or played a musical instrument with more power than artistry. If someone needed their services, they showed up around midnight and began a chivaree that often lasted, with frequent resort to stimulants, from forty-eight to seventy-two hours. The result was usually an outbreak of recriminations from fellow tenants and the landlord—and a broken lease.

On at least one occasion the Lease Breakers performed an unwanted service. A writer named Percy Crocker had just moved into an apartment on Fifth Avenue and decorated it in handsome style. He intended to settle down there for years. When he gave a housewarming party, he unwarily invited the members of the Lease Breakers Union as individuals, not to practice their avocation. Wilson and his colleagues were so warmed by Crocker's hospitality and stimulated by his liquor that in gratitude and refusing to heed their host's pleas that he hadn't planned a musicale, they launched into their cacophony with their accustomed vigor. Police, summoned by the neighbors, came and went. The concert continued for two nights and days. When Crocker recovered from the effects of the housewarming, he found a notice from his landlord ordering him to vacate the premises within ten days. Henceforth anyone in Wilson's circle giving a party took care not to invite more than one or two members of the Lease Breakers.

Aside from lease breaking and other social activities, Wilson put in most of his time from his thirty-fifth to forty-fifth years, a decade when most men are intent on providing for their future, as a high-rolling gambler, roisterer, and big spender. For several years after his collaboration with Paul

Armstrong ended, he received substantial royalties from
their plays. But he was never solvent. His career as a
womanizer saw to that. He was an easy mark for theatrical
beauties who felt deprived of diamonds and furs. The money
flowed in, from both the plays and successful gambling
ventures, and it flowed out in slightly greater volume. Not
to worry. The federal income tax wasn't enacted until 1913,
and at least he wasn't bothered by the revenuers.

His carefree attitude toward money was the wonder of
Broadway, many of whose habitués liked to pose as sports
and wine buyers but who clandestinely fingered their bank-
rolls with a miserly caress. Wilson's theory was that you had
to treat money with contempt in order to keep it coming at
you. Parsimony, in his view, was the deadliest of virtues.

Shortly after he returned from England in December,
1912, he became involved in a marathon poker game with
three other high rollers in a Times Square hotel. They had
sequestered themselves with the purpose of genially ruining one another, and there were tens of thousands on the
table before Wilson and his opponents, John Shaughnessy,
George Bauchle, and Nat Evans.

When they were all getting bleary from the nonstop
action, as the New York *World* reported in an exclusive story
on page one (the times were still tranquil enough, but not for
long, that a poker game could rate such journalistic attention), Wilson yawned and told the other three men; "I can't
bear to spend Christmas in New York. If I win this hand, I'll
take you all to Europe and show you around as long as the
money lasts. But only provided you go to the boat with me as
soon as the hand is played."

He won the hand and kept his word. The four men caught
a liner leaving for England that afternoon. Their subsequent
adventures were described by Wilson himself for

the benefit of one of the smaller New York dailies, which couldn't afford to send a correspondent over but persuaded Wilson to cable an account of the quartet's wanderings.

They left so hurriedly that, according to Wilson, whose fondness for hyperbole was notorious, they only had one toothbrush and a mustache cup between them as luggage. Arriving in London on Christmas Day, as Wilson cabled the newspaper, they found "all stores and theaters, not excepting Westminster Abbey, are closed." Somewhat shabby and travel-stained, they were nevertheless invited to a large Christmas party. One of the voyagers, John Shaughnessy, was a belligerently patriotic Irishman who, under the impact of much free booze, felt himself surrounded by hereditary foes. Shaughnessy clambered up on a chair and bellowed the challenge "If there's any battle of the American Revolution that remains undecided, I'd like to fight it over again."

Somewhat shaken by that experience, Wilson whisked his guests off to less controversial France and escorted them around the best restaurants. By now a number of newspapers had assigned their European correspondents to keep an eye on the junket. They reported that a certain amount of rancor arose when Shaughnessy, Bauchle, and Evans complained that Wilson was trying to get rid of them before all his winnings were spent. Whenever, clinging to Wilson's coattails, they walked into a cabaret, Wilson would bribe the orchestra leader to play "Home, Sweet Home" over and over again, but they refused to succumb to nostalgia for the New York streets. His guests, in fact, dogged Wilson until there was only enough money left for their passage home.

It was during that European sojourn that a new German process for reproducing old masters caught Wilson's opportunistic eye. With that process, even the imperfections were reproduced, and he was assured that only an expert could tell the difference between the original and the copies. With his strictly commercial interest in art, Wilson was determined to secure the American franchise for the process and was immediately reassured about the worth of the schemes which were beginning to ferment in his brain when customs officers in New York ruled that some of the reproductions he brought with him were, in fact, the originals and it took lengthy proceedings to regain custody without paying a large impost.

Immediately after obtaining the American rights to the process, recalling a similar venture during his marriage to Mrs. Yerkes/Mizner, he opened shop on Fifth Avenue. The Old Masters Art Society, as it was called, was established opposite the Astor Library near Fifth Avenue and Forty-second Street in the spring of 1913. For some months the enterprise prospered as New Yorkers were enchanted with the idea of buying a reproduction so exact that anyone with $100 could display a Rembrandt and defy anyone but an expert to dispute its provenance.

Then cheaper processes were developed, and the Old Masters Art Society found itself undersold by the competition. Aside from the undercutting by his rivals, Wilson's business suffered from his high-handed attitude toward customers and his ignorance of modern merchandising methods. His salon looked something like a Chinatown rookery with small, dimly lit rooms and dog-leg corridors in which a customer could easily fear he might be mugged, a fear substantiated by the rather menacing attitude of the proprietor and his chief assistant, a former bartender, whenever the customer showed a tendency to haggle. Wilson felt that art was too sacred to be subjected to the methods of an Egyptian bazaar. One prospect who tried to bargain with Wilson aroused his anger to the point that

Wilson gestured toward the master switch and shouted at
his assistant, "Bert, turn off the lights and let this son of a
bitch find his own way out!" That wasn't the manner prescribed for the proprietor of a Fifth Avenue salon.

Wilson's temper grew testier as the competition beat
prices for Old Masters, once removed, still further down.
He was outraged when he had to sell copies of Leonardo da
Vinci's "The Last Supper" for $65 a throw. It was an insult to
da Vinci, to the holiness of the painting's subject matter,
and, most of all, to Wilson himself.

"I'll be damned," he fumed, "if I'll sell 'The Last Supper'
for less than five dollars a plate."

Furthering the cause of art appreciation, he found, was
not adequately appreciated by the public, and he closed
down his gallery in 1914. It was merely a sideline, something Wilson was doing for the sake of mass culture. He
must have reflected that his service to that cause, beginning
with his attempted diversion of the Yerkes collection into
the broader channels of the art world, had been ill rewarded. There was so much rancorous envy in that world
that a man with ambitions to let a little fresh air into the
musty ateliers and galleries would always suffer for his originality.

So he concentrated his energies, for the most part, in the
gambling world at a time when it was recovering from
successive shocks caused by the reform element which had
been struggling for decades to "clean up New York." District Attorney William Travers Jerome had been successful
for a time in clamping down on the Tenderloin and closing
down organized gambling. Governor Charles Evans
Hughes, another stern moralist, had persuaded the state
legislature to pass a bill outlawing the activities of bookmak-
ers so numerous they seemed to haunt every doorway in the

metropolis. But, as usual, enforcing such laws in New York City was another matter, and by 1913 it was again a wide-open town. Even before the Old Masters Art Society folded, Wilson had plunged into the gambling rackets as one of the bolder and more inventive operators. From the exquisite style of his tailoring and the luxury of his accommodations in an apartment on West Forty-third Street near Sixth Avenue—a short lurch from Jack Dunstan's—it appeared that he was prospering. The diamonds worn by his girlfriends also attested to his success at figuring the odds, then tilting them ever so slightly in his own favor.

One of his short-term enterprises was a deadfall called the Millionaires Club. Wilson was its senior partner, but he posed as a mere member who could be persuaded by visiting outlanders to obtain a guest card entitling them to associate with the best people in New York. The club's chief attraction was a walrus-shaped fellow who closely resembled William Howard Taft, who had departed from the White House in favor of Woodrow Wilson not long before the Millionaires Club opened its doors. He was stationed in an oversized chair in the club's reading room and instructed to keep himself partly concealed behind a newspaper. Strangers steered into the club by Wilson or one of his confederates were allowed to guess that the fat old fellow was indeed ex-President Taft, without anyone's actually saying so. They were told not to approach the man or embarrass him with their attentions. Most were so impressed by the supposed Presidential presence that they dropped considerable sums of money in the adjoining cardroom without a murmur of protest.

One night when Wilson had just steered in the fleeciest of lambs for shearing, "President Taft" suddenly pulled a knife

and stabbed the waiter who kept him supplied with highballs, shouting in an unstatesmanlike manner that he was
sick of being served drinks with only a tincture of whiskey.

Wilson's prospect fled in dismay, but when they met on
the street a few days later, Wilson blandly said, "Can you
beat it, the way they hushed up that story about Taft stab-
bing a waiter and kept it out of the newspapers?"

Such establishments as the Millionaires Club were necessarily quickie operations from which one made a score and
then closed up shop before there were too many complaints
to the authorities. Many of Wilson's bigger coups resulted
from the exercise of his agile mind, his insight into human
behavior, with which a professional trickster is likely to be
more familiar, on the practical level, than most academic
specialists in psychology. When Jack Johnson was matched
to fight Jess Willard in Havana in 1915, Wilson was certain
the fix was in. The heavyweight title had to change hands, be
returned to the white race after so long and painful a hiatus,
to build up the gate. A white champion was now necessary
for businesslike procedure; Johnson was still the best fighter
in the world, but his box-office potential had dissipated.
Still, Wilson preferred a sure thing to a hunch bet. Before
laying down all available cash on Willard, he decided to seek
confirmation about the fix from Johnson, with whom he had
been on friendly terms ever since the Ketchel fight. If
Johnson was being paid to take a dive, he'd tell Wilson his
chances were first-rate. So he cabled Johnson in Havana the
terse question "What shall I do?" When he received no
reply, he knew the champ was telling him something: The
fix was in. Wilson bet his shirt on Willard. And when Johnson succumbed in the Havana ring under the brassy Cuban
sunlight and while the referee tolled the ten-count, Johnson

casually raised his arm from the canvas to shade his eyes
from the sun, letting everyone who mattered know that he
had sold, not lost, the championship.

During the period just before World War I broke out,
Wilson and some of his colleagues were annoyed by the rise
of Arnold Rothstein as a kingpin of the gambling world.
Rothstein emerged from the respectable background of a
Lower East Side immigrant family, poor but hardworking,
to become a highly successful gambler. Eventually he made
himself the country's biggest bookmaker, pioneered union
and industrial racketeering through forging links among
politicians, the police, and the underworld, and supervised
the beginnings of the international traffic in narcotics. His
career as mastermind of the New York underworld ended in
1928, when he was shot in a room at the Park Central Hotel
by rivals who quickly divided his empire among them.

If they could have had their way, Wilson and his friends
would have cooled Rothstein long before that. They resented his "pushiness" and no doubt deplored his success in
exploiting his friendly, almost filial relationship with Tim
Sullivan of Tammany Hall. Rothstein would swagger into
Jack Dunstan's and without invitation plunk himself down at
the No. 1 table over which Mizner presided, which violated
protocol. Rothstein's personality also worked against him in
that atmosphere of predawn bonhomie. For one thing,
Rothstein would be sober while Mizner and his friends
would be high on one thing or another. And, his most recent
biographer noted, "Because Rothstein was not a good
mixer, because he had a supercilious twist to his lower lip,
he irritated many people. They didn't like a man who appeared to be self-sufficient, whose attitude they felt was
superior. Certainly Rothstein was given to being dogmatic.
And he had a habit of referring to other people as

'chumps.' " Presumably "chump" was more offensive coming from Rothstein, if only because of his scornful manner,
than Wilson's hearty greeting of "Hello, sucker."

Wilson and several of his cronies—Tad Dorgan, the car-
toonist, Hype Igoe, the sports columnist, and gambler Jack
Francis—decided to arrange Rothstein's comeuppance,
teach him that *hubris* wasn't the name of a Greek restaurant
owner. Rothstein's weakness, they decided, was his vanity.
One of the talents which Rothstein was chestiest about was
his pool playing. So Wilson and his friends decided to im-
port Jack Conway, a "gentleman sportsman," amateur jockey, and expert pool player who had defeated a number of
professionals in matches at the Racquet Club in Philadelphia. Since Conway was a Philadelphian, they were sure
that Rothstein wouldn't know he was a ringer.

Wilson knew that only the indirect approach, rather than
a challenge, would trap Rothstein. One night at Jack's
Rothstein joined Wilson's table and should have been put on
his guard by the unusual cordiality with which he was
greeted. His opinions on forthcoming prizefights and horse
races were tenderly solicited. Then, very casually, Jack
Francis expressed his opinion that Jack Conway was the best
amateur pool player in the United States.

Rothstein snapped at the bait. "Wrong," he said, "a
hundred and ten percent wrong."

"Name someone who could beat him," Wilson suggested.

Rothstein began to suspect that he was being lured into a
trap but knew he couldn't back down in front of all these
big-time sports without a disastrous loss of face.

"Me," he said, pulling out a roll of bills, wetting his thumb
and peeling off greenbacks. "I'll bet five hundred I can take
this Conway."

The details were settled with an alacrity that further

aroused Rothstein's suspicions. They would play a 100-point game, the site of which would be McGraw's Billiard Parlor near the old Herald Building.

Conway was brought up from Philadelphia, and the set-to began one evening at eight o'clock. Word had spread of the epic quality of the Rothstein-Conway match, and there was a sizable audience gathered around the green baize arena at McGraw's.

From the outset it was apparent that both men were masters with the pool cue. Conway won the first game by a few points. Rothstein, with a painful smile, paid off and suggested another. This time Rothstein won. A rubber match was proposed to settle which was the better player. Rothstein won the third game and was prepared to pack it in, but Jack Francis had a better idea.

"How about another set of three games?" he suggested.

"Hell," Rothstein replied, "I can play all night."

The billiards academy was jammed now as reports spread around Broadway that Rothstein would either be buying a Duesenberg next morning or would be bankrupted. So many people had crowded into the pool parlor that the proprietor, John J. McGraw, whose daytime occupation was managing the New York Giants, ordered that the doors be locked.

The seesaw struggle between Rothstein and Conway continued for several hours, with Rothstein $2,000 ahead on bets, but when closing time arrived McGraw said they would have to suspend the contest until the following night. Wilson was furious at the thought of his plot falling through and infuriated by the spectacle of Rothstein strutting around and chalking the tip of his cue with the dainty precision of a craftsman confident of his skill. He offered to pay the attendants overtime if McGraw would let the contest continue, and the latter agreed.

By dawn Rothstein was still stroking away with masterly skill and timing and had won another $3,000, making him the winner at that point by $5,000. Conway won occasionally, but Rothstein was more consistent.

"Just one more," Conway kept saying after losing a round. Rothstein would grin, stretch, and yawn, and pick up his cue again.

With an occasional time out for black coffee and sandwiches, the play went on all that morning and afternoon and continued into the second night. Rothstein and Conway had been bashing away for more than twenty-four hours, goaded on by Wilson and his confederates, who began to mutter about breaking someone's head with a pool cue if any suggestion was made that the marathon game be called. Both players were beginning to reel with exhaustion. Wilson and the anti-Rothstein clique were suffering from a severe case of financial debility.

It was four o'clock in the morning, thirty-four hours after the balls had been racked for the first match, when McGraw finally began snapping off the lights and demanding that everyone clear out of his joint.

"If I let this go on, I'll have dead men on my hands," he was reported saying by the New York *Daily Mail*.

Wilson and his friends whisked Rothstein and Conway off to a Turkish bath to make plans for a rematch. It was agreed that they would meet again, this time in Philadelphia, but Conway backed off before the rematch could be held, his friends explaining that it would be "degrading" for a gentleman sportsman to keep on playing with a professional gambler.

Mizner & Co. had dropped a reported $10,000 trying to teach Rothstein the meaning of *hubris*.

Usually his efforts to educate humanity in the folly of taking too much on faith were more successful. He divided his time between gambling on any proposition, in which he could discern an unfair edge for himself, and trimming any suckers that came into view. Certainly the intelligence and careful planning that went into his schemes, the hair-trigger wit he displayed, and the diligence with which he pursued a mark could have made him richer and more respectable in any other occupation. He once told a Hollywood friend that he and a couple of confederates pursued a wealthy prospect around the world, slowly winning his confidence, before they moved in for the fleecing. His quickness to seize upon a profitable opportunity became legendary around Broadway. Once a rich young wastrel from Seattle complained that he'd guzzled so much champagne the night before that he couldn't remember where he had been or what he had done. Wilson quickly decided to fill in the blank spaces for the playboy. He arranged with the night manager of a Broadway lobster palace to draw up an itemized bill for almost $2,000. Then he looked up the playboy and told him he had thrown the wettest and wildest party in recent memory in a private dining room. Wilson and the restaurant's night manager split the proceeds.

He continued his profligate course throughout World War I, quite unaffected by the atmosphere of moral earnestness which gripped most of his fellow citizens as they joined in the crusade to make the world safe for democracy. The prevailing idealism, the mood of sacrifice, the surge of patriotism that overcame his fellows did not penetrate the cocoon of Wilson's self-interest. Men who marched off

under whipping banners were, in his view, the greatest
suckers of all. He had turned forty by the time the United
States entered the war and did not have to be restrained
from rushing to join the colors.

Wilson kept right on gambling, smoking opium or sniffing
cocaine when he felt in the mood, drinking the nights away,
and doing his best to tap some of the wartime prosperity.
One day in November, 1918, he and some friends were
hitting the pipe in a Times Square hotel room with a wet
bedsheet draped over the door to keep the opium fumes
from leaking into the corridor and annoying the other
guests. One of the smokers complained that he kept hearing
a distant ringing of bells, but Wilson suggested he was
afflicted with "head noises," the current euphemism for a
disordered psyche. Hours later Wilson went out for a breath
of fresh air and learned that the ringing in his friend's ears
had been the celebration attending the signing of the armis-
tice.

That year Wilson had been having his troubles with the
law, which in a seizure of wartime purity had been making it
tough on the professional gamblers. A John Doe investiga-
tion of such matters was held in the Court of General Sessions in March, 1918. One of those said to be knowledgeable
in gambling activities was Wilson Mizner, who was subpoenaed to appear on charges that he had won $35,000 from
a German baker in a chemin de fer game. German-
Americans weren't very popular just then, so the baker's
troubles were treated with facetious humor in the newspaper accounts of Mizner's court appearance. One paper
reported that the baker had started paying off Wilson with
products from his bakery. Wilson's apartment, it added, was
filled with thousands of doughnuts.

"How long," an assistant district attorney asked Wilson, "have you been playing chemin de fer?"

"Since infancy," he replied.

Equally flippant was his appearance in Magistrate's Court the following August on charges brought by an actor named Herman Frank who complained that Wilson assaulted him in a Broadway restaurant when he accused Wilson of having stolen a Ziegfeld showgirl from him. The prosecution demanded to know whether it wasn't true that Wilson was a sinister character who made his living off gambling and other illegal pursuits.

A foul insinuation, Wilson loftily replied, adding that he owned a half interest in a New Jersey tannery and occasionally wrote scenarios for one of the lesser New York film studios. (The latter assertion, at least, was true. He resorted to composing scripts for silent films when he had nothing else better to do.)

The assistant district attorney tried to pin him down on the exact nature of his literary efforts.

"Well, I didn't actually write the script," he testified in regard to a film for which he had received a writing credit. "I phoned it in."

"Do you mean to say that you gave that to the motion-picture company by telephone?"

"Yes—and they paid me by telephone."

Wilson proved such a slippery witness that the charges against him were dropped by the prosecution in a fit of petulance.

On the whole, however, Wilson's luck was beginning to run out on him. The times were changing and not, from his viewpoint, for the better. All forms of crime were being tightly organized, and Wilson was not an organization man.

He could only operate as a free-lance in the gambling racket; acting under the direction of a Sicilian executive did not appeal to him.

One of the harder blows which struck Wilson and his fellow bon vivants was the imposition of the Prohibition laws. Among other things, they killed the Broadway of his salad days; speakeasies were a poor substitute for the red plush and crystal chandeliers of the lobster palaces. The difference was that between drinking champagne at Rector's and downing shots of illicit rye at one of the places called Tony's. On the night of January 26, 1920, just before the dry laws took effect, Wilson and other mourners gathered in a private room at Jack's for the wake. For once Wilson could produce no witticisms—the parched years stretching ahead like the Great American Desert were a prospect too dehydrating for easy joking. Wilson and his companions in distress drank the night away in dead earnest.

The times were out of joint, all right. In 1919 he had been arrested on a charge of operating a gambling house on Long Island, and this time he wasn't able to josh his way out of court. He was convicted and given a suspended sentence. Bootlegging might have provided a new career, as it did for many of his old colleagues but he considered that a man in his forties was a little too old to shoot it out with hijackers or outrun the Coast Guard cutters on Long Island Sound.

He must have known the good times were over—at least in the New York sector—when he was beaten up and left for dead in a midtown alley. The reason for the assault was never disclosed; if Wilson knew, he obeyed the code he had so often praised and kept his mouth shut. He couldn't have talked if he wanted to, in fact, because his assailants had left him with multiple fractures of the jaw and internal injuries.

The Broadway rumor was that he had crossed someone influential, either over a bet or over a girl.

"What did they hit you with?" a detective asked him when he had recovered sufficiently to receive the police.

"St. Patrick's Cathedral."

11

A SUCCESSOR TO
PONCE DE LEON

FOR many years Wilson regarded trifling with narcotics as an endearing foible, no worse than an addiction to gumdrops.

He could take the stuff or leave it alone, he maintained. So could most people before morphine and heroin became more widely used. An occasional pipe of opium was not addictive in the sense of harder drugs. Nor was cocaine, a stimulant rather than a depressive like the opium-based drugs, considered addictive. Wilson believed there was nothing more companionable than a group of good fellows passing the bamboo pipe; the way he saw it, there were more brawls and crimes of violence in a bottle of whiskey than a whole bale of opium.

As the philosopher-humorist-propagandist of the drug-taking milieu, he was credited with coining the elliptical term "user." Far from making his habit a closet vice, he boasted about it and probably magnified his devotion to the

poppy and its by-products. Once he was presiding over a
faro layout in a Times Square hotel room when a newcomer
came in shaking the snow off his fur collar. Snow was the
user's term for cocaine. Wilson immediately summoned a
bellboy. "Boy, take my nose and hang it out the window."

But even Wilson, whose knowledge of narcotics was not
as far-ranging as he fancied, eventually found himself
hooked, and it was no longer something to joke about.
During the hospital stay occasioned by his encounter with
thugs, he was given morphine to quiet the pain of his
fractured jaw. Morphine, being ten times as potent as
opium, was nothing to trifle with. After leaving the hospital,
Wilson, less lightheartedly, continued to take morphine.
Then, adding immeasurably to his psychological problems,
his mother died. Though he concealed the fact under a hard
glossy veneer of cynicism, he was always, secretly, Mama's
Angel Birdie. A stirring rendition of "Mother Machree"
would leave him quietly sobbing. Mrs. Mizner's death was
such a blow that, according to his friends, he suffered something akin to a nervous breakdown and had to surrender
himself to a sanatorium.

During the early twenties, when the country was going
jazz-mad and whooping it up in the speakeasies and generally rejoicing in the flapper era, Wilson was fighting off his
demons and watching life turn sour on him. He had passed
his forty-fifth year. A seizure of excessive virtue had struck
the constabulary, and he was unable to make a living at
gambling and confidence games. Once so debonair, once
the *beau ideal* of the gentleman's outfitters, he had reached
the frayed-cuff and soiled-collar level, and many of his ill-
wishers were predicting he would soon be sleeping under
the El on the Bowery.

At that low-water mark in his career he had to resort to

writing scripts for the ragtag of the film industry. Most of the moguls-to-be, Ince and Griffith and Lasky and Goldwyn and Laemmle, had already hit the high road to Southern California, but there were still studios grinding out two-reelers on the Lower East Side, in the Bronx, and over at Fort Lee, New Jersey. They needed story material in quantity. In response to that need, a new subliterary craft had developed. A writer who couldn't make the grade even with the pulps could turn his hand to scenario writing. The formal screenplay was still far in the golden future, along with $5,000-a-week salaries for their authors. A scenario was a sketch of a film story, a few pages of plot and character descriptions, which the director stuffed into his pocket and used as he saw fit. Even the greenest of tyros, if equipped with an agile story mind, could make a living turning out scenarios for $100 or thereabouts. Anita Loos, the pixyish San Franciscan who had admired the Mizner legend from afar ever since childhood, broke in as a scenarist and recalled in her autobiography that in four years she produced 105 scripts and sold all but 4 of them. A somewhat better paid craft was that of writing titles ("Came the dawn. . . . Another redskin bit the dust") for the finished product, for which the specialist was paid $1,000 a reel on feature films.

Wilson had been flirting with the nascent film industry for some years. Back in 1916, he had been offered $2,500 a week to write the story of his life and enact the leading role, but he rejected it after a film test, he claimed, made him "look like a bloodhound with the mind of a Pekinese." Now the flickers seemed the only alternative to panhandling. Gone were the high-spirited, idol-smashing, practical-joking years when the world seemed to reverberate with Mizner-generated laughter. Such as the fairly recent gag he had pulled at a patriotic celebration at the Polo Grounds,

which Charlie Chaplin would fondly recall in his memoir.
Seven brass bands were to parade before the governor of
New York (Alfred E. Smith, whom he came to admire
greatly). Equipping himself with a gaudy, beribboned, but
entirely fraudulent badge, Wilson stopped each band as it
entered the arena and instructed the leader to strike up
"The Star-Spangled Banner" as it passed the governor's
reviewing stands. By the time Governor Smith had been
forced to stand up for the fourth time he profanely ordered
that the national anthem be played somewhere well past the
reviewing stand.

Wilson was so close to down-and-out that he hired out as a
scenario writer for the Oliver Film Company, which was
producing quickies in an East Side studio, all of them so
forgettable the company is not even mentioned in standard
histories of the film industry. Such film companies sprang
up with a fluttering of iridescent wings, then died like
dragonflies in a summer afternoon. The Oliver company was
also short-lived, and Wilson decided to try his luck in Hollywood, though he had the native San Franciscan's contempt for Los Angeles and all its suburbs, including Bur-
bank, Culver City, and Hollywood, where the film studios
were springing up. The tales he had heard of orgiastic
life-styles in what the newspapers were calling the "film
capital of the world," however, made it irresistible. "That,"
he later explained, "was before the bankers had got into the
saddle and the inmates were still running the asylum. I had
heard so much of the menace of the movies and the terrific
tug of Hollywood vice . . . but I crashed into the dullest and
best lighted madhouse in America.

"That was the silent period in which movie heroes were
hand-kissers as opposed to the later era in which the gentlemen socked the ladies with tender brutality. There is

nothing more awful than a hand-kisser with poor lighting and all over the streets of the cinema capital were gents so soft and sweet that you worried with their mothers.

"I had no objection to my own platinum chains, but within a week it was clear that the majority of the body-and-soul merchants knew how to buy brains but failed to use their own, once an intellect was captured. Lazy as I had always been, the complete indifference with which they paid me tall dough for nothing left me doubly nonplussed.

"My first assignment was a picture which no one was ever destined to see called 'Yukon Days.' All I had to do was to have the Yukon flow over the silver screen in some dramatic fashion, and having been told this I was placed in a small cubicle to worry and fret. As no one came near me, I just sat there for the first week or two wondering what I was thinking about.

"Before the first story conference I had been paid two thousand dollars. At the conference I learned that another picture so similar to the one we had in mind had been released that I'd better think up something else. So I went back into my cubicle and said to myself, 'Bill, don't you worry,' and since no one else spoke up I answered, 'No, sir, I won't,' and I didn't."

When that term of salaried loafing in Hollywood ended, Wilson returned to New York and continued to scrabble for a living and to contend with the increasingly heavy burden of his narcotics addiction.

The monkey on his back was assuming a menacing aspect. The habit was no longer something to joke about. A rather gruesome end was foreseeable when the guardian angel of his youth, his brother Addison, learned that Wilson was going downhill and would have to be saved from himself.

Instead of a bed in Bellevue and a nameless plot in

potter's field for one of life's more assiduous comedians,
Florida in the mid-twenties boom years reached out for
Wilson.

It was another Klondike, but in a warmer and more
salubrious setting, with hammocks substituted for Arctic
tundra, and much more profitable. The craze for subdivid-
ing Florida and raising pastel cities out of the swampy
lowlands was one of those recurrent phenomena that jiggle
and almost unhinge the American economy. For a time the
rush for Florida land, even those sections below water,
threatened to depopulate the other forty-seven states. The
boom in real estate spread from Miami to Palm Beach to
Boca Raton—the Mizner brothers' highly lucrative
development—and elsewhere as soon as the alligators could
be dislodged from their muddy nests.

Among the literary figures whose talents were enlisted to
glorify the Southern paradise was Rex Beach, who was
employed to produce an advertising brochure for the hopeful small city of Coral Gables. He scouted the sections of the
state being boomed by the real estate developers and later
reported: "Roads were black with scouts, binder boys,
speculators, investors and homeseekers; it was difficult to
find accommodations in any town large enough to have a
hotel for most of them were growing like toadstools and
were ablaze with excitement. Passenger buses rushed prospects hundreds of miles to this development or that, bands
played, auctioneers and spellbinders did their ballyhoos,
groundfloor land offices, decorated with potted palms and
cut flowers, were open most of the night; lawyers engaged in
searching titles kept awake on black coffee." As a native son
Beach could only regret that the boomers were trampling
over the inland hammocks which were "Florida's native
beauty spots, her green mansions of palms, hardwood, fern

and undergrowth; they were the favorite hunting grounds of the Seminoles and still a refuge for deer, turkeys and an occasional panther. . . ."

Ben Hecht and J. P. McEvoy, both writers of later eminence but presently teamed up to gather material for a W. C. Fields silent film loaded with Florida land-boom humor, journeyed down there and promptly dropped their cinematic chores to become press agents for one of the more spectacular developers.

"The City of Miami," Hecht recalled, "had turned itself into a real-estate cornucopia. A hundred thousand people were getting rich selling building lots to each other. They raced up and down the hot sidewalks in bathing suits, bathrobes and jiggling sweaters. A colored boy had sold his newsstand for ten thousand. The news of great profitable sales spread like the arrival of a Messiah. Straw-hatted salesmen waved 'new development' maps in the air and chanted the names Silver Heights, Coral Gables, Picture City, Montezuma Manors, Sea Cove Crest, Biscayne Bay, like the signal towers of a Promised Land. Symphony orchestras played in salesrooms. Buses full of bonanza hunters roared through the streets and down the coral dusty roads. Tumbling out of their tallyhos, these Argonauts looked at rubbish heaps and reeking swamps and visioned the towers of new Babylons.

"Everybody was trying to get rich in a few days. Nobody went swimming. Nobody sat under the palm trees. Nobody played horseshoes. Seduction was at a standstill. Everybody was stubbing his toe on real-estate nuggets. People who had been worth only six hundred dollars a few weeks ago were now worth a hundred thousand dollars—not in money but in real estate. . . ."

And one of the principal authors of that essay in frenzied

finance was Addison Mizner. He had come to Florida in
1916 and established himself as the premier architect and
decorator for wealthy people who migrated to Florida in the
wintertime. His speciality was a fake-Spanish Renaissance
style of architecture which seemed to fit the landscape and
which appealed especially to the tastes of the newly rich.
Addison soon prospered. He not only was running up mansions all over the place but had also established a workshop
in Palm Beach which produced the roof tiles and ornamental
terra-cotta so necessary in converting Florida into a fever
dream of Granada.

Addison had become associated with Paris Singer, a tall,
blondbearded fellow who had cut a wide swath through
international society. He was one of the twenty-five children of Isaac Merrit Singer, the sewing-machine magnate,
only eight of whom were legitimate. Paris Singer was one of
the seventeen illegitimate offspring but inherited a large
share of the Singer fortune. In 1908 he had attracted the
libidinous eye of Isadora Duncan. The famous dancer had
just lost her patron, the Prince de Polignac, and needed a
new sponsor for her ambitious plans to revolutionize the
dance. Isadora met Paris Singer at the prince's funeral and,
with her usual disregard for the conventions, latched onto
him before the funeral party disbanded at the cemetery
gates. Paris, who was so named because he had been born in
the French capital, then took up the burden of paying for
Isadora's expensive schemes.

Eight years of living with the tempestuous dancer on
various French and English estates so debilitated Paris
Singer that in 1916 he decided to flee for his life. He arrived
in Florida so ill and exhausted that he had to be carried off
the train on a stretcher. Isadora's absence proved the tonic
he needed, along with the stimulation provided by a friend-

ship he formed with Addison Mizner, who was inspiring him to undertake another and less exhausting form of artistic patronage: the transformation of Florida. Isadora caught up with him and indulged in her usual alcoholic escapades —causing Addison to rechristen her "Is-a-bore when drunken"—but eventually she turned her attention to a mad Russian poet and let Paris and Addison get on with their Florida renaissance.

The idea which seized Mizner and Singer was converting the Florida coastline, with its ramshackle villas and shingled cottages, into something approximating the luxury and architectural ambiance of the Mediterranean coastal resorts. There was no reason Miami Beach should not resemble Cap Ferrat, that the resort hotels with their rocking chairs and tacky verandas should not be swept away and replaced by the more admirable aspects of European culture.

One afternoon in January, 1917, Singer, dressed as usual in his Côte d'Azur trousers, striped Riviera shirt, Basque beret, and purple espadrilles, was sitting on the porch of the Royal Poinciana in Palm Beach with Addison Mizner. Both men, surveying the stodgy scene through the shimmer of afternoon heat, the spavined old millionaires, and the wattled dowagers, were suffering from a severe case of boredom.

"Mizner, you know I came here expecting to die, but I'm damned if I feel like it."

"What are you going to do about it?"

"What would you do about it," Singer asked his current cultural adviser, "if you could do anything you wanted?"

Addison swelled like a Venetian master builder receiving a commission from one of the more generous doges. He had been waiting a long time for a well-heeled patron to say something like that. With an expansive gesture that took in the Royal Poinciana and its dowdy surroundings, he replied, "I'll tell you what I'd do. I'd build something that wasn't made of wood, and I wouldn't paint it yellow."

So Addison Mizner was started on his way. Both a patriot and a philanthropist, Singer first commissioned him to design a convalescent home for American soldiers wounded in Europe. This was to become the celebrated Everglades Club, a purely social headquarters, after wounded servicemen showed little interest in recuperating so far from their homes (only thirty-three responded to Singer's invitation to come to Palm Beach at his expense for their recuperation). It was lavishly appointed, with paths cut through the surrounding brush for wheelchairs and docks built for houseboats. "A little bit of Seville and the Alhambra, a dash of Madeira and Algiers," a local newspaper described it.

That was a fair summation of Addison's architectural efforts. Everyone was so pleased with the Everglades Club that the commissions started pouring in. For the Stotesburys of Philadelphia he built El Mirasol, a sprawling estate which extended from Lake Worth to the Atlantic beaches and included half a dozen patios and a private zoo. The main building started out "along the lines of a Spanish convent and ended up as a Spanish castle," one commentator noted, and that was characteristic of Addison's grandiose improvisations. He was a Method architect. With El Mirasol he had not neglected to build a forty-car garage, but he forgot to include a kitchen until he was reminded of his negligence. With his freehand style, he often soared above practical matters. During the construction of one lordly villa he forgot to provide a staircase. To retrieve that grievous error, he hastily added a turret to the house—and damn the effect on its lineaments—around which he placed an outside spiral staircase.

Success did not greatly change Addison, who had inherited the curious strain of combined arrogance and fecklessness of the Mizners which had flowered even more fully in Wilson. His high-handedness soon became legendary. It was said that he bought an old Oriental rug in Spain for $2 and sold it for $2,000 in Palm Beach to a client. Even such socially elevated clients as Mr. and Mrs. E. T. Stotesbury were treated as commoners by Addison. One day he lured Mr. Stotesbury away for a pinochle game during one of Mrs. Stotesbury's celebrated musicales. Mrs. Stotesbury tracked the truants down, and she shrieked at Addison, "You sneak away when Rachmaninoff is playing!" "Oh," Addison replied, "I thought it was the piano tuner."

Once he and Wilson became embroiled with Captain Alistair Mackintosh, who had been the royal equerry at the Court of St. James' before he migrated to Florida. Addison was building a house for Captain Mackintosh, and while he was an expert adapter of medieval Spanish architecture, his training, so concentrated on graceful lineaments, had included little indoctrination in the matter of plumbing. Addison was weak on bathrooms. In a Spanish palace, after all, the bathroom had been a thunder mug behind an elegant Moorish screen. Mackintosh tried to enlighten Addison on the necessity of providing for modern plumbing in his Florida dream house, but Addison roared with defiance, "You, you have stood in line for hours in the corridors of Buckingham Palace waiting for your weekly chance at the tub—you dare to come over to this country and tell us about bathrooms?" And Wilson chimed in with one of his lightning epigrams. "An Englishman never bathes," he intoned. "He is born wearing a sack suit, which they have to pry off him after death with a cold chisel."

Before the land boom had really revved up, and while

Addison was congratulating himself on having made his first million as cultural adviser to those who wintered in Florida just before the 1924 Republican victory in the national elections provided a surge of economic overconfidence, Addison imported his younger brother. Wilson wasn't needed as an executive assistant, but Addison was worried about reports he had received of Wilson's rapid decay.

The moment Wilson seedily manifested himself in Palm Beach, Addison summoned specialists to cure him of morphine addiction. They tried to wean him away from the needle in gradual stages but he kept backsliding. One of his favorite tipples was a highball laced with laudanum (an opiate). Finally Wilson shrugged off the specialists and kicked the habit by taking the cold-turkey cure. He suffered the agonies of withdrawal, but eventually the drug was cleaned from his system, and he never again succumbed to the addiction. It was evidence that, when called on in a dire emergency, there was a residue of iron in the Mizner character.

A few months after he had been teetering on the brink of the lower depths, bright-eyed with larceny and bushy-tailed with energy, Wilson was now capable of confronting the largest challenge of his career. He and Addison within a few years would be worth, on paper, between $10,000,000 and $50,000,000. The gap in the estimate testified not only to the looseness of their accounting methods but also to the elasticity of Florida boom fortunes. No man who struck it rich in Florida worried about decimal points.

Wilson's first assignment as Addison's executive assistant was to take charge of the largely black work force at the latter's Palm Beach workshop. His record as a labor expediter was not something which would have wrung admiration from Comrade Stakhanov; it will be recalled that as a boss of his brother Edgar's miners he had encouraged marathon poker sessions and as a Guatemalan banana planter he had constantly advised his workers to stay out of the sun and get plenty of rest. As manager of Addison's workshop, his brother soon learned, Wilson presided over a downward curve in production statistics. He had learned that many of his black workers possessed beautiful voices. Soon he had formed them into a choral group which rehearsed on company time while Wilson accompanied them on a portable organ. Wilson was removed from the workshop and brought into the offices.

He not only served as secretary-treasurer of the Mizner Corporation, but rapidly made himself one of the social lions of Palm Beach. As usual, he capitalized on his misdeeds. When he learned that rumors were circulating around the fashionable colony that he had recently served time in a New York penitentiary on gambling charges—a canard, for once—he assumed a hangdog look and greatly irked Addison by entertaining dinner parties with tales of his life as a felon. For purposes of verisimilitude he invented a cellmate, an Australian who had deserted his wife and child when he migrated to America. Wilson claimed that the deserted wife cabled his cellmate that she and her baby were starving and that the Australian cabled in reply, "Eat baby."

One who was particularly nauseated by Wilson's fables about his imprisonment was Paris Singer, a fastidious fellow who was revolted by the crudity of Wilson's recollections.

The Duchess of Richelieu, who had taken charge of the decorating end of Addison's business, asked him, "Do you believe Wilson was ever really in prison?"

"I think he must have been," Singer replied. "He has such an intimate knowledge of the plumbing."

The Mizner brothers began dabbling in the purchase and sale of real estate just as the boom began assuming extravagant proportions. Otherwise sensible persons were predicting that Florida would become the greatest bonanza ever known. The conservative economist Roger W. Babson forecast a state subdivided and populated in every inch of swamp and tidal land from the Georgia border to the Keys. Another economist foresaw a population of 20,000,000 in a few years, with $40 billion worth of housing going up. Florida became a rage, then a delirium, and finally a madness. Tales of sudden wealth flashed from Miami to every corner of the nation: the barber with a nest egg of $80 who made a fortune in a few weeks, the schoolteacher who made $6,000,000 on an investment of $3,500.

The Mizner brothers, with greater capital than any barber or schoolteacher, jumped in with both feet. Their corporation acquired a large tract of land covered by swamps, thickets, and a few bemused Seminoles and promoted it into the snobbish resort of Boca Raton. They built it from the waterlogged ground up in a few hectic years through Addison's architectural talent (geared to the mass production of Iberian fantasies), Wilson's swivel-tongued ability as a spieler (first developed as a pusher of Dr. Slocum's miraculous vermifuge), and the spectacular achievements of Harry Reichenbach, the masterful press agent, whom they hired the moment they knew they were going to need large amounts of speculative capital.

Boca Raton, they proclaimed, would rise from the bayous to become *the* place for wealthy aristocrats to spend the winter or retire. A few miles south of Palm Beach, it would (they said) soon outshine that rest home for millionaires with tired blood and fish-faced First Families who clung to their trust funds and were afraid of new splendors. Palm Beach would soon merely be the service entrance of Boca Raton. With its network of canals and motorized gondolas, it would revive the water-girt glory of Venice, only Boca Raton would be new and hygienic and offer all modern conveniences. To enhance Wilson's spieling and Reichenbach's uninhibited prose, Addison drew sketches of what Boca Raton would be when its builders finished their task—and those gaudy watercolors, according to those who were privileged to peep into the prospective paradise, offered visions of a tropical pleasure dome that would have caused Kublai Khan to behead his chief architect.

Behind all the razzle-dazzle was Reichenbach's dictum: "Get the big snobs, and the little ones will follow."

So Addison and Wilson worked their social connections, dating back to their youth in San Francisco and Addison's days in New York as grand vizier to the matriarchs of the Four Hundred, with a shameless enthusiasm. They wanted no part of the middle-class migration, homely folk clutching their life savings and looking for a few last years under a kindlier sun. No one but a multimillionaire was deemed fit to settle down on the Mizner subdivision.

Among the wealthy or celebrated bellwethers whom the Mizners advertised as Boca Raton pioneers, and whose names were used to lure in the fleecier sheep, were several Du Ponts, H. H. Rogers of the Standard Oil directorate, Harold Vanderbilt, Elizabeth Arden, Herbert Bayard Swope, Matthew C. Brush, James M. Cox, and two old friends of the Mizner brothers, Irving Berlin and the musical comedy star Marie Dressler. In addition to the Duchess de Richelieu, they also welcomed the Rumanian Princess Ghika and such high-born Britons as Lady Diana Manners, Charles Spencer Churchill, the Duchess of Sutherland, and Lord Glenconner. Titles were regarded so important as boob catchers that Harry Reichenbach hurried to Europe to track down royalties from defunct Balkan kingdoms and crowned heads sent into exile as a result of the upheavals of the First World War. But American celebrities were also reckoned good for business, and the Mizners contested with the other promoters for the presence of Paul Whiteman, the bandleader; Evelyn Nesbit Thaw, who had become a nightclub singer after starring in the Thaw-White murder case, Madame Alda and Chaliapin of grand opera. Ruby Keeler, Fritzi Scheff, and Elsie Janis also raised their voices in celebration of the new paradise. Wilson, in particular, realized the importance of music to ream the suckers by; he brought in songwriter Grant Clarke to compose his development's anthem, "Boca Raton, You Have a Charm All of Your Own."

Marie Dressler would look back upon her Florida experience with a bitter philosophy. She had known Addison Mizner when he was a court favorite of Mrs. Stuyvesant Fish, who was also a friend of Miss Dressler's. A few years before the Florida boom she had been associated with Harry Reichenbach in making a series of European travelogue films. That venture had foundered, however, when Reichenbach proved so inept as a film producer that she wouldn't allow the product to be released.

Despite that experience, she succumbed to Reichenbach's urging that she make her headquarters in Boca Raton, buy real estate there herself as an investment, and help sell it to people impressed by her luster as a film and stage performer. "The Florida boom was then at its height," she wrote in her memoir. "I accepted it as gospel what I was told about the value of land down there. I had sold a good deal of it before I realized that not only was I a sucker, but that I was making suckers of those who bought through me. Almost beside myself with distress, I did what I could to straighten things out. This experience was one of the most humiliating of my life." Like many others, she would learn that it was foolish to "be drawn into a game of which I did not know the first rule."

A startling new Wilson Mizner was born in the Florida boom. The scent of all those millions in fresh money cascading into the state galvanized the man. Gone, suddenly, was the lackadaisical charmer, the exemplar of indolence, who viewed business hours, office work, and commercial procedures as the obsession of dullards.

Wilson was now secretary-treasurer of the Mizner Corporation, which often had millions in its bank accounts from real estate transactions. He was a certified tycoon, at least when he was on the job; what he did after dark, as he and J. P. Morgan knew, was his own business. He had played the role before, as an impersonation, so he knew what was required of him. Around the corporate offices his manner was dynamic, commanding, and occasionally verged on the satirical. He rushed around barking orders at the help. He studied sales charts with a gravity worthy of the Harvard Business School and adopted a manner compatible with that of the chairmanship of United States Steel.

This was the Mizner brothers' chance to make a real killing, and he wasn't going to blow it through tomfoolery. The rest of the family—a court of tribal opinion which was the only restraining influence on a Mizner—had always regarded the younger two brothers as lacking in fiber, Addison a gaudy eccentric, Wilson a prospective gallows bird. Now, by God, they were running a real estate kingdom in a manner worthy of all those antecedent empire-building Mizners who had done so well in and by Northern California.

In his state of tentative respectability, Wilson even resisted the temptation to tap the till; after all, as he kept reminding himself, he was part owner of the till. And he was rather touched by the fact that Addison, who knew all about his frequent essays in grand larceny, trusted him enough to place him in charge of the exchequer.

If there was any corporate hanky-panky involving Wilson, it concerned the private sale of a new block of lots just before they were offered to the public. Wilson would invite his friends to study the location of the lots in the new offering and pick out ones likely to gain in value. In Boca Raton, as in other Florida subdivisions, one didn't buy a lot merely to build a house on it. The speculative value of such property, during the height of the boom, was so great that often it had doubled in value before the transaction was completed. Boca Raton was among the gaudiest of the speculations, thanks to the promotional talents of Wilson and Harry Reichenbach; a visitor to the development often was greeted by Irving Berlin, America's No. 1 songwriter and an old pal of Wilson's, and invited to tea by Marie Dressler, better known now as the "Duchess of Boca Raton." The price of Mizner Corporation stock, under such stimulus, shot up $100 to $1,000 a share.

Wilson was carried away by euphoria and boasted to his friends that inside a few years, unless someone pricked the bubble, he was going to be a hundred times a millionaire.

He and his architectural-genius brother, he explained, weren't merely crass little Babbitts creating some new Zenith in the Florida bogs. They weren't simply promoters selling real estate hand over fist. No, he would add, banging his broken-knuckled hand on his mahogany desk top, they were Noahs with a gilded Ark, founding fathers of a walled-in civilization, creating an enclave where the rich and famous could frolic without danger of rubbing elbows with the lesser specimens of humanity.

Occasionally, of course, the stern empire builder's mask would slip and reveal the impish, Nibelungen grin of the old Wilson, the prankster, rounder, and professional cynic. Then he would descend to self-caricature. At times it seemed ridiculous for Wilson Mizner to find himself, wearing his treasurer's hat, signing perfectly legitimate checks for hundreds of thousands of dollars. He would stare at the amount, then the signature, and wonder when the law was going to clap its hand on his shoulder.

Once he shouted to Bess Hammons, his secretary, who had just brought him a sheaf of checks to sign, "Oh, hell, I'm tired of autographing this chickenfeed. Bring me a million-dollar check to sign."

Undoubtedly his tongue was lodged firmly in his cheek during the giddier and more grandiose moments when the Mizner brothers were establishing the city-state of Boca Raton. Like many of the other real estate promotions, it announced that Boca Raton would become a cultural center and the home of a university. The Mizner academy would be known as Upton University and would put Old Heidelberg to shame for the purity of its scholarship. Inquiries from the Better Business Bureau, however, forced Boca Raton and its rivals to admit that their colleges were merely airy aspirations and that no faculties had been engaged or ground broken for university buildings. There were so many dream schools existing only in the real estate promoter's literature that Seth Clarkson, a former New York newspaperman (and author of the celebrated headline proclaiming that British

forces had occupied Jerusalem during the war, BRITISH
ENTER CHRIST'S HOME TOWN) and ex-drinking companion of
Wilson's, poked at them with a satirist's pen. Clarkson, as
resident humorist of *Miami Life*, recorded intimations he
had of the last football game between teams from phantom
universities in the Ghost University League. The stands
were crowded with alumni selling each other parcels of real
estate; the cheerleaders' yells were slogans coined by the
subdividers. The game broke up when the opening of a new
subdivision was announced, and both teams raced off the
field to join the spectators in a stampede to the site of the
bonanza.

As Seth Clarkson and others have recalled, Wilson did not
spend all his time presiding over the corporate offices,
roping in prospects, inspiring his salesmen, and swanking
around in the highest social circles. True, he was the social
guardian of Boca Raton, who examined credentials, lips
pursed, with as much hauteur as any dowager queen of
society screening out the parvenus and climbers. Under
Harry Reichenbach's inspiration a committee was organized
to govern the admittance of persons applying for residence
in Boca Raton. If you didn't have a title or your name in one
of the social studbooks, you might have some difficulty in
buying property. A fistful of money wasn't the sole qualifica-
tion at the height of the euphoria.

Wilson, whose career as a cotillion leader had been
largely confined to mining-camp hoedowns and whores'
balls on the Barbary Coast, had absorbed some understanding of his responsibilities at his mother's knee. And there
was no one with a sharper eye for a phony. Wilson himself
had posed often enough as a traveling steel magnate in his
days as one of the "greyhounds" coursing through the luxury
liners' cardrooms to spot another pretender. It was ob-

served that Wilson enjoyed his work as the Ward McAllister of Boca Raton.

After almost half a century emulating Peck's Bad Boy, however, Wilson could not transform himself into a round-the-clock model of respectability. Even while weeding out unworthy applicants for residence in Boca Raton, he was joyously holding reunions with old friends more likely to be found on police blotters than in social registers. Florida had become a con man and gambler's paradise; they went, as always, with the sucker money. Such old acquaintances and confederates from his grifting days in New York as Jack French, John Henry Strosnider, and Mr. and Mrs. Earl, who had plied the Atlantic as cardsharps with Wilson, had joined the rush to Miami and Palm Beach. French, it was reported, cleared $348,000 in one week during the height of the boom. Naturally these sharpers stayed away from Boca Raton, which they recognized as the biggest con of all, a really breathtaking "score" to which Wilson had exclusive territorial rights.

Wilson entertained some of his old friends from his less respectable years in his own home, the novelist Arthur Somers Roche recalling that Mizner once phoned him to say, "I want you to come over to my house and meet an old girl friend of mine. Greatest pickpocket in the world. She can steal the grand piano from your drawing room and you'll never miss it." For those old pals who were suffering from the shorts, or indigence, he sometimes found employment to tide them over. He persuaded one friend in the present (Boca Raton) to hire another from the past (Barbary Coast) as his butler. The butler was fired when his employer learned that Wilson's old pal had just finished a sentence for manslaughter in California.

Wilson was too busy building the Mizner Corporation

into a giant among enterprises, on paper, to shower the
scene with his usual barrage of witticisms, but a number of
them were lovingly collected and preserved by Alva Johnston. Regarding one of his migrant friends from the New
York underworld, Wilson remarked, "He couldn't dip his
hand in the Hudson River without knocking over the
Palisades." A prizefighter from the old days who stopped
Wilson on a West Palm Beach street and woozily asked if
Wilson thought he'd ever amount to anything in the ring was
advised, "Hang up your gloves. You'll never be anything but
a catcher. If you don't quit, you'll be walking along the street
slobbering out of both sides of your mouth instead of only
one."

In his memoir, brother Addison revealed that Wilson,
even while guarding the corporate treasury and busying
himself with schemes to enlarge it, could not entirely con-
tain his boisterous wit. Addison was always his No. 1 fan;
even while tut-tutting his younger brother's more outrageous behavior, he could not stifle his appreciation of Wilson's
acidulous style. Once when Wilson and several of his friends
were on a Florida tour, they stopped at a Sebring hotel, and
soon their merrymaking was disturbing the more sedate
guests. The manager called Wilson's suite to complain.
"Listen," Wilson bellowed into the mouthpiece, "if you
bother us again, you officious bastard, I'll take a pair of
scissors and cut your goddamn flophouse to pieces." Regarding a Palm Beach contractor noted even among his piratical
breed as a greedy fellow, Wilson quipped, "He's so crooked
he'd steal two left shoes." Of a former carpenter who had
enriched himself and was making a splash in resort society
but who could hardly open his mouth without dropping a
malapropism, Wilson said, "Every time he opens his yap, a
handful of shingle nails drops out." A tainted canapé passed

to him at a cocktail party drew his comment that "Those anchovies died of convulsions in a septic tank."

The old rough-and-ready Wilson Mizner, despite prolonged immersion in more polite surroundings, also asserted himself when the circumstances seemed to require brisk executive action.

One of the Mizner developments in Boca Raton was the Mizner Mile, which was supposed to become the classiest strip of territory this side of the Côte d'Azur. Its centerpiece would be a $10,000,000 hotel in Addison's most exuberant bastard-Spanish style. Above and below the Mizner Grand would be estates of lordly dimension running down to the wide white beaches. The only trouble with that plan was that the projected Mizner Mile was bordered by a colony of Finnish farmers, a stubborn breed, who could not be persuaded that their homely presence detracted from property values in a gold-plated subdivision. Furthermore the Finns had cajoled the state into building a highway which Mizner's clients would have to cross to reach the beaches.

Wilson wanted the old highway torn up and a new one constructed, at the expense of the Mizner corporation, farther inland. As he saw it, people with a lot of money had a lot more rights and privileges than a nest of simple folk grubbing away at their cabbage patches.

One dark night Wilson stole a march on the Finns by moving in heavy equipment to tear up "their" highway and start work on his own. (Florida in those days did everything it could to please wealthy people from the North, who had first call on the state's resources.) The Finns rushed to the scene with whatever weapons came to hand, and reports of a riot in the making reached the Palm Beach newspaper. A lady journalist named Emilie Keyes was dispatched to investigate and found the mob of Finns on one side of the barricades, and Wilson Mizner, in white tie, tails and top hat (perfect representation of the capitalist oppressor), on the other. His machines were tearing up the "Finnish highway" while he stood on a tractor and shook his fist at the rabble. Wilson had learned a certain amount of Finnish, all the naughty words, associating with Finnish prospectors in the Yukon. Being cursed in their native tongue so startled the Finns that they refrained from carrying out their assault, though Miss Keyes later confessed that she had been hoping someone would at least put a bullet through Wilson's silk hat. The Finns eventually took their case to court, but by then the Mizners had made their highway a *fait accompli*, and residents of Boca Raton's Gold Coast could stroll down to the beach without hindrance.

Brushing aside such minor opposition to their plans, Wilson and Addison became almost delirious in their determination to build a new Byzantium washed by the tepid waters of the Gulf Stream. They were gouging the earth to build the widest road on the planet leading into their kingdom, bisected by a canal with genuine gondolas and bordered by Venetian balustrades and arcades; they were creating a cuckooland of hybrid architecture; they were selling corner lots in the choicest locations for $100,000, and for once their imaginations, which had always run to the rococo, were given free play.

To all the other attractions they offered, the Mizner brothers added the lure of "pirate gold," which has always had a powerful, unsettling effect on the American imagination.

All over Florida the new subdivisions were claiming that chests of maritime loot had been buried on their land by Captain Kidd, Sir Henry Morgan, Sir Francis Drake, Gasparilla, Black Caesar, and other pirate captains. Newcomers to Florida were told that, though it might cost them a lot of money to buy a homestead, they could more than recoup by digging up their backyards or digging along the nearby beaches and uncovering masses of doubloons, pieces of eight, jewelry, and bullion in their spare time. The pirate-gold craze was helped along immensely when a fisherman found two crocks of gold coins near Key Largo.

The Mizner Corporation was quick to join the clamor. Wilson, after all, knew a lot about salting gold mines. Along with drumbeater Reichenbach, he promoted Boca Raton's claims to being a veritable Golconda of buried treasure. Boca Raton's publicity bureau began whirring with mimeographed releases alleging that it had once been the shore base of Captain Teach, alias Blackbeard, one of the more formidable buccaneers on the Spanish Main. The whole area, it was asserted, had been used as an underground vault by Blackbeard and his associates.

Obviously that assertion needed a little reinforcement. One dark night Mizner and Reichenbach buried some replicas of the artifacts of Blackbeard's career around Boca Raton Inlet, along with doubloons fabricated by Addison's artisans. Discovery of the hoard was announced as the climax of Reichenbach's campaign in the newspapers, and the lambent air was filled with the smoke of photographers' flash powder and the plaintive cry of the human pack scrabbling for gold. Wilson had always deprecated the Klondike gold rush as a sissified affair, but he must have shaken his head over his own stampede with women in knickers and sunshades and elderly clubmen clawing away at the beaches.

The real gold rush, he realized, was in the pockets of the Northerners coursing into the state to buy real estate.

It was the principal task of the Mizner Corporation, as its

secretary-treasurer saw it, to make Boca Raton the most alluring of all the developments springing up, jerry-built, a wasteland-to-be of pink stucco and green lumber, up and down the Florida coastline.

The crowning glory of Boca Raton was to be the Camino Real (King's Highway) which led into the city. As Reichenbach's press releases and promotional brochures endlessly reminded the public, this was the widest road in the world—twenty traffic lanes, 219 feet wide, capable of funneling in 100,000 people and their vehicles in a few hours. It wasn't merely the most capacious traffic artery in the world—a preview of the Los Angeles freeways—but the most ornamental. Along its verges ran a series of parks, plazas, and gardens. Down the center of Camino Real ran a masterpiece conceived on Addison Mizner's drawing board, a re-creation of the Grand Canal of Venice. Better, in fact, because newer; the Grand Canal would be a Venetian sewer by comparison.

There was trouble with the more conservative faction on the board of directors over the Mizner brothers' perfectionism. Addison was obsessed with the color of the water in the canal, Wilson with the gondolas, some of the other directors with cutting costs. The brothers had acquired some of the lordlier tastes of the Venetian doges whom they were aping. Addison insisted that the canal water had to be a clear blue to serve as a reflecting pool for the architectural ornaments he was designing for the banks of the canal, marble landing stages, voluptuously curved balustrades, and the like. The water in the canal, however, kept filling up with silt. Addison kept a crew of workmen busy dredging it out, but his grand canal was the same brackish brown as Venice's.

Wilson, on the other hand, was determined that the

Venetian-built gondolas, which would be driven by battery-supplied electricity, would be manned by genuine gondoliers, preferably ones who could carol "O Sole Mio" in a vibrant tenor. One gondolier would steer the craft and operate the engine while the other stood in the prow with his pole and bayed picturesquely at the semitropical moon. One niggling director pointed out that the man with the pole might push the boat in the opposite direction to that taken by the man at the wheel in the rear. Then the electrified gondola would be run aground. "Give the man in the front a *fake* oar," was Wilson's prescription for that problem. "Besides, the son of a bitch will be too busy singing to worry about navigation."

Artistically, the Camino Real was a triumph, but as an example of highway engineering it would rate with those boulevards in African capitals which start magnificently from the government buildings and peter out a few miles away in the jungle.

Indubitably it was the widest thoroughfare in the world but it was also one of the shortest, running only about half a mile from the Dixie Highway to Lake Boca Raton, where it became a sandy track through the piny woods. It served its main purpose, however, which was to indicate the coming glory of the city built by a modern Romulus and Remus. Up went the Cloister, a hotel later renamed the Boca Raton, and other edifices haphazardly modeled after the masterpieces of Moorish Spain and the Italian Renaissance. Not to mention golf courses, an airport, a yacht basin, and a polo field. Nor was God, as represented by their pious brother the Reverend Henry, entirely neglected in all the offerings to Mammon. In a rare outburst of brotherly esteem, they built a church for Henry.

12

THE BURSTING OF
THE BUBBLE

IN 1925, the vintage year of the Florida boom, there were almost 6,000 people registered in Miami as dealers in real estate, all of them attended by scores of touts, scouts, and high-powered salesmen. There must have been more than 50,000 engaged in the business of peddling real estate in the Miami area alone.

The statistics should have suggested something to anyone as boom-wise as Wilson Mizner. During his years in the North Country, he had cleared out of Dawson, then Nome, when those places were overrun by fortune hunters. In Florida there were so many thousands of people dealing in real estate that inevitably they would soon outnumber the available prospects for their merchandise. Lots were sold and resold so many times, for speculative reasons, that property had lost any intrinsic value; it was a scrap of paper grubby from passing through so many greedy hands. If not the statistics, then the febrile atmosphere, the unqualified

hope which always degenerates into panic, should have
alerted the sensors of Wilson's preternaturally alert nature.
But the Florida boom was a virulent fever indeed, and
Wilson and his brother, for all their experience, were as
delirious as the rest of them.

Very few were equipped with the prevision of Ben Hecht,
one of the livelier chroniclers of the boom. As he recorded in
his autobiography, he received $2,500 a week for turning
out coruscating prose on the splendors of Key Largo City.
He not only refused all temptations to get in on the ground
floor and buy choice real estate parcels, but also distrusted
Florida banks and kept his money on his person. He was
convinced that the boom would burst with the sudden splat-
ter of the old Mississippi Bubble and wanted to be ready to
evacuate at a moment's notice. When he left Florida, at the
stately pace of a winner contrasting with the midnight flights
of so many of the bigger plungers, his clothing was padded
with about fifty pounds of United States currency.

That Wilson Mizner and his brother were not equipped
with the same twenty-twenty vision in economic affairs
testified not to their lack of foresight so much as their total
involvement in an artistic, as well as financial, enterprise.
Boca Raton was their baby. The figures on the balance
sheets were entrancing, of course; they indicated that their
paper worth was something close to $40,000,000, but their
obsession was not with columns of figures, but with the
rococo skyline of their budding city. They were creators, not
mere entrepreneurs. Boca Raton would be their monument, their pension fund, the capstone of their careers.

They did not take intimations that the upswing might be
trending in reverse without putting up a fight. Wilson's wits
had not grown so larded with prosperity that they could not

supply him with an old con man's answer to the dilemma of slackening enthusiasm for bits of Florida landscape.

When business began slacking off, Have-Faith-in-Florida Clubs were organized, and real estate promoters from all over the state gathered in West Palm Beach for a spiritual rally they called the Inventory Congress, a designation which presumably stemmed from their need to take stock of their prospects. It was to be a sort of boosters' revival meeting. The Mizner brothers, of course, were among the leading evangelists. Wilson produced a German baron, impeccably turned out to the glitter of his shaved head and his monocle. The Prussian, who could have passed for Erich von Stroheim's brother, informed the delegates that he had the backing of a consortium of German financiers eager to invest in Florida real estate. If the delegates hadn't been so quick to snatch at any hopeful augur, they might have paused to consider that the German economy had been wrecked by inflation, with Germans carrying their walk-around money in suitcases, and there was barely enough venture capital to keep German industry going. Nevertheless, Wilson's friend served his purpose, and the realtors went back to their hutches filled with optimism.

Months after that optimism proved to be strikingly ill founded, one of the delegates slipped into a Miami speakeasy for solace. Presiding behind the bar, without a monocle, was the "baron" Wilson had produced. He readily explained himself: "Sure, I pulled that caper as a favor to Mizner. We met when I was a steward on the Hamburg-American liners and he made many crossings. He was sure a generous tipper. When we met down here, he loaned me the money for a seaplane to smuggle rum in from the Bahamas. He asked me to show up at that meeting rigged out as a big businessman from Germany, and I was glad to do it."

Inside the Mizner Corporation, even before the boom began losing steam, there was a certain amount of high-level friction. The board of directors, composed of men who had supplied the Mizners with financial transfusions to keep Boca Raton flourishing, included such bigwigs as General T. Coleman du Pont, Matthew Brush, and Jesse L. Livermore, whose speculations had kept other Wall Streeters in a swivet for several decades.

Brush and Livermore were docile enough, but Du Pont was a mercurial fellow whose temperament did not jibe with the Mizners'. He was one of the Du Pont poor relations, an offshoot of the Kentucky branch of the family rather than the main root in Delaware, and thus did not inherit a high place in the Du Pont munitions industry. He had started out as a small-time coal-mine operator in his native state, branched out into the traction business, and made a specialty of buying up and reviving companies close to the bankruptcy court. It wasn't until 1902 that he began taking a direct interest in the affairs of the gunpowder mills that made the Du Pont family a mighty dynasty. That year the Du Pont Company was foundering, with no wars on the horizon and munitions makers in despair. With two of his cousins the General (a courtesy title stemming from a National Guard commission) bought a controlling interest in the family enterprise. He initiated a diversification of its activities to protect the corporation during those glum periods when there was no war to create a demand for high explosives of the military type. For a dozen years he devoted most of his energies to making Du Pont a giant among American corporations, and family historians credit him with having been one of the several Du Ponts most influential down through the generations. Whatever time he could spare from high-level decision making was diverted into prankish attempts at keeping non-Du Ponts on their toes and striving for the greater glory of the corporation.

He would call a department head into his office, steal his watch, and then innocently inquire what time it was. After allowing the man to fumble around for a few moments, he would hand him his watch with the stern injunction "Here it is. You'd better keep a closer eye on your department than you do on your watch."

Handing out loaded cigars was another of the General's diversions. After watching one explode in a victim's face, he would guffaw, "I never thought the powder business would be so much fun!"

He won an intrafamily fight for control of the company and then announced an astonishing project: "I'm going to build a monument one hundred miles high and lay it down on the ground." What he meant was the Du Pont Highway (U.S. 13 to Dover and U.S. 113 from Dover to Shelbyville), which cost $4,000,000 and which he presented to the state. It still links the Delmarva Peninsula with Wilmington. A little later, with Lucius M. Boomer, he built up a chain of first-class hotels, buying some and building others, including the McAlpin, the Waldorf-Astoria, the Sherry Netherland, and the Savoy-Plaza in New York, the Willard in Washington, the Bellevue-Stratford in Philadelphia, and the Du Pont in Wilmington.

Wall Street was even more impressed with the General when he bought control of the Equitable Life Assurance Society from J. P. Morgan and thus acquired the power of decision over how Equitable's $600,000,000 were to be invested.

Then came the event that changed his acquisitive outlook

on life. In 1915 he was hauled off to the Mayo brothers' clinic after specialists told him to make out his will. Complications had followed an abdominal operation. From his supposed deathbed he directed the sale of his Du Pont interests for $14,000,000. Then he learned that, after all, he was going to live and laughed off the panic sale of his holdings in the family corporation. From then on, he announced, he was going to enjoy himself, "burn up the pike," as he put it.

The General continued to take an interest in business affairs but made the process as painless as possible by surrounding himself on all occasions with beautiful women, most of them recruited from the New York theater. His parties were fabulous routs in the full-blooded style of Diamond Jim Brady and other magnificoes of the Gilded Age.

Du Pont, who was sojourning in Florida when the real estate boom began gathering full force, was attracted to the promised amenities of Boca Raton by the fact so many celebrities had been induced to join the Mizner brothers' venture. Soon he was the biggest outside investor in the Mizner Corporation and a member of the board of directors, thus associating himself with Wilson Mizner whose previous corporate experience had been with the Hotel Rand, the Old Masters Art Society, the Millionaires Club, and other enterprises of dubious legality.

It may have seemed at first that General du Pont and Wilson were fated to be bosom buddies. For one thing they both loved practical jokes, and they both kept themselves surrounded by desirable females. In practice, however, they approached each other like a couple of strange dogs in a dark alley. Du Pont suspected there was something irregular about Wilson's background, his extraordinary knack for rounding up prospects and talking them into deals. And Wilson wasn't greatly attracted by the Du Pont personality.

As a practical joker, Wilson insisted on a certain amount of artistry in his pranks. They had to point, if deviously, a moral. The victim of his jokes was supposed to deserve his discomfiture as punishment for his pomposity, arrogance, or stupidity. And the payoff was engineered with all the craft of an ex-playwright concocting a second-act curtain.

The General, on the other hand, was a joker on the wholesale scale, using crudely mechanical devices, unselective about his victims. An exploding cigar convulsed him in a frenzy of knee slapping. He was in the top drawer of American tycoons, but in Wilson's jaundiced view he lacked class, his tall rawboned figure invariably clad in white knickerbockers and knee-length silk stockings. His escape from the deathbed had turned the General into something of a clown. He emptied joke shops of dribbling highball glasses, asbestos-tipped cigarettes, electrified chairs, water pistols, the whole array of the inveterate funster, but the centerpiece of his collection was a plaster bulldog kept in a dimly lighted room. By remote control the General would activate the bulldog for a visitor, causing the thing's eyes to glow like a tiger's and mechanical growls to issue from its throat.

Wilson could only shake his head at the Du Pont idea of fun making and yearn for the day when he could be bought out and sent on his prankish way.

His opinion of Du Pont as a screwball, a peasant who'd got lucky and made the most of his family connections, was one of the more serious miscalculations of Wilson's career. Long as he had been sizing up boobs and measuring suckers for the payoff, astute as he was about assessing human frailties and the uses to which they could be put, he underestimated the General. The fact that one of Du Pont's favorite tricks was to attract the attention of a gold-digging blonde, build up her expectations of diamond bracelets and mink coats, then introduce her to his daughters and nieces at a stuffy family party and watch her hopes evaporate, didn't mean that he was merely a senile sadist. The General was fun-loving, but he hadn't lost his wits.

Not where money was concerned. Du Pont had invested in the Mizner Corporation for what he regarded as sound business reasons, not as an outlet for money he had no use for. Furthermore, he wasn't going to see his investment evaporate in the outlandish projects dreamed up by Addison and Wilson Mizner, and he fought them tooth and nail when they wanted to lavish corporate funds on grand canals, motorized gondolas, marble piazzas, and all those folderols. He secured the support of other conservatives on the board to thwart the brothers' more grandiose visions. Hell, this was a business proposition, not an architectural dream factory.

Alert as he was to other aspects of the Boca Raton operation, he didn't realize for some time that his gilt-edged name was being used by Wilson's staff of high-pressure salesmen as their biggest come-on. Wilson instructed his salesmen that they were to emphasize in their pitches that Du Pont, the cagiest of financiers, had invested millions in Boca Raton. Prospects were led to believe that the whole Du Pont fortune was pledged to the enterprise, that every cloudy promise regarding the worth of Boca Raton real estate was supplied by Du Pont with a silver lining.

The General didn't twig until one spring day, when he was up in New York on business, he read a Harry Reichenbach publicity release stating that T. Coleman du Pont and other bigwigs had decided to build hotels, theaters, and other structures in Boca Raton and make it the most magnificent resort south of the Mason-Dixon line.

The General exploded in wrath, sensing that his name was being used to exploit the Mizner brothers' schemes. He wired the corporate headquarters that his name wasn't to be used in such a manner, that Reichenbach's release was to be counteracted "with as much or more publicity as was given false statement. Am deeply chagrined by statement and fearful of outcome of a concern that does business this way. Kindly wire me Waldorf that adequate denial has been made." Addison telegraphed an apology and promised that the General's name would not be misused. Du Pont followed up his telegram with a letter lecturing the management on the virtues of truth in advertising and warning that despite the giddiness of the Florida business climate, there might be a legal accounting for any false promises made to the buyers of swampland who were led to believe that swank suburbs would rise from the bogs.

The General's suspicions had first been aroused in May, 1925, but were dormant again all that summer. Then, in September, he read in a Palm Beach newspaper that Reichenbach's prose factory, no doubt inspired by Wilson Mizner, was at it again. The Mizner Corporation, he read, was announcing a multimillion-dollar development program that would put Miami in Boca Raton's shade. Nor was he pleased that Reichenbach was grossly exaggerating in his claim that no other resort in the world could compare with Boca Raton, that "The Riviera, Biarritz, Mentone, Nice, Sorrento, Egypt—all that charms in each of these finds consummation in Boca Raton." He was further upset by the proclamation that "yachts discharge directly at the lake entrance to this hotel," when that hotel was only a series of airy sketches on Addison Mizner's drawing board for the

development of Lake Boca Raton and the pier referred to
was a rickety wooden platform barely strong enough to
support an undernourished fisherman.

There were a couple of highbinders, Munchausens, in the
Mizner organization who would have to be weeded out, he
saw, before it could operate on sound business principles.
What thoroughly alarmed him was the fear that his name
and the names of other well-heeled directors of the corporation were being used in such a way that if the enterprise
went aground the victims of the financial shipwreck could
sue the hell out of the stockholders on the grounds that they
stood behind the Mizners' glittering promises.

His best hope of clearing himself of future liability, he
decided, was to arrange the dismissal of Wilson Mizner and
Harry Reichenbach. The departure of Reichenbach was
necessitated, he felt, by an advertisement headed "A Decla-
ration of Responsibility," in which it was asserted that the
financial sponsors of Boca Raton guaranteed every statement made in its advertising and promotion campaigns.
Since the Boca Raton ads promised practically everything
under the sun—and the sun's daily performance, too—Du
Pont considered that the company's directors would be held
financially responsible if the project collapsed. And while
Boca Raton was growing, its growth was easily outpaced by
Reichenbach's imagination.

Reichenbach and his evil genius, Wilson Mizner, had to
be thrown out, Du Pont argued, or the directors faced the
possibility of spending years in the courts. He enlisted the
support of the more conservative directors, including
Livermore, after producing a photostat of a newspaper clip-
ping which reported Wilson's conviction for operating a
gambling house on Long Island in 1919.

Wilson knew how to fight back. He paid a visit to the

county jail and persuaded one of the female inmates to write General du Pont a letter, of which Wilson had copies made, stating, "You are responsible for my pregnancy." But dirty tricks didn't work with a man of Du Pont's flinty character. They only reinforced his determination to escape the consequences of the collapse of the House of Mizner, which he loudly predicted would happen all the sooner if Wilson weren't sent packing.

His riposte was a blistering statement issued under his name and published not only in the Florida but also in the New York newspapers condemning the Mizner/-Reichenbach promotional methods. Wilson's answering broadside was not entirely effective: He charged that the General was sore because he wasn't permitted to add a number of Du Ponts to the Mizner Corporation payroll.

Historians of the Florida boom differ on whether T. Coleman Du Pont's statement was the needlepoint that burst the bubble. Certainly it abruptly ended the Mizner's recordbreaking sales of real estate, and Wilson's booming laugh no longer rang out from the executive offices. Rats were seen climbing down from Boca Raton palms.

All over Florida, within days after Dr Pont's diatribe was published, it seemed, people stopped besieging real estate offices and darted up alleyways rather than be buttonholed by the ubiquitous salesmen.

Some chroniclers, foremost among them Kenneth Ballinger, believed that deflation had set in at least three months before the Du Pont broadside. In Miami it was noted in August, 1925, that a lot sold for $50,000 was dumped on the market for half that price. Many who invested in Florida real estate were discouraged by a Treasury Department ruling that even paper profits were subject to the federal income tax. During the autumn of 1925, too, hundreds of buyers who had made the down payment had begun defaulting on the succeeding installments of the money due the seller. People had begun to recall other booms and ponder their lesson: Each one was punctured sooner or later. And they were taking a closer look at what they had bought, bramble and bog, and wondering what guarantees they had that the developers would live up to their promises.

Second thoughts, obviously, are disastrous to the promoters of a boom. Euphoria must be kept at a high level. The rose-colored glasses must never be allowed to slip down an investor's nose. After Du Pont lowered the boom, the Mizners redoubled their efforts to lure in the prospects. Pedigrees were no longer required, and Wilson's committee on social qualifications ended its labors. Almost anyone who had not been released from the penitentiary in the last year was welcomed by Wilson's squad of salesmen. And Harry Reichenbach's publicity bureau became downright frenzied in its claims that Boca Raton was an earthly paradise in the making, that nothing on earth had seen its compare since the topless towers of Ilium tumbled.

None of the ballyhoo brought a fresh influx of buyers down the broad but brief Camino Real. Boca Raton had turned into a pastel-tinted nightmare for its proprietors. Grass began growing in the cracks between the marble paving of its canalside arcades, and Wilson expected to see the first vulture circling overhead any day.

Everything seemed to go wrong at once. It almost appeared that General du Pont had pulled out the props from under the Mizners' extraordinary run of luck. A gourmand to command the respect of a Trimalchio, Addison Mizner now weighed in at 280 pounds. The doctors warned him that he was straining his heart by climbing nightly into his

Spanish bed, which stood on stiltlike legs and (according to Addison) had once belonged to Ferdinand and Isabella. Sure enough, Addison suffered a heart attack.

At the same time the corporation was defending itself in court proceedings brought by the Finnish colony which had had its highway more or less stolen by Wilson. The plaintiffs alleged that the Mizners had persuaded an outgoing municipal administration in Boynton, the nearest town, to announce it was willing to scrap the old highway and accept the new one built by the Mizners as a convenience for the owners of their estates on the beachfront.

The prosecutor at the subsequent trial subpoenaed Wilson but found him an evasive witness, experienced as he was in confrontations with the law. The former tried to get Wilson to admit that he was covering up for his older brother.

"You love your brother, don't you?" the prosecutor roared. "You have a great affection for him, don't you?"

"I have a vague regard for him," Wilson replied.

The jury apparently was fascinated by Wilson and returned a verdict of acquittal.

During the sunny but gloomy winter of 1925–26, as he convalesced from his heart attack, Addison occasionally had reason to believe Wilson's regard for him was vague indeed. Wilson, like the Viennese in contemplating their postwar situation, considered the situation hopeless but not serious. He may have been bemused by the continuing evaporation of their fortune but had decided to treat it as a trifling matter. He had come to Florida broke and would probably leave the same way; he had the fatalism of the veteran boomer.

One day their literary friend Arthur Somers Roche found Addison in his towering Spanish bed, alternately weeping and cursing. Roche asked him what the trouble was. "Oh, it's my dear little baby brother . . . Mama's Angel Birdie," the architect replied.

"What's he done now?" Roche inquired.

Addison, as he related, had persuaded a wealthy New Yorker, an old friend from his Manhattan days, to come down to Florida with his wife and look over the Boca Raton development with a view to pumping in some fresh money. The New Yorker was impressed by what he saw and was about to buy into the Mizner Corporation when Wilson dropped by. It turned out that Wilson and Addison's friend's wife had known each other in the past—how well, neither Addison nor the husband suspected. Wilson invited the couple over to his house for dinner. It turned into a bibulous evening, they ran out of liquor, and the New York financier volunteered to make an emergency run to the nearest boot-legger. He returned quicker than expected. His wife was sitting on Wilson's lap. Wilson had an icepick in his hand and was trying to pry the large emerald out of one of her rings. The financier was not amused by the tableau and stormed out of Wilson's house dragging his wife behind him. Naturally the stock-buying deal was canceled. Wilson was unrepentant, merely shrugging and saying, "If he'd only been a little slower afoot, I'd have got that goddamn emerald out of its setting. These days a rock like that is worth more than all the real estate in Florida."

By then, in fact, the Florida bubble had burst, though in later decades it would become apparent that the real estate boom was merely premature.

When their Boca Raton hotel opened in February, 1926, the Mizners made it a splashy affair, but it was all a bluff. Real estate all over the state was selling, if at all, at panic prices. There was an outburst of recriminations all around, as in a gambling house where it had been discovered that the wheel was fixed. The languid air seemed to be quivering with the plaints of the bilked, and lawyers' offices were thronged with injured parties seeking redress. As Wilson later recapitulated those stormy days, the little suckers were all hunting down the big suckers with baseball bats. They were, in his opinion, bad losers—and there was nothing he hated worse than a spoilsport. The real test of a man's character was how gallantly he took the news that he was wiped out. The Florida boomers, on his scale of values dating back to the Klondike gold rush, were a bunch of rubes who couldn't take their beating with any show of class.

Hundreds of lawsuits—the exact number was never compiled—were filed against the Mizner Corporation and everyone connected with it. General du Pont's timely disavowal protected him from involvement in the collapse of that enterprise, but the Mizner brothers were showered with writs and suits of all descriptions. No good to explain that the treasury was empty. Ordinarily, Wilson would have disentangled himself, as always in the past, by a hasty decampment. But Addison was determined to weather the storm, face his accusers, and Wilson couldn't desert him. He had always been impatient with the processes of litigation, but he stood it as long as he could.

"I never open my door but a writ blows in," he wrote Arthur Somers Roche. "When the bell rings, I open the door, automatically stick out my hand, admit being Wilson Mizner, and accept service. I spend my evenings shuffling these fearsome documents and can cut to any complaint I desire. This proficiency may prove valuable, should the judge wish to decide by chance what case to try next."

He spent enough time in Florida courtrooms that year to conclude that flight would have to be the better part of discretion, if not valor. He quoted to Roche the valedictory of a Confederate general with a game leg whose sense of timing he admired: "Boys, things look tough, but remember the eyes of Dixie are upon you. The beauty and chivalry of the South know our desperate plight and thank God for it, as only in extremity are heroes made. The damn Yankees are preparing to charge. Let them come. A volley at such close range should wreck havoc. Then take to the bayonet and fight it out hand to hand until the case is hopeless. Then you can retreat—but seeing as how I'm lame, I'll start right now."

Early in 1927 Wilson himself judged the case was hopeless. As in the Klondike, he said, "It was a place where I learned from my scars." Boca Raton would have to return to its tropical slumber.

The last Florida saw of Wilson Mizner he was streaking northward in the huge Packard he called "the stonecrusher" and heading for greener pastures.

13

THE SAGE OF
BOOTH 50

SCORCHING over the highways of America in his
huge and clanking Packard, fleeing the fallout from the
collapse of the Mizner Corporation and its paper empire on
the Florida strand, and undoubtedly cursing his failure to
cash in before the joint had been raided, Wilson Mizner was
arrowing westward for his last stand against adversity.

There was no temptation for him to stop anywhere short
of California because he was strictly a littoral man who had
lived by or on the sea all his life. The 3,000 miles between
the coasts were a wasteland so far as he was concerned, a
great mental vacuum in which America raised corn, hogs,
bumpkins, and Bible bangers.

Wilson had turned the half-century mark and was looking
for surcease at the moment. He had participated in enough
booms, rushes, and stampedes to last him for the rest of his
life, had worn out his welcome from the Florida Keys to the

249

Bering Strait, and he was not the sort of man who retraced his footsteps or would stoop to playing the prodigal son.

There was one place left for an aging and financially depleted desperado: Hollywood. It was one place in which the past had been abolished, one place where the authorities would not riffle through their rogue's gallery photographs when they heard his name, because his previous stay in the film capital had been brief, inconsequential, and had been devoted entirely to labors in a writer's hutch.

Hollywood was the place for new beginnings. If he was remembered at all, it was for a bit of japery he had committed at the premiere of some forgotten film. Even then it had been the fashion for Hollywood to celebrate an opening with searchlights playing against the sky and the currently famous filmmakers showing up in ermine wraps and limousines half as long as the theater. Wilson had not been able to resist the temptation to satirize.

He had agreed to escort a young and beautiful actress named Cecile Evans and to appear in evening dress, but nobody had specified that he show up in the back seat of a Duesenberg or Pierce Arrow. He chose to drive up at the wheel of a battered and rachitic Model T Ford.

While he helped Miss Evans out of the flivver and haughtily ignored the dismay of the hosts of the occasion, the doorman, costumed as a Ruritanian field marshal, asked him, "What shall I do with your, uh, automobile, sir?"

"Do with it, my good man?" Wilson roared. "That's not my car. It's yours. I'm giving it to you. And you can do with it whatever you like."

He then stalked away with Miss Evans on his arm.

Now Wilson, his nose as keen as ever in scenting the perfume of opportunity, was streaking westward at a propitious moment. Hollywood was shortly to be in turmoil, one of its periodic upheavals, in which a nimble mind could always seize the advantage. 1927 was a landmark year, underscored by the production of the first talking picture, and Al Jolson singing "Mammy" on the sound track was the requiem for the old Hollywood of D. W. Griffith and other geniuses of the silent screen. Actors would be required to speak, rather than mouth, their lines before the suddenly audible camera. Writers would have to compose dialogue to be spoken rather than indicated.

Technology had shaken the dream factory out of its preoccupation with giant motorcars, new crops of starlets, party giving, and recurrent scandal and made it cope with the problems of recording sound on film. Suddenly there was a demand for stage-trained actors and for writers with an ear for the spoken word.

On arrival in Hollywood Wilson checked into the Ambassador on Wilshire Boulevard and settled down in a suite there for the rest of his days. He had nothing, he said, to "fall back on but my battered backside," plus his colossal gall, his ability to charm, his social desirability as an informal entertainer and raconteur. For some months, with his Florida wardrobe intact and highly suitable for Southern California, he dined out at the best tables and amused the elite with tales of the Florida crash, which was not mourned in the Golden West. He was one fellow who could jest at his own wounds—a valuable trait in Hollywood at the moment famous actors were learning their voices were too squeaky for the sound tracks and celebrated directors were told they were passé—and Hollywood dinner tables rocked with empathetic laughter over his tales of courtroom battles arising from the collapse of Boca Raton. The general favorite was the story of how a plaintiff's lawyer angrily demanded

whether or not he had promised a buyer of Boca Raton real
estate that he could grow nuts on his land. "No," Wilson had
replied, "I said you could GO nuts on it."

He couldn't go on serving as the unpaid comedian of
Beverly Hills dinner parties indefinitely. Employment
worthy of his self-esteem was hard to come by, though with
the advent of the talkies it appeared that a man who had
coauthored several Broadway hits and was said to have an
acute ear for realistic dialogue might be useful in the
studios. Wilson was handicapped by his aversion to writing
anything more intellectually taxing than his name on stock
certificates. But not all Hollywood writers actually wrote;
some served more or less as script consultants or were
valued for their narrative abilities in story conferences. Out
at Metro-Goldwyn-Mayer an odd little man named Robert
Hopkins spent most of his working days lounging around the
commissary or propping up one of the sound stages, yet his
name often appeared among the writing credits on MGM
productions. Hopkins was never known to have written a
line and regarded a typewriter as an impossibly intricate
piece of machinery. Whenever a director needed a sight gag
for his comedy, or a team of writers got bogged down and
needed a new plot turn, however, Bob Hopkins was summoned on the double and usually solved the problem instantly. That was the sort of consulting job, Mizner and his
advisers figured, that Wilson could do.

An old Broadway friend of his, Lew Lipton, was a producer on the RKO lot and got him an office in the writers'
building, along with $500 a week and a portfolio as script
doctor. That studio had recently been reorganized under
the RKO trademark by the New York financier Joseph P.
Kennedy, the father of a future President, from three other
production and distribution companies: Keith-Albee-

Orpheum; FBO (Film Booking Office), which made low-budget films; and Pathé Studio, long a producer of comedies. Kennedy had blossomed out as a Hollywood mogul partly through his interest in the career of Gloria Swanson, but as the boss of the RKO lot, and as a tightfisted Boston Irishman (known in the old country as a gombeen man), he was determined to make RKO pay its own way. Six hundred thousand dollars of Kennedy money went down the drain in making *Queen Kelly*, in which Erich von Stroheim directed Miss Swanson, because many of its scenes were too lurid to pass censorship. That meant an eagle eye was kept on other RKO productions and on that invisible monster labeled "overhead."

So Wilson didn't fall into a sinecure on the RKO lot. He was called in as script doctor on a number of productions and was credited with contributing most of the dialogue to an exposé film, *Gambling Ship*, which made full use of his knowledge of gambling and the underworld. The critics praised the crisp reality of its scenes.

Confinement, whether in a writer's cubicle or a jail cell, irked Wilson immeasurably, but he left RKO at the expiration of his contract on good terms with his former employers. Kennedy may never have heard of the middle-aged scapegrace who had been drawing a salary from the Kennedy till, but several years later he bought a house on North Ocean Boulevard in Palm Beach which Addison Mizner had designed and built in 1923, a house which figured largely in the brief history of the Kennedy Presidency.

Wilson had turned his attention by then to another project. Hollywood, it seemed to him, needed a restaurant operated along the lines of Jack Dunstan's in pre-Prohibition New York. There were a few good restaurants in downtown Los Angeles, and there was the old Montmartre

on Hollywood Boulevard, but otherwise there were few
places people could go on the servants' night out. The food
wasn't so important; what such a place would need was the
social cachet and the intellectual authority Wilson could
confer.

Naturally the money would have to come from other
pockets. He had recently made friends with Herbert K.
Somborn, whose present claim to public attention was as a
recent husband of Gloria Swanson, who had dropped him in
favor of the Marquis de la Falaise de Coudray, more familiarly known in Hollywood as Hank. Somborn owned a piece
of property on Wilshire Boulevard opposite the Ambassador
Hotel. That became the site of the first of the several Brown
Derby restaurants, named by Wilson in honor of the
headgear worn by two men he admired, Bat Masterson and
Governor Alfred E. Smith.

The financial backing came from Jack L. Warner, whose
fortunes had bounded upward with his production of *The
Jazz Singer*. With Wilson providing the atmosphere, Somborn the real estate, they inveigled Warner into becoming a
third and silent partner, who agreed "there was no really
first-class restaurant where actors of lofty eminence could
dine in relative privacy and also get the service to fit their
special needs. . . . The proposition appealed to me because
there was a need for a rendezvous point, especially during
the late hours, and I put up the money."

The cuisine at the first Brown Derby, and at its successors
on Vine Street, on Los Feliz Boulevard and out in Beverly
Hills, was never anything to win the congratulations of a
Cordon Bleu chef. It ran the gamut from hamburgers to chili
con carne, standard Southern California fare, and a strange
type of enchilada made with a sort of pancake instead of the
traditional tortilla. That didn't matter, because most of its

patrons had only recently been elevated from the hot-dog stand and luncheonette. The people from the studios needed a place to hang out, a center for gossip and shoptalk, among their peers. "Happily," as Jack Warner recalled in his autobiography, "it was one of the few hunch investments I made that did not go into the red. The Derby was an instant success, and even the poorest movie fans, who could barely afford a hamburger there because it was made of expensive top ground round, came to gawk at the stars and get their autographs. It was not uncommon to see Gloria Swanson in one booth with her newest mate and her former husbands, Wallace Beery and Herb Somborn, in Booth 50, where Mizner regularly held court."

As the sage of the Brown Derby, Wilson rapidly became a leading figure in Hollywood during its transition period. His brief but lucrative experience as an associate playwright on Broadway was sufficient to make him a caustic commentator on show business with a lofty disdain for its less capable entrepreneurs. Certainly he did not win his place as a shepherd of the "picture people," as the stuffier Angelenos called them, through any consistent display of politesse. His role as boniface of the Brown Derby did not, he felt, compel him to bow and scrape before just anyone able to pick up a dinner check; that was for headwaiters and busboys. Instead of flattery, which he believed was the function of Louella Parsons and the fan magazines, he laid down a nightly barrage of insults, character assassinations, and imprecations. It soon became an honor, of sorts, to have been insulted by Wilson Mizner. Until the Academy Awards reached a dignified stature, they were a singular form of recognition. The only compliments he passed out were to himself. People who had risen to worldwide fame on the strength of a chiseled profile or a startling configuration of

the torso needed the corrective supplied by his acidulous
tongue.

Thus a small but overbearing studio executive was loudly
informed one evening, "You had rubber pockets in your
pants so you could steal soup. You were sixty years old
before you knew what a bathtub was for. You prove one
thing—the marvelous persistency of the uninspired."

He was the first of a line of Hollywood iconoclasts who
jeered at the studio bosses and their claim to inventing a
new art form. Soon it became fashionable for anyone claiming to be a genius to announce his superiority to the job that
paid him so well. The writers and directors who migrated
from New York to teach Hollywood how to put the spoken
word on sound tracks were loftily scornful of the pharaohs,
many of whom had originated in the New York garment
district. It was an uneasy time in Hollywood, and the posture of artistic superiority assumed by the imported helpers
had to be tolerated until it was possible to send them back
East muttering how insufferable it was to be indentured to
employers with the intelligence quotients of cretins. How
surprised both the self-styled geniuses and their employers
would have been to learn that three decades later the films
they produced in that harried time would be resurrected by
European and American intellectuals and crooned over
polysyllabically as authentic masterpieces of the cinematic
art.

Wilson's scorn for the film industry was genuine, however, and stemmed not only from a natural perversity but
also from his naysaying attitude toward most of the great
events and hallowed personalities he had studied at close
range. Born irreverent, he refused to be impressed by
anyone's pretensions; it was his chosen role to be a mocker
and idol smasher. He wasn't merely adopting an intellectual

pose when he said, "I don't know anything at all about this town. To me, Doug [Fairbanks] and Mary [Pickford] are just a mule team. But after seeing some of the new pictures, I'm convinced that all the movie heroes are in the audience. Oh, the place almost made a good picture once, but they caught it just in time." Then he added, with a poisonous smile, "But don't get me wrong. I love Hollywood."

Early every evening Wilson strolled to the Derby from his hotel suite across the boulevard and conferred briefly with Bob Cobb, the manager, and out in the kitchen with the head chili maker. Then, impeccably dressed, he took his place in Booth 50, which was always reserved for his coterie. It was observed that Booth 50 resembled the imperial divan of a Turkish sultan, to which only the current court favorites were invited. In his middle years, in a slightly more kinky and much less conventional way, Wilson had come to resemble Mama Mizner in her role as a social arbiter. A culling of gossip columns of the period indicates that in one fairly typical week, Mizner would share Booth 50 with Douglas Fairbanks, Sr., Darryl Zanuck, the governor of California, George Jessel, Charlie Chaplin (who spoke of Wilson as a fellow prince of comedians), a recently deposed maharaja, Mae Murray, and whichever Prince Mdivani she was married to at the time. Hollywood boasted that the quality of wit that flashed around his table could be favorably compared to that of the Round Table at the Algonquin in New York.

Wilson's booth was surrounded by caricatures of film stars long since shuffled into the discard. "Why," Jack Warner asked him one night, "do you want to sit here when all those people on the wall are out in Forest Lawn?"

"I'll tell you," Wilson replied. "This is just one of my whims. While I'm living I want to be among the dead. And vice versa."

There were times when he felt uneasy with his present respectability and yearned for the days when he had had to sharpen his wits on Pinkerton detectives and Florida lawyers instead of stropping them on the Hollywood ego. "It's getting so people no longer count the silverware when I come to dinner," he grumbled. "Why, someone even asked me for my autograph. I don't know if I can bear up under that. I was never cut out to be the darling of the peanut munchers who make up this world."

Old crooked friends and confederates from New York or the Barbary Coast days, no matter how far down in their luck, were always invited to join him in Booth 50 and rub elbows with the elite of the studios. The roguish Stanley Rose, who oddly combined the roles of Hollywood's No. 1 bootlegger and operator of a Hollywood Boulevard bookstore which served as the way station for literati in town to write a screenplay, often conferred with Wilson late in the night when most of the studio people had gone home. In the darkened restaurant Wilson became a different man, brooding over the past, expressing a melancholy philosophy. The wit that flew off the tip of his tongue like sparks from a flywheel was mostly for public consumption. With friends like Stanley Rose and the downtown sports columnist Mark Kelly, Wilson dropped the Samuel Johnson role and talked about old times with a nostalgia that would have surprised and disgusted his younger self.

"This," he remarked one night, waving an arm around the empty restaurant, "isn't life. It's just serving time."

All the best people, he felt, were dead and gone, except for his brother Addison, and Addison wasn't long for this world either. During the late hours when he coddled his insomnia in proven company, old pals down in their luck sidled into the Derby and made their hangdog appeals for temporary assistance. "He was the softest touch in the world," Stanley Rose recalled. "Every night he showed up at the Derby with a roll of bills. By the time he left he would be broke. There wasn't a moocher in the world who couldn't make a score off him. He once explained that he had 'borrowed' or misappropriated so much money in his harumscarum years that he figured he had to pay off his debts in his own way, that there was a scorekeeper up there who was crediting him with his repayments."

During those late-night semiprivate sessions in Booth 50, he occasionally jousted with Jack Barrymore, whom he had known since the pre-earthquake days in San Francisco, and W. C. Fields, both rounders of ripe experience whose cynicism and world-weary humor matched his own. It was said to have been in Booth 50 that Barrymore, the veteran of so many matrimonial disasters, delivered his classic apothegm: "The only way to fight with a woman is with your hat. Grab it and run."

One night Fields told Mizner, "You could steal a herd of elephants in a canoe. If I looked under your coat I would find two hot glaciers."

"Your ninety-proof breath," Wilson replied, "could start a windmill in an old Dutch painting. If I put a wick in you, you would burn for three years."

He freely dispensed advice and criticism in Booth 50, as on the night Mark Kelly, the *Examiner* sports editor, brought in young Adela Rogers St. Johns, whom he had persuaded to take up sportswriting, after they had attended the wrestling matches at the Hollywood Legion. It was unclassy, Wilson observed, to take a nice girl to something so redolent of knavery as the wrestling matches. "Wrestling is not a sport," he added, forgetting his own brief career as the manager of a boxing bear; "it is an inferior brand of

Shakespearian comedy. If you had any guts as a sportswriter, you'd close up that fraudulent fandango."

His friends testified that lotus eating in Hollywood had not larded his wits. One night he insisted on driving the actor Pat O'Brien home in "the stonecrusher." When they entered the Derby parking lot, they found a thief making off with a tire from the old Packard. "Come back!" Mizner shouted after the thief. "Anyone who can change a tire that fast can be my chauffeur." On another occasion late at night he was leaving the Derby with Sammy Finn, another actor, when they noticed that they were being followed by two men evidently intent on robbery or assault or both. "You take the big guy," Wilson told his companion, though the two footpads were only dim figures in the fog, "and I'll take the little guy with the knife." It wasn't until hours after they had outpaced the would-be muggers that Finn realized Wilson couldn't possibly have seen whether the "little guy" had a knife.

Jim Tully, the barrel-shaped writer who had made literary capital out of his earlier career as a hobo and roustabout, was another lusty fellow who helped Wilson while the long Hollywood nights away. Tully would recall him as "a vast and grandiloquent pimp to whom all of life was a house of prostitution."

Wilson shared with Tully his prescription for dealing with people intent on violence: "Always hit the man with a catsup bottle. Then he'll think he's bleeding to death." Mizner and Tully were sitting in Booth 50 one night when the handsome but hot-tempered John Gilbert, then Greta Garbo's leading man, headed their way with blood in his eye. Tully had written a magazine piece to which Gilbert stormily objected. As Gilbert approached, Wilson handed Tully a cat-

sup bottle, but Tully refused the weapon and flattened
Gilbert with one blow.

Wilson rarely lapsed into sentimentality in public, Tully
observed, and when he did, the results were usually discouraging. He did allow himself to be lured into presiding
over a dinner for surviving members of the various scofflaw
worlds he had inhabited, old Klondikers, veterans of
pre-1914 Broadway, ex-desperadoes of all kinds. Wilson
didn't realize he was being set up for an elaborate practical
joke when he arose to make the keynote address of the
evening. "We," he began his speech with a grandiloquent
gesture, as his fellow diners smirked expectantly, "are the
last of a magnificent old school. . . ." Just then he felt a
scorching sensation in one of his feet. Jack Dempsey was
under the table expertly administering a hotfoot. Wilson
hastily concluded his speech by referring to his old pals as
"dirty sons of bitches," and he didn't smile when he said it.

Unwittingly—otherwise he doubtless would have demanded his share of the proceeds—Wilson served as the
inspiration of one of MGM's most successful films.

For years Anita Loos, the San Franciscan who had written
Gentlemen Prefer Blondes, had worshiped the Mizner
legend and had been fascinated by his slightly sinister reputation. She was only a child when he was the toast of the
Barbary Coast, but her journalist-father was a sometime
drinking companion of Wilson's. In her autobiography Miss
Loos wrote that she had "never encountered America's most
fascinating outlaw" in her girlhood, but she caught up with
him in Booth 50 of the Brown Derby and found him even
more fascinating in the flesh. "Never," she heard him say
one night, "try to get rich in the daylight."

Miss Loos was then employed as a writer at Metro-Goldwyn-Mayer and was commanded to concoct a screenplay, with the nonwriting writer Bob Hopkins as her collaborator, about the Barbary Coast just after the turn of the century. The Mizner legend came to her assistance. Her collaborator also had some firsthand acquaintance with that subject. "Hopkins," she wrote, "had been a messenger boy on the Coast in its heyday, when Wilson Mizner was a young dandy in silk hat, white tie, and tails, who gambled with rich suckers for big stakes. Our movie was called *San Francisco*; its leading character was inspired by Wilson Mizner and played by Clark Gable, whose performance suggested much of Wilson's insouciance and illicit charm."

Miss Loos still treasures a photograph of Wilson Mizner signed by its subject. It was taken of him as he attended a costume party given by Darryl Zanuck and shows him, in a cowled monastic costume, as a rather frazzled and larcenous Little Brother of the Poor clutching a huge brandy inhaler. H. L. Mencken had signed a similar photograph of himself "Pax vobiscum. Brother Heinrich." Wilson went him one better and signed his "Pox vobiscum."

There was a temporary slump in receipts at the Brown Derby as the Depression worsened early in the thirties, and as a result, Wilson finally yielded to entreaties that the silver screen needed some of the wit and humor he casually flicked away like cigarette ashes nightly at the Brown Derby.

As his new employer Jack Warner explained, he wouldn't have to write full-fledged screenplays with all the boring details of camera placement, two-shots, close-ups, dissolves, and montages, which could be left to other craftsmen. "I knew Mizner could write the sharpest dialogue in the business," Warner expalined, "and that he could earn

$2,500 a week on any lot in town. But money was scarce, and I told him frankly that we couldn't pay what he was worth. 'Name your own price, kid,' he said. 'Okay, we start at five hundred a week,' I said. He grinned at me and extended a hand as big and swollen as a fighter's glove. 'I'll be there tomorrow.'"

Warner Brothers then was embarking on a long and lucrative series of gangster pictures, prison films, underworld melodramas for which it developed a stable of tough-guy stars, including James Cagney, Edward G. Robinson, Humphrey Bogart, Barton MacLane, Pat O'Brien, and George Raft. Warners obviously got Wilson Mizner, as a specialist in the speech and atmosphere (slightly outdated) of the underworld, at a bargain-sale price. And though his manicured fingers never touched the keyboard of a typewriter, the studio got its money's worth in the salty dialogue and authentic criminality he was able to contribute to its cycle of underworld melodramas.

Given the content of the studio's product during those years, it was fitting that the working conditions at Warners, according to the few remaining survivors, resembled somewhat those of a penitentiary. The actors' dressing rooms were periodically searched for liquor to prevent undue interference with the shooting schedules. In the writers' building the atmosphere was something like that of the jute mill at San Quentin, with front-office supervisors prowling the corridors to make sure the hired hands weren't just doodling, daydreaming, or taking a nap. The one privileged character, or trusty, was Wilson Mizner, for whom rules and regulations had never applied, or existed only for the purpose of providing a challenge for his lawless nature. "Mizner was in poor health during the later years of his life," Jack Warner recalled, "and because he was inherently lazy he

spent most of his waking hours lounging in the most comfortable chair he could find. At the studio he usually
sprawled half asleep in a big red plush chair which so closely
resembled a churchly throne that his friends nicknamed him
'the Archbishop.' He never cared much for interior decorating or other fancy trappings, and had an exasperating habit
of flicking cigarette ashes into a ten-gallon hat."

Slumped on his archepiscopal throne, with the debilitated manner of one of the later Byzantine emperors, he
made himself available for consultation. Sometimes he contributed only the outline of a situation, a gag, a wry exchange
of conversation, to the screenplays being fabricated. On
others he dictated whole stretches of dialogue and action.
He was credited with considerable collaboration on such
memorable films of the era as *Little Caesar*, still regarded as
a classic of its genre with Edward G. Robinson in a Capone-
like role, *Five Star Final*, and *20,000 Years in Sing Sing*.

Wilson occasionally became restive and "insisted more
than once that writing picture scripts was as much of a dead
end as whoring in the Yukon," Warner wrote, but he stayed
on the studio payroll "if only because he wanted a refuge in
his twilight years."

Wilson was not about to slouch off into the twilight without a last few hurrahs, however. Those who saw him in
action, a pale reflection of the Barbary Coast and Klondike
scuffler he once had been, maintained that he was an awe-
some spectacle. One witness to a Mizner brawl—which had
little in common with the ordinary Hollywood fistfight emblazoned on front pages, in which the contestants were
supremely concerned about their peerless profiles and
could depend on friends and bodyguards to stop the hos-
tilities before claret was tapped or expensive dentistry

ruined—was Cecil Beaton, the British society photographer, court favorite, and travel writer. The elegant
young Mr. Beaton was introduced to Mizner by Anita Loos
as the most picturesque character in America.

Late in December, 1930, he and Anita Loos, with Mizner
and Irving Berlin, dined together at El Cholo, a Mexican
restaurant in downtown Los Angeles. The occasion, Miss
Loos told the British visitor, was the reconciliation arranged
for Mizner and Berlin. Wilson and the songwriter had been
friends for a quarter of a century, but there had been a frost
on their relationship for the past several years because, as
Beaton learned, "each lately thought the other was trying to
high-hat him." More likely the coolness had come about as a
result of the collapse of the Mizner real estate empire in
Florida; just possibly Berlin had resented being used as
sucker bait. At any rate friends had persuaded them to
forgive and forget, and the songwriter arrived at the restaurant bearing a bottle of Napoleon brandy "as a loving cup."

Berlin was celebrated for writing lovely lyrics and Mizner
was supposed to be a master of the *mot juste*, yet when the
two wordsmiths got together, according to Beaton, the only
thing that came out of their mouths was a string of expletives
customarily exchanged by two American males meeting
after a long hiatus. As transcribed by the bemused Mr.
Beaton: "Well, you old son of a bitch. Ha, ha! Haw, haw!
Oh, you old bastard, you old son of a bitch. Haw, haw! . . .
why, Willy, you old son of a bitch do you remember. . . .
Jesus Christ, you old bastard! You son of a bitch. But I've
always liked you, haven't I, you old son of a bitch!"

Mizner and Berlin blessed their reunion with episcopal
flourishes of the brandy bottle. "Anita, very gay, screamed
with laughter. The bottle of Napoleon brandy quickly became empty, the profanity more raucous. Wilson broke out

in a running sweat, mopped his head and chin with a quivering hand, drew in his breath with a whistle and guffawed more asthmatically than ever."

Then appeared two standard menaces of any Hollywood gathering, a couple of intruders attracted by the scent of celebrity. Both were drunk, but Wilson had a tender feeling for people in that condition and made them feel welcome until boredom set in. The drunks were not amusing, and Wilson suggested that they depart because he and his friends had something to discuss. The two drunks turned nasty at that point, and one of them began shouting, "Where are those Anaconda Copper bonds?" as though suspecting Wilson of grand larceny.

In that suddenly curdled atmosphere, Beaton observed, Wilson did his best to keep the peace. He kept uttering soothing phrases to the two belligerents: "Don't be silly. Go home and be quiet. We're among friends." Then the drunks began cursing Berlin as a "dirty Jew," and Wilson had enough. Beaton recalled:

"Old Wilson, his white face pouring with sweat, rose and stood to attention in all his giant height. Anita got up from the table. We all clustered around, weakly advocating, 'Now be quiet.' "

One of the drunks aimed a haymaker at Wilson, which he easily sideslipped, "but it was enough to start the melee. Wilson, with blood in his eyes, fumbled quickly for a beer bottle and cracked it over the side [of his assailant's] head. Crash! The glass fell in smithereens."

A battle royal ensued, a scene out of a Eugene O'Neill forecastle, with Mizner as the Hairy Ape. Wilson and his two opponents were bombarding one another with bottles and glasses. "Wilson, the old tough, stood in the doorway dividing shop and back parlour. His face deadly white and pouring with sweat, his eyes darting out of his head, he threw bottles at the enemy while the enemy responded with other bottles, tumblers and heavy glass water carafes that whizzed through the air past his head. . . ." Wilson barked an order for Berlin and Beaton to get Anita out of the place. A large mirror was shattered. Retreat from the establishment through the rear was cut off by a locked door, for which the panic-stricken proprietor could not locate the key.

Beaton realized now that the Wild West had not been entirely a myth. "Wilson would surely be killed," he wrote in a memoir years later. "It seemed useless for the rest of us to join the battle. We were sober, and didn't want to kill the drunks. We only wanted the fight to cease. . . .

"Then suddenly the fight stopped: the drunks had mysteriously retreated. . . . Irving and Anita dragged a reluctant Wilson out through the kitchen while I hurriedly paid at least the food bill. [Irving Berlin settled all damages with the proprietor the next day.] The shop was entirely wrecked. No picture remained intact upon the walls; every mirror had been broken; pieces of glass lay strewn about. Beer and water ran down the walls and along the floor."

Anita and her three escorts made a dash for her limousine just as the two drunks suddenly reappeared in a mood to resume the battle. They made their getaway, with Anita chiding her friends, "Really, boys, we might all have landed on the front page."

Wilson, his breath still coming in tortured asthmatic gasps, turned to the visiting Britisher and said, "Well, young Beaton, now you've seen the social life of Hollywood."

In the recently published second volume of her fascinating autobiography, titled *Kiss Hollywood Good-by*, Miss Loos revealed that Mizner was the great love of her life.

While married to John Emerson, she met him during the lush years in Florida and found him fascinating, despite the fact that he was a "badly preserved giant of fifty-one." After she moved to Hollywood a few years later, "we would be together practically every day until Wilson died." Part of his fascination for the much younger Miss Loos, admittedly, was "the aura of his reckless past . . . his air of tranquil assurance, which, as a rule, exists only in men of genius." That type of sex appeal, she explained, was sometimes shared by "aging gangsters . . . certain Greek tycoons and a few popular entertainers like Frank Sinatra." No doubt the brawl at El Cholo only reinforced Miss Loos' impression of Mizner as a figure of hell-roaring legend.

Wilson may have been declining physically and tasting the dregs of a hectically misspent life, the booze and dope with which he had insulted his system taking their toll, but his wit was still honed to a fine edge, at least by Hollywood standards. Jimmy Cagney once inspected his broken knuckles and asked how he got them. "Slugging broads in the Yukon," Wilson replied.

When he was assigned to work on the screenplay of *20,000 Years in Sing Sing*, the autobiography of Warden Lewis E. Lawes, he was introduced to Lawes and remarked, "Warden, I never expected to meet you without an iron grille between us."

One film in which the Mizner personality was clearly visible was *One Way Passage*, in which William Powell and Kay Francis appeared in the leading roles. The Powell character was a crook being extradited to the United States, most of the action occurred on a luxury liner, and it was clear that the suave and sophisticated outlaw was modeled after Wilson himself. The dialogue often reflected his rueful at-

titude toward the human condition, his conviction that
nothing, even the best planned and most skillfully executed
capers, ever worked out right, his eventual conclusion that
"Maybe Easy Street is only a blind alley." Certainly one of
the lines which Wilson put in the mouth of the Mizner-like
hero could have served as his epigraph: "I went a long way
and I walked a wide mile."

With his failing health and his certainty that his best years
were long behind him, he succumbed to what he had once
regarded as the vice of dotards, nostalgia. He closed out
many nights at Jane Jones' tiny nightclub, where tear-
jerking ballads were the specialty of the house, and draped
himself over the piano there to exercise his rusty baritone in
such lachrymose numbers as "The Curse of an Aching
Heart" and "The Chairs in the Parlor All Miss You." It could
be said that he wallowed in the role of an "old-timer,"
though he was only in his middle fifties. And the sentimentality with which he viewed old friendships he would once
have cursed as a sure sign of senility. It was Wilson's own
kind of tribute that he memorialized Hype Igoe, a fellow San
Franciscan graduated to a New York sports column, who
had aided and abetted him in several ventures, by having his
name echo on the sound track of *20,000 Years in Sing Sing*.
In a Death Row scene, he had a condemned man being led
to the electric chair; the other inmates called after him, "So
long, Hype." And when the aging old champion Jack Johnson was cast in a bit part in a Warner Brothers film, Wilson
greeted him with open arms and kissed him on both cheeks,
then hauled him around the lot to make sure the bosses
knew what a great man was honoring their studio.

The idea of winding up such a picturesque life as a quill
driver on a film studio's assembly line was something he
found it difficult to reconcile himself to. Cannibalizing his

career for the amusement of popcorn-munching rubes who
had to find satisfaction in vicarious adventures flickering on
a screen—that was what it amounted to. How could they
understand the pulse-quickening pleasures of a life lived
outside the law? And he was disgusted by the inequities of
the Hollywood system, the industry that called itself an art
form but served as a stamping mill to pulverize talent and
convert it into box-office gold.

There were times when he sounded like a social reformer,
if not quite a Bolshevik, as he meditated on the injustices of
the film industry and the crass overlordship of the "pointed
heads" in the executive offices. Only occasionally, he observed, did the right people come out on top. He often cited
one incident as an example of things working out right:

"I was sitting in my office one day, balmy with the tropical
heat, watching a colored man I knew paint an elephant
yellow. The elephant was going to be featured in the durbar
sequence of one of those Gunga Din-type of pictures, and
Slim, the colored man, was having a hard job applying the
yellow paint, which would show white on film.

"As fast as Slim put it on the paint, because of the
elephant's oily hide, would run down and come right off. His
boss was a fellow named Hyde, a natural slave-driver, and
he raged at the black man even though he was working as
hard as possible to get the elephant painted in time for the
scene to be filmed. Finally Slim got some powder and
smeared it all over the elephant. The powder stuck all right,
but Hyde was displeased with the effect. He knocked Slim
aside and took up the paint brush himself. This time the
paint stayed on because of Slim's ingenuity. While Hyde
was working on the elephant's side, the elephant took a deep
drink from the paint bucket. He didn't much like it. The
elephant turned and let Hyde have a stream of yellow paint

right in the face. They drycleaned Hyde for weeks but he still looked as though he were suffering from jaundice.

"That was the quickest instance of Hollywood justice I can remember. And needless to say, up in my lonely cubicle, I did not work on my story *that* day. I just sat around humming to myself."

There were few such incidents to gladden his days, and Jim Tully, the hobo turned novelist, observed that in his last years Wilson was prematurely aged and "seemed like an immense leprechaun who must laugh at a world that deserved tears."

14

EXIT LAUGHING

"A bum ticker" was Wilson's explanation to friends for his haggard features and the shadow that seemed to have fallen over him. His heart was faltering, his footsteps dragged, and in his fifty-seventh year he looked ten years older. He may even have regretted not having paid more attention to the strictures of his pious brother Henry. In public, however, he maintained his devil-may-care posture. Perhaps he remembered his hard-boiled—but soft-centered, when you thought about it—remark when he was told that his lion-hearted gladiator Stanley Ketchel was dying. "Tell 'em to count ten over him," Wilson had said, "and he'll get up."

Nobody had to give Wilson the ten-count. The old scuffler and scofflaw, unregenerate, kept coming out of his corner with his fists up.

Though he gallantly concealed the fact, Wilson had known his days were numbered ever since the year following his arrival in Hollywood.

He had suffered a heart attack late in March, 1928, and collapsed in the lobby of the Ambassador where he lived throughout his Hollywood career. Reporters who converged on his sickbed several days later were told that he had "done a tailspin down in the lobby," leaving the implication he might have collapsed from overindulgence, but his doctors confirmed that he had suffered a heart attack.

From then on he knew he had been dealt the queen of spades, but refused to regulate his life in accordance with his doctors' suggestions or to cut the late hours, the liquor and cigarettes, which were part of his style of living.

The deaths of old friends provided further intimations of mortality. Less than a year after his first heart attack, his old friend Wyatt Earp died—in bed, unlike several members of the Clanton tribe who encountered the Earp brothers one bitter dawn at the O. K. Corral—leaving a fat portfolio of Los Angeles real estate parcels, Colorado copper mines, and Bakersfield oil property. Wilson was one of the pallbearers, along with the cowboy film stars Tom Mix and William S. Hart, and listened grimly as a tenor sang "Beautiful Isle of Somewhere," which seemed a bit treacly for a man who had parlayed a six-shooter into a sizable fortune.

Three years later, in the midsummer of 1932, Wilson collapsed again after driving home from a party at Tallulah Bankhead's in an open car on a foggy night. He came down with bronchial pneumonia and had to be confined to his suite at the Ambassador for several weeks.

Against the advice of the "croakers" as he called them, he kept commuting between the writers' building on the Warner lot and Booth 50 at the Brown Derby.

And he could still respond spiritedly to a challenge to his ability to talk his way out of a tight corner. Some of his fellow writers, as a prank, arranged to have him invited to address a group holding its convention in Los Angeles and topping it off with a tour of Warner Brothers' studio. It wasn't until he mounted the platform that Wilson noticed that the audience was dressed in blue uniforms—and they weren't survivors of the old Seventh Cavalry holding a reunion, but delegates to the convention of police chiefs. Wilson gazed down on all those hard constabulary faces and snarled, "The last time I saw so many cops they were chasing me."

His erratic heartbeat did not prevent Wilson from mixing it with his fists whenever the proper, or improper, occasion arose. He was among the guests at a dinner at the Ambassador given in honor of Eddie Mannix, a bull-like, hot-tempered Irishman who had once been a bouncer in an amusement park, but was now Louis B. Mayer's chief lieutenant at Metro-Goldwyn-Mayer. Wilson was one of the guests. Another was his employer, Jack L. Warner, who recalled that Mannix "got himself stoned before we even got to the soup course." The MGM executive could not be prevented from mounting the bandstand and taking over the drums. Though he was the guest of honor, it was decided not to humor Mannix, and an earnest effort was made to extract him. When persuasion failed, another guest tried to drag Mannix off the bandstand and got knocked unconscious for his pains.

"The blow touched off a wild brawl," Warner wrote, "and in an instant the Warner men and the Metro men—who had never been able to work off their mutual animosities in open combat—were happily socking each other in little groups all over the ballroom." Warner admitted that like any sensible general, he encouraged his troops from a safe vantage point, having sought refuge behind a large potted palm. "Mannix was yelling joyfully at the same time, flattening every man within reach, and Ben Frank, the hotel manager, was close

to rigor mortis as dishes, glasses, and furniture flew in every
direction.

"Enter Wilson Mizner, playwright, adventurer, and lovable con man. Six feet four, two hundred and twenty
stripped. He confronted Mannix, measured him with an
experienced eye, and gave him a longshoreman belt on the
button. Mannix went into a triple somersault and was carried away, and Mizner went to the hospital to have the
broken bones in his hand set."

Given his weakened condition, as he often warned his
intimates, Wilson was no longer able to engage in protracted
brawls, but he could still muster a Sunday punch of poleax
quality. If that failed to take out his intended victim, his
friends were instructed to intervene.

Soon even such minor exertions would overtax his
strength. His asthmatic heart condition and other complications caused by a strenuous fifty-six years were sapping his
vitality to an alarming degree, though he insisted on staying
on the job at Warner Brothers. He was working on a film for
Jimmy Cagney titled *Hard to Handle*, which the studio
executives felt was an appropriate designation for both writer and actor.

His friends were convinced that he was toughing it out
and knew that it would soon be time to cash in his chips.
Irvin S. Cobb, an old friend from the days when Park Row
seemed to run straight up Broadway to Times Square, who
was out in Hollywood on a writing contract, remembered
the shock he felt at seeing Mizner for the first time in years.
"For months before the end he dragged himself about Film-
land so consumed by the mysterious illness which racked his
wasted body that his skin, which had always shown a curious
pallor, was now of a ghastly lifeless cast. His naturally sepul-

chral voice had become a forced graveyard croak and his
great staring brown eyes burned with a febrile fire. Yet his
customary hailing cry for friend or foe of 'Hello, sucker!' was
as explosive as ever and his tongue as keenly barbed."

As always, Wilson treated death, even the prospect of his
own, with ribald contempt. Even the deaths of those close to
him tapped not his tear ducts but his vast resources of black
comedy. When their oldest brother, Lansing, died while he
and Addison were in Florida, Wilson grumbled to Addison,
"Why didn't you tell me *before* I put on a red tie?"

In January, 1933, Wilson received word from Florida that
Addison, who had stayed on the scene of the misadventures
in high finance and fanciful architecture, was dying. Wilson
was then polishing the script of a film titled *Merry Wives of
Reno* and telegraphed Addison, "Stop dying. Am trying to
write a comedy." Addison had been failing ever since the
crash of their fortunes, but his death was a shattering blow to
Wilson, who loved his brother more than any other man and
all women but their mother. But he managed to conceal his
grief, believing such conventional feelings were for lesser
mortals.

The croakers, as he called them, kept advising him to quit
work and give up late hours, but he had "walked a wide
mile" all his life and wasn't going to be confined to a sick-
room without putting up strong resistance.

But Addison's death had struck him a mortal blow and in
mid-March, 1933, not long before his fifty-seventh birth-
day, he suffered a heart attack in the writers' building at the
studio. An effort was made to place him in the hospital, but
he insisted on being taken to his suite at the Ambassador,
where he was immediately placed under an oxygen tent.
The jokes kept coming from his bluish lips. A nurse who

asked him if he wanted a priest to administer the last sacra-
ment was told, "I want a priest, a rabbi, and a Protestant
minister. I want to hedge my bets."

Even on what proved to be his deathbed, according to the
recollection of Irvin S. Cobb and other reliable witnesses,
Wilson felt the continuing compulsion to wear the mask of
comedy. Hollywood, which takes death seriously, if the
ornate memorials at Forest Lawn may be accepted as evidence, marveled at the flippancies which issued from his
bedside.

A pious woman friend insisted on bringing a clergyman
renowned for the deathbed conversions of various pagans
and scoffers to Wilson's side. He had already started slipping in and out of coma, and the balance of his life was
measured in hours, but he still felt that he owed life a few
more witticisms. Cobb said, "Literally, Mizner died laughing," but it would be more accurate to say that he died trying
to make other people laugh.

The clergyman leaned over him and said, "Part of my
trade is giving such spiritual consolation as I may to those in
extremity. Without offense, please let me say that if there is
anything I can tell you in this hour or anything you'd care to
say to me, I shall be only too glad to serve."

"Much obliged, Padre, much obliged," Wilson replied.
"But why bother? I'll be seeing your boss in a few minutes."

His last words could be taken as the *mea culpa* of a man
who had never believed in repenting a misdeed the moment
a cop's hand was laid on his shoulder. "I don't expect too
much," he added in a rattling breath. "You can't be a rascal
for forty years and then cop a plea the last minute. God
keeps better books than that."

A few minutes later, at 11:04 P.M. on April 3, he died.

Hollywood hoped to give him a grand funeral, though most writers go to their graves with no more than a final paycheck from the studio. Wilson Mizner was more than a writer, he was a "personality," a legend, and he deserved at least the funeral of a film star of the second magnitude. Wilson, however, had thwarted such plans in his will—a deck, predictably, stacked with one or two extra jokers.

Wilson had made it clear that he would tolerate none of the posturing and crocodile tears of the usual Hollywood funeral. There was a brief memorial service at which Gene Fowler sensibly eulogized him as a man who "will be remembered for his lovable faults long after we are forgotten for our virtues." Then he was cremated, and his ashes were removed to a crypt at Cypress Lawn, near San Francisco, to rest briefly beside those of his brother Addison. Finally, still in accordance with the terms of his will, they were flung into the winds blowing through the Golden Gate.

His will further dictated that $1 each was to be given his two nieces, one the daughter of his sister, the other the daughter of the Reverend Henry Mizner, and the residue of the estate was left to "my friend, Florence Atkinson." Eyebrows lifted in lecherous surmise. Was Florence Atkinson a back-street romance he had kept concealed for years? Not at all, his last testament made clear; she was a platonic friend whom he had known for fifteen years, back in New York and Florida as well as later in Hollywood. That Wilson was capable of such a relationship, with all his hard-bitten attitudes toward women and sex, came as a blow to his fellow cynics. To Miss Atkinson he left his manuscripts, his interest in screenplays and stage plays, a small amount of stock, and his share of Addison's estate, valued at more than $10,000. Reporters found Miss Atkinson in a modest home on a street remote from the glamor with which Hollywood laminated itself. A former film actress and interior decorator, she told them Wilson had been the "best and dearest friend I ever had in my whole life. . . . You see I knew Addison almost as well as Wilson. We were like three brothers. . . ."

The Wilson Mizner she knew was a striking contrast with the image of himself he had so sedulously fostered. "Only a few ever pierced the gay and cynical armor and learned of the kindly, thoughtful, understanding man beneath it. . . . He was like a small boy, really, who needs to be looked after so that he won't get his feet wet and hurt himself."

Probably Wilson would have enjoyed the bewilderment of people who had taken him at face value as a jeering, hard-boiled, iconoclastic observer of human frailty; it is equally possible that he would have been annoyed that his sentimentality, his need of uncomplicated affection, had been exposed. He had always been the kind of man who did good in stealth, as if fearful of ruining his reputation.

Neither the postmortem revelations from Florence Atkinson nor any pious reflections from a biographer can conceal the fact that he had been a rogue straying from the herd, a rascal who lived by his wits for most of his life, and sometimes a scoundrel. His life could hardly be offered as an inspiring example to youth. Indeed it was only possible for him to have lived it, in his damn-your-eyes style, in a time when Americans could afford to laugh at themselves.

His victims may have numbered in the thousands, and he left in his turbulent wake the outcries of the bilked and insulted, but their plaint has been drowned out by the laughter he caused. No matter how nefarious his activities, they were always plotted with hilarious consequences in mind. It could justly be said that he gave more than he got, licitly or illicitly.

The wisecrack may not be the most sanctified form of humor, but it is quintessentially American, and Wilson Mizner was its foremost exponent. "Generations yet to come will be quoting Mizner without ever having heard his name," his admiring friend Anita Loos has written, though full credit has been given him for his contributions to the American lexicon, to that vast body of legend known generically as Americana, by H. L. Mencken and other experts.

He saw life as a comedy of pain and punctured pretensions, and unlike most comedians, he had the courage to keep the laughs coming no matter how racking the effort. There could be no greater tribute to his raffish spirit than the fact that people are still, innocently, stealing his stuff. Only a thief as boastful of his vocation as Wilson Mizner could appreciate that ironic stroke of justice.

NOTES ON SOURCES

THE complete listing of many sources indicated below under their author's surname may be found in the Selected Bibliography, which follows.

1. MAMA'S ANGEL BIRDIE

Wilson Mizner's family background and his boyhood are sketched in his brother Addison's memoir, *The Many Mizners, passim.* Additional material may be found in the California Historical Society's Mizner file, particularly on his mother's social career and his father's political career. Mrs. Mizner's social activities are also covered in the memoir of Arnold Genthe, the San Francisco society photographer—*As I Remember, passim.*

Charlie Chaplin, a friend of the Mizner clan, recalled the incident of Minnie's burning trash to annoy her neighbors in his *My Autobiography,* 383.

Details of the Corbett-Choynski fight and events surrounding it were described in the San Francisco *Examiner,* May 30, June 1, 5 and 6, 1889; also in James J. Corbett's autobiography, *The Roar of the Crowd, passim.*

Wilson's brief career as a gold miner in Grass Valley was detailed by the Los Angeles *Examiner,* April 4, 1933.

His adventures after being expelled from Santa Clara College with Dr. Slocum's medicine show were related by him to a reporter for the New York *Press,* which published a lengthy account of Mizner's youthful career on January 22, 1911, when he was becoming well known as a playwright.

His travels as Kid Savage's second in the ring, Los Angeles *Examiner*, April 4, 1933.

The historian of the medicine shows quoted was Stewart H. Holbrook, *The Golden Age of Quackery*, 6, 13, 208.

Mark Kelly revealed Mizner's impersonation of The Golden-Throated Salvini, illustrated-song artist, in his Los Angeles *Examiner* sports-page column, February 20, 1934.

2. WILSON'S ONE-MAN GOLD RUSH

Much of this chapter was drawn from Addison Mizner's memoir, *The Many Mizners*, which was published shortly before his death.

Soapy Smith's background was detailed by Forbes Parkhill, *The Wildest of the West*, 87–95.

Incidents involving the Mizner brothers on the trail through the Chilkoot Pass and beyond, Richard O'Connor, *High Jinks on the Klondike, passim*.

Wilson's experiences in Dawson as a gold weigher and singer, New York *Press* interview, *op. cit.*

His partnership with Rena Fargo and its disastrous end, Addison Mizner, *op. cit.*, 38.

Sid Grauman's recollection of Wilson's robbery of a candy store, Bill Kennedy's column, Los Angeles *Herald-Express*, June 21, 1964.

Mizner's promotion of the Slavin-Hoffman grudge match was related by Pierre Berton, *The Klondike Fever*, 379–380.

3. AT HOME IN NOME

Wilson's disillusionment with stampeding is recounted by O'Connor, *High Jinks on the Klondike*, 219.

The quotation from Berton on the mass evacuation from Dawson, *op. cit.*, 412.

Rex Beach's recollection of Nome in earliest phase as a gold-rush center, his autobiography *Personal Exposures*, 27–28.

The activities of the Wag Boys were described in some detail by Beach, *op. cit.*, 111–19.

Mizner's victimization of Key Pittman and his involvement in prize-fight management, O'Connor, *High Jinks on the Klondike*, *passim*.

The story of Diamond Jim Wilson's position in the Nome underworld and his last night on earth, as well as the dividing up of his estate, was related by Jack Hines, *Minstrel of the Yukon*, *passim*. Hines was a sort of protégé of Mizner's.

Mizner's use of the tomato can as a temporary aid in working the badger game, New York *Press* interview, *op. cit.*

Addison recalled his trip to Nome to investigate Wilson's activities in his memoir, *op. cit.*, *passim*.

Wilson's morale-raising activities aboard the icebound *Portland*, O'Connor, *High Jinks on the Klondike*, 222–23.

The complete story of the Nome Claim Steal is told in the memoir of an Alaskan federal judge, James Wickersham, *Old Yukon*, *passim*.

Mizner's indulgence in pinochle on the return from Alaska, Bill Kennedy's column, Los Angeles *Herald-Examiner*, June 21, 1964.

4. THE ADVENTURES OF THE CANDY KID

A description of Wilson's activities as a man-about-San Francisco may be found in Evelyn Wells' *Champagne Days in San Francisco*, 109, 124, 142.

The reunion of Wilson and Addison in New York and its marital consequences for Wilson, Addison's memoir, *op. cit.*, *passim*, and Edward Dean Sullivan, *The Fabulous Wilson Mizner*, 179.

Charles Yerkes has never attracted the attention of a biographer, only that of novelist Theodore Dreiser, in whose novels he became a powerful, commanding, but understandable figure. Some indication of his financial dealings may be found, however, in Emmett Dedmon's *Fabulous Chicago*, 259–61, 274; Richard O'Connor, *Courtroom Warrior*, a biography of William Travers Jerome, 266–68.

Chicago historian quoted on Yerkes' operations as a traction magnate, Dedmon, *op. cit.*, 260.

Addison Mizner's views of Myra Yerkes are contained in his memoir, *op. cit.*, *passim*.

The headline over the story of Wilson's crosstown elopement with

Myra Yerkes was from the New York *Morning Telegraph*, February 2, 1906.

Accounts of Wilson's introduction of his bride to the press and his calculating approach to taking over as master of her household were published in the New York *Press*, *Evening Sun*, and *Evening Telegram*, February 3, 1906, and the *Morning Telegraph*, February 4, 1906.

5. HIGH JINKS ON FIFTH AVENUE

Addison Mizner recalled his visit to the bridegroom several days after Wilson's marriage to Myra Yerkes was revealed in his memoir, *op. cit.*, 100-5.

Johnny Bray's service as Wilson's gentleman's gentleman and his serving a hypodermic needle on a silver tray were recalled for the author by the late Stanley Rose, of Matador, Texas, and Hollywood, California. Rose was Hollywood's pioneer bootlegger, a character possibly more colorful than Mizner himself, though less celebrated, and the operator of a bookstore on Hollywood Boulevard which served as an aid station for visiting literary men employed in the film studios. Rose was a friend of Mizner's throughout the latter's half dozen years in Hollywood.

Mrs. Mizner's letter to Wilson and Addison relating her experiences during the San Francisco fire and earthquake was quoted by Sullivan, *op. cit.*, 196-99.

Wilson's operations as an unofficial administrator of Charles Yerkes' estate were detailed by Alva Johnston, *The Legendary Mizners, passim*.

Wilson's blasting away at a cuckoo clock with a shotgun was disclosed by Myra in an interview with the New York *Press*, June 16, 1906.

Her complaints about Wilson's turning her mansion into a training camp for Willus Britt's pugilistic stable, *ibid.*

6. "NO OPIUM SMOKING IN THE ELEVATORS"

A celebration of Ned Greenway's career as the king of San Francisco wine bibbers may be found in Wells, *op. cit.*, 98-100.

Irvin S. Cobb's characterization of Wilson is from his autobiography, *Exit Laughing*, 499.

The ambiance of the Hotel Rand may be gathered from Johnston's sterling chronicle of the Mizner family, *op. cit.*, 112, and an article in the New York *Morning Telegraph*, March 10, 1926. A story on Wilson's managerial appointment and his services as boniface of the Rand was published by the New York *Press*, August 10, 1907. The files of the *Press* constitute a running account of Mizner's New York years; likewise the *Morning Telegraph*, a daily then devoted to sporting and theatrical news.

The story of Doc DeGarmo's service as house physician of the Hotel Rand and its occasionally disastrous consequences is told by Gene Fowler, *Skyline*, 69-71.

The Broadway chorus lines' reaction to Wilson's resignation was reported by the New York *Press*, October 8, 1907.

Wilson's activities as an oceangoing cardsharp were related by Johnston, *op. cit.*, 176-77.

The quotation on Wilson's role in trimming the suckers on luxury liners, *ibid.*, 208.

Frankie Dwyer's brawl on the *Mauretania* and its consequences were covered by the New York *Times*, June 12, 1908, and subsequently by the other New York journals. None of the accounts mention Wilson as a participant in the fracas.

Wilson's misadventure with the multicolored rats was recalled in Bill Kennedy's column, Los Angeles *Herald-Express*, September 2, 1954.

The John Barrymore anecdote in which Wilson figured was included in Gene Fowler's *Good Night, Sweet Prince*, 107-8.

7. IN STANLEY KETCHEL'S CORNER

The White Hope craze was studied with scholarly detachment and considerable humor by the late John Lardner, *White Hopes and Other Tigers*.

The first meeting of Wilson Mizner and Stanley Ketchel was recorded by Sullivan, *op. cit.*, 202-3.

Ketchel's career in the Butte smelters, saloons, and prize ring, *ibid.*, 206.

The sportswriter who charged that Ketchel was "hitting the hop" was Wurra Wurra McLaughin, in the New York *World*, February 4, 1910.

The quotation on Wilson's benign influence in keeping parasites from Ketchel, Sullivan, *op. cit.*, 213.

Ketchel's weeping over the picture of a lost lamb in the entrance hall of a bordello, Johnston, *op. cit.*, 144.

The account of the Ketchel-Langford fight was abstracted from the story in the New York *Morning Telegraph*, April 18, 1910. It was written by the *Morning Telegraph*'s sports editor and boxing expert, William B. Masterson. Better known as Bat, the sheriff who (temporarily) cleaned up Dodge City and other centers of gunplay, Masterson had retired from gunfighting and taken up a career in journalism. He was probably the most perceptive, if not the most polished, writer, among a notable band of fight experts on the New York newspapers.

The choreography of the Ketchel-Lewis fight was carefully explained by Johnston, *op. cit.*, 152-53.

Bat Masterson criticized Ketchel's indulgence in sartorial display in the *Morning Telegraph*, June 11, 1910, in reporting on what turned out to be Ketchel's last fight.

Mizner's maneuvers before the Jeffries-Johnson fight, Sullivan, *op. cit.*, 207-10.

The Rex Beach observations were included in his autobiography, *op. cit.*, 85.

Mizner and Ketchel on a spree with Jack London, Richard O'Connor, *Jack London*, 319.

8. WITH PIPE AND PEN ON BROADWAY

An account of drug addiction in the United States before World War I may be found in George E. Pettey's *The Narcotic Drug Diseases and Allied Ailments*.

The Mark Sullivan quote is from his magisterial history, *Our Times*, Vol. II, 128.

Howard Emmett Rogers recalled his first meeting with Wilson Mizner for Johnston, *op. cit.*, 68-70.

The theatrical historian quoted on the "new" playwrights was Allen Churchill, *The Great White Way*, 150-51.

Glimpses of George Bronson Howard's personality were provided by Johnston, *op. cit.*, 166-67; Sullivan, *op. cit.*, 230-31.

Wilson Mizner's comments on Howard's appalling energy were published by the New York *Dramatic Mirror*, August 2, 1909.

The affinity for opium shared by Mizner and his first collaborator, Johnston, 169-70.

Reviews of *The Only Law* cited were from the New York *World* and the *Morning Telegraph*, September 11, 1909, and the *Dramatic Mirror*, September 16, 1909. The play reopened in Chicago on March 8, 1910, but closed within a week.

Howard's novelette "The Parasite" appeared in *Smart Set*, August, 1912. It also was published as part of a collection of Howard's stories, *The Birds of Prey*, New York, 1913.

Mizner's counterattack against Howard was quoted by Sullivan, *op. cit.*, 230-31.

9. SHAKESPEARE OF THE UNDERWORLD

The background and personality of Paul Armstrong were drawn from Churchill, *op. cit.*, 152-53; H. L. Mencken's *Newspaper Days, passim*, and George Tyler's *Whatever Goes Up*, 176-77. Mencken was an observer of Armstrong's early career as a playwright, Tyler was the producer of most of his plays.

The account of Armstrong's difficulties with directing and producing his own play, *St. Ann*, was drawn from Mencken's memoir, *op. cit.*, 115-16.

Armstrong's curtain speech at the opening of *Salomy Jane* was recalled by Tyler, *op. cit.*, 175-76. The circumstances under which he wrote it were recalled by Eleanor Robson Belmont in her memoir, *The Fabric of Memory*, 60.

The collaborative difficulties experienced by Mizner and Armstrong were recorded by Sullivan, *op. cit.*, 222.

Tyler recalled how Armstrong choked up over his curtain speech at *The Deep Purple Opening* in his memoir, *op. cit.*, 176-77.

Colgate Baker's interview with Wilson was published by the New York *Review*, October 10, 1911.

Irving Berlin dedicates a song to Wilson, Sullivan, *op. cit.*, 225.

Alva Johnston's analysis of Wilson's problems with creative writing, *op. cit.*, 174-75.

Lansing Mizner's comment on his son's efforts, Churchill, *op. cit.*, 154.

Stories on Wilson's operation and the quips from his bedside were published by the New York *Morning World* and the *Morning Telegraph*, September 21 and 22, 1912.

Mizner's remarks on his play-doctoring job on the London revue, *Come Over Here*, were quoted by Sullivan, *op. cit.*, 222-23.

Mencken's comments on Armstrong's earning power in his last years and his plans for the future, *op. cit.*, 117-18.

10. "HELLO, SUCKER!"

The ambiance of the Times Square area was strikingly described by Irvin S. Cobb, *op. cit.*, *passim*.

The membership of the Broadway Poultry Club was listed by Sullivan, *op. cit.*, 146.

The big-stakes poker game involving Mizner and several of his friends was reported in the New York *World*, December 19, 1912.

A partial account of Wilson's trip to Europe with the poker-game losers as his guests was published by the New York *Press*, January 4, 1913.

Wilson's carefully calculated bet on the Johnson-Willard fight was related by Johnston, *op. cit.*, 199.

The plot to humiliate Arnold Rothstein in the marathon billiards match was recorded by Leo Katcher, *The Big Bankroll*, 53-56, and Donald Henderson Clarke, *In the Reign of Rothstein*, 122-27.

The Rothstein biographer quoted on his repellent personality was Katcher, *op. cit.* 53.

Wilson's pursuit of a mark around the world was recalled for the author by Stanley Rose, who got it from Mizner himself.

Wilson's role as a witness at the John Doe inquiry into gambling, New York *Sun*, March 15, 1918.

His appearance in court on the assault charge was reported by the New York *World*, August 29, 1918.

The obsequies at Jack Dunstan's attending the closing of the saloons, Katcher, *op. cit.*, 227.

11. A SUCCESSOR TO PONCE DE LEON

Some indication of the haphazhardness of writing for films around the time of World War I was conveyed by Anita Loos, *A Girl Like I*, 71-72.

Wilson's practical joke on Governor Smith was related by Chaplin, *op. cit.*, 219.

His recollection of his first experience in the Hollywood studios, Sullivan, *op. cit.*, 280-81.

The background to the Florida boom and the Mizners' participation was drawn from Addison Mizner's memoir, *passim*, Ben Hecht's *A Child of the Century*, 417-23; Beach, *op. cit.*, 266-67. For Addison Mizner's collaboration with Paris Singer, Cleveland Amory, *The Last Resorts*, 352-55.

The "big names" used by the Mizners to lure prospects to Boca Raton were listed by Johnston, *op. cit.*, 221.

Marie Dressler's bitter recollection of her experiences as the "Duchess of Boca Raton" were included in her memoir, *My Own Story*, 187, 213.

The late Seth Clarkson's satiric deflation of the Florida boom was recalled for the author by Clarkson.

The activities of the confidence men, many of them old friends of Wilson's, were recorded by D. W. Maurer, *The Big Con*, *passim*.

Development of the "pirate gold" gimmick as a lure for Florida land buyers was described by Hecht, *op. cit.*, 417-24.

The expansive building program launched for Boca Raton was described by its chief engineer, Addison Mizner, in *op. cit.*, *passim*.

12. THE BURSTING OF THE BUBBLE

Ben Hecht recalled his foresight in leaving Florida with all his takings in cash in *op. cit.*, 430-31.

The background of General T. Coleman du Pont was drawn from William H. A. Carr's family history, *The Du Ponts of Delaware*, *passim*.

Anecdotes concerning Du Pont's lively career and personality, *ibid.*, 281, 285-86.

The causes of General du Pont's quarrel with the Mizner

Corporation's management were explored by Johnston, *op. cit.*, 281, 285-86.

The plans which excited General du Pont's wrath were announced in the Palm Beach *Post*, September 11, 1925.

Du Pont's condemnation of the Mizner advertising and promotional methods was published in various New York and Florida newspapers during the last few days of November, 1925.

The collapse of the Florida boom may be traced in Kenneth Ballinger's *Miami Millions, passim*. The resultant lawsuits filled the columns of Florida newspapers for half a dozen years afterward. To many it seemed as though the collapse of the state's real estate boom heralded the Wall Street crash of 1929.

The letter from Wilson Mizner to Arthur Somers Roche, a highly successful magazine writer who had settled in Florida, was quoted by Johnston, *op. cit.*, 298.

13. THE SAGE OF BOOTH 50

Joseph P. Kennedy's overlordship of the RKO studio during Mizner's employment there is related in Richard J. Whalen, *The Founding Father*, 87-99.

The story of Wilson's driving up at a film premiere in a Model T Ford was recounted in the Los Angeles *Examiner*, April 3, 1933.

Jack Warner told the story of his partnership in the Brown Derby enterprise in his autobiography, *My First Hundred Years in Hollywood*, 159-60.

Stanley Rose's reminiscences about Wilson Mizner were provided the author before his death in 1954. Similarly, those of the late Mark Kelly, who was sports editor and columnist of the Los Angeles *Examiner* during Mizner's Hollywood years, and Louis Stevens, a San Francisco contemporary of Mizner's who had sold newspapers on the old Barbary Coast and later was one of Hollywood's most highly paid writers.

Adela Rogers St. Johns recalled how Mizner criticized Mark Kelly for taking her to the wrestling matches in *The Honeycomb*, 218.

The Pat O'Brien and Sammy Finn anecdotes were published in Bill Kennedy's column, Los Angeles *Herald-Examiner*, June 21, 1964.

Anita Loos' recollections of Mizner and his serving as the model for the Clark Gable character in *San Francisco*, *A Girl Like I*, 22, 30, 331.

Mizner's employment as a writer at Warner Brothers, Warner, *op. cit.*, 225-26.

The restaurant brawl in which Wilson stood off a pair of bottle-hurling drunks was recalled by Cecil Beaton in his memoir, *The Wandering Years*, 190, 212-15.

Wilson's fondness for singing tearful ballads at the Little Club, Johnston, *op. cit.*, 206.

His philosophic reflections on the elephant-painting incident, Sullivan, *op. cit.*, 282-83.

14. EXIT LAUGHING

Wilson's participation in the brawl with Eddie Mannix was recalled by Warner, *op. cit.*, 136-37.

The circumstances surrounding his first heart attack were reported by the Los Angeles *Herald*, March 29, 1928, and the Los Angeles *Times*, March 30, 1928.

His attendance at Wyatt Earp's funeral as a pallbearer, Los Angeles *Examiner*, January 15 and 16, 1929.

Wilson's ghastly appearance during the last months of his life were recalled by Cobb, *op. cit.*, 500.

Wilson's attitude toward death was explored by Johnston, *op. cit.*, 303.

Wilson on his deathbed, Cobb, *op. cit.*, 500; Los Angeles *Examiner* and *Times*, March 28 and 30, 1933.

His death was reported in detail by the Los Angeles *Herald-Express*, *Times*, and *Examiner*, April 4, 1933.

The contents of his will were reported by the Los Aneles *Examiner*, April 6, 1933.

The interview with Florence Atkinson revealing her long and platonic friendship with Wilson, Los Angeles *Examiner*, April 7, 1933.

Anita Loos' quotation, *A Girl Like I*, 21.

SELECTED BIBLIOGRAPHY

AMORY, CLEVELAND, *The Last Resorts*. New York, 1952.

BALLINGER, KENNETH, *Miami Millions*. New York, 1952.

BEACH, REX, *Personal Exposures*. New York, 1940.

BEATON, CECIL, *The Wandering Years*. Boston, 1961.

BELMONT, ELEANOR ROBSON,*The Fabric of Memory*. New York, 1957.

BERTON, PIERRE, The *Klondike Fever*. New York, 1958.

CARR, WILLIAM H. A., *The Du Ponts of Delaware*. New York, 1964.

CHAPLIN, CHARLIE, *My Autobiography*. New York, 1964.

CHURCHILL, ALLEN, *The Great White Way*. New York, 1962.

CLARKE, DONALD HENDERSON, *In the Reign of Rothstein*. New York, 1934.

COBB, IRVIN S., *Exit Laughing*. Indianapolis, 1941.

CORBETT, JAMES J., *The Roar of the Crowd*. New York, 1922.

DEDMON, EMMETT, *Fabulous Chicago*. New York, 1953.

DRESSLER, MARIE, with MILDRED HARRINGTON, *My Own Story*. Boston, 1934.

FOWLER, GENE, *Good Night, Sweet Prince*. New York, 1944.

———, *Skyline*. New York, 1961.

GENTHE, ARNOLD, *As I Remember*. New York, 1936.

HECHT, BEN, *A Child of the Century*. New York, 1954.

HINES, JACK, *Minstrel of the Yukon*. New York, 1938.

HOLBROOK, STEWART H., *The Golden Age of Quackery*. New York, 1959.

JOHNSTON, ALVA, *The Legendary Mizners*. New York, 1953.

KATCHER, LEO, *The Big Bankroll*. New York, 1958.

LARDNER, JOHN, *White Hopes and Other Tigers*. Philadelphia, 1951.

LOOS, ANITA, *A Girl Like I*. New York, 1966.

———, *Kiss Hollywood Good-by*. New York, 1974.

MAURER, D. W., *The Big Con.* New York, 1947.

MENCKEN, H. L., *Newspaper Days.* New York, 1941.

MIZNER, ADDISON, *The Many Mizners.* New York, 1931.

O'CONNOR, RICHARD, *Courtroom Warrior.* Boston, 1963.

———, *High Jinks on the Klondike.* Indianapolis, 1954.

———, *Jack London: A Biography.* Boston, 1964.

PARKHILL, FORBES, *The Wildest of the West.* New York, 1951.

PETTEY, GEORGE L., *The Narcotic Drug Diseases and Allied Ailments.* New York, 1925.

ROGERS, W. R., and WESTON, MILDRED, *Carnival Crossroads.* New York, 1960.

ST. JOHNS, ADELA ROGERS, *The Honeycomb.* New York, 1969.

SULLIVAN, EDWARD DEAN, *The Fabulous Wilson Mizner.* New York, 1935.

SULLIVAN, MARK, *Our Times*, Vol. II. New York, 1905.

TYLER, GEORGE, *Whatever Goes Up.* Indianapolis, 1934.

WARNER, JACK L., with DEAN JENNINGS, *My First Hundred Years in Hollywood.* New York, 1964.

WELLS, EVELYN, *Champagne Days in San Francisco.* New York, 1939.

WHALEN, RICHARD J., *The Founding Father: The Story of Joseph P. Kennedy.* New York, 1964.

WICKERSHAM, JAMES, *Old Yukon.* Washington, D.C., 1938.

ACKNOWLEDGMENTS

THE AUTHOR is greatly indebted to the Lincoln Center branch of the New York Public Library and its theatrical collection; the New York Newspaper Library; the Athenaeum in Boston; the Bangor, Maine, Public Library and its head, Robert Woodward; the library of the California Historical Society in San Francisco; and the libraries of the Los Angeles *Herald-Examiner* and the San Francisco *Examiner*.

INDEX